B1+

STUDENT'S BOOK

BEYOND

Robert Campbell
Rob Metcalf
Rebecca Robb Benne

MACMILLAN

	LISTENING & VOCABULARY	GRAMMAR (2)	LANGUAGE & BEYOND	SPEAKING	WRITING
	I did it! ***Take notes*** **Vocabulary (2):** Achievements and challenges	Past tenses review ***Talk about past achievements***	Know yourself: ***Consider the positive and negative aspects of taking risks***	At the sports centre ***Start and change topics in a conversation*** By the way	History of a sport (article) ***Edit and proofread a text***
	Record. Stop. Play. ***Use the audio type, grammar and pronunciation to help you understand*** **Vocabulary (2):** Negative prefixes: *un-* and *in-*	Present perfect continuous ***Talk about activities in progress before or until now***	Get thinking: ***Deal with peer pressure***	Be very careful ***Give warnings and prohibitions*** Watch out!	Keep in touch (email) ***Organise information in informal emails and letters***
	Survival stories ***Focus on important information*** **Vocabulary (2):** Noise verbs PRONOUNCE Consonant combinations	Sense verbs + *-ing* or infinitive ***Talk about things that you see, hear, feel and smell***	Respect others: ***Understand another person's feelings***	That's not true ***Contradict facts and opinions*** I don't think so	It happened to me (story) ***Link ideas in a story***
	Film credits ***Infer meaning when you listen*** **Vocabulary (2):** Film jobs	Defining and non-defining relative clauses ***Add extra information to a sentence***	Get organised: ***Think ahead and make plans***	Have you got the idea? ***Check and correct understanding*** That's not what I meant	My job application (letter) ***Write a formal letter***
	Sand sculptures ***Recognise general statements and exceptions*** **Vocabulary (2):** Words to describe art	Question tags ***Ask questions and confirm ideas using question tags*** PRONOUNCE Intonation in question tags	Respect others: ***Value the art and culture of different societies***	So do I ***Agree or disagree with an opinion*** I totally agree	I recommend it (review) ***Use linking words***

	LISTENING & VOCABULARY	GRAMMAR (2)	LANGUAGE & BEYOND	SPEAKING	WRITING
	No place to hide ***Recognise turn-taking*** **Vocabulary (2):** Types of evidence	*Can't have, could/may/might have, must have* ***Talk about possible explanations for things in the past*** PRONOUNCE Stressed and unstressed words	Know yourself: ***Take responsibility for your actions***	You shouldn't have done that ***Give and react to criticism*** It won't happen again	In my opinion (opinion essay) ***Use paragraphs and topic sentences***
	If … ***Predict what a story will be about*** **Vocabulary (2):** Adjectives ending with *-ful* and *-less*	Third conditional ***Talk about imaginary situations in the past***	Communicate & cooperate: ***Adapt to changing situations***	At the post office ***Send letters and parcels at the post office*** How much will it cost?	Join our appeal (poster) ***Use persuasive language***
	Need to talk? ***Understand hesitation*** **Vocabulary (2):** Reporting verbs PRONOUNCE Stress in two-syllable words	Reported speech review ***Report what other people say***	Communicate & cooperate: ***Give and accept feedback***	Don't worry about it ***Express regret and forgiveness*** It doesn't matter	My role model (description) ***Add detail to a description***
	Teen habits ***Understand the speaker's attitude*** **Vocabulary (2):** Services	*Have/get* something done ***Talk about things you pay someone else to do***	Get thinking: ***Make decisions***	Get your hair cut ***Ask for advice at the hairdresser's*** I'd like a haircut	Our school report (report) ***Write a report***
	Futurology ***Understand paraphrase*** **Vocabulary (2):** Prefixes of size, quantity and degree	Future continuous and future perfect ***Say if actions will be in progress or completed in the future***	Get organised: ***Rate your progress***	We'll miss you ***Express hopes, wishes and promises*** Look after yourself	You choose! (email) ***Present options***

UNIT 1 BE EXTREME!

IN THE PICTURE Extreme sports

Talk about different adventure sports

RECALL AND READ

1 Work in pairs. Do the Sports Challenge. You have three minutes.

THE 5-4-3-2-1 SPORTS CHALLENGE

A Write the names of the sports.
1 Five team sports.
2 Four sports that use a bat, stick or racket.
3 Three water or ice sports.
4 Two sports that don't require any special equipment.
5 One sport that uses animals.

B Which three sports in *A* are the least and most challenging? Why?

2 Read Alison's description and match it to the correct photo (a–f). Who does she thank and why?

WORK WITH WORDS

3 a 1.01 Name the sports in the photos. Use the words in the box if you need help. Then listen and check.

base jumping free running rock climbing
skateboarding skydiving windsurfing

b 1.02 Listen to the people talking about the sports. Which sports are they talking about?

4 Read the descriptions (a–f) of six more extreme sports. Then match and complete the names using the words in the box.

a travelling down a snow-covered hill while standing on a board
b jumping from a tall structure while connected to a large elastic cord
c climbing frozen waterfalls, cliffs and rocks covered with ice
d riding a wave without using a board
e racing up staircases inside skyscrapers or other tall structures
f diving underwater without any equipment

boarding climbing diving jumping running surfing

1 bungee ______ 3 free ______ 5 body ______
2 tower ______ 4 ice ______ 6 snow ______

5 1.03 Listen and check your answers to Exercise 4. Then listen and repeat all the extreme sports.

d

First we're told what to do. One tap on the shoulder means open your arms, a second tap means bring your arms to your chest as the parachute opens, and don't forget to keep your knees bent for landing.

Now we're sitting on benches inside the plane and I'm looking down at the Spanish Costa Brava 12,500 feet below. It's too late to turn back now. This is it! My first skydive.

Jump! I'm attached to my instructor, spinning in the sky as we fall towards the Earth at 180 km per hour. How can I describe it? You know how it feels when you hold your arm out of the window of a moving car and the air runs through your fingers. Think bigger!

It's amazing. Nothing beats this; not snowboarding; not diving; nothing. Thanks Mum, thanks Dad. It's the best birthday present ever. *Alison x*

HOME » ABOUT US » BE EXTREME

6 a 1.04 PRONOUNCE **Listen and repeat the words, paying attention to the /ɪ/, /iː/ and /aɪ/ sounds.**

wind /wɪnd/ ski /skiː/ dive /daɪv/

b 1.05 **Listen and write the sounds you hear: /ɪ/, /iː/ or /aɪ/. Then listen and repeat the words.**

1 extreme	3 bike	5 free	7 ice	9 cliff
2 climb	4 equipment	6 hill	8 bungee	10 sky

EXTEND

7 **Write a sentence describing each of the extreme sports below. Use a dictionary to help you.**

abseiling hang-gliding kayaking mountain biking

Mountain biking involves riding over rough tracks, rocks and hills.

8 THE MOVING PICTURE **Watch the video. What's the extreme sport? Why do you need to wear protective clothing?**

GO BEYOND

Do the Words & Beyond exercise on page 130.

SPEAK

9 **Work in pairs. Create an unusual extreme sport of your own. Use the names in Exercises 3 and 4 to help you.**

What other surfaces can we do a boarding sport on?

We could combine bungee jumping and rock climbing to make bungee climbing.

Workbook, page 4

READING Choose a sport

>>> Recognise and understand idioms

SPEAK AND READ

1 Work in pairs. Answer the questions.

1 Which extreme or adventure sports do you do or watch?
2 Which extreme sport would you most or least like to try? Why?

2 (1.06) Read the magazine feature and follow the instructions.

FIND AN EXTREME SPORT THAT'S RIGHT UP YOUR STREET. READ THE QUESTIONS AND CHOOSE THE ANSWERS THAT REFLECT YOUR CHARACTER AND ABILITIES.

1 Do you like heights?
a I don't mind heights.
b I don't really like heights.

2 How do you feel about the water?
a I'm a strong swimmer.
b I'm not a very confident swimmer.

3 What do you normally do?
a walk up the stairs
b take the lift

4 Which sentence describes you?
a I'm a team player.
b I prefer my own company.

5 You need to cross a frozen river. It's six metres wide and the ice is 20cm thick. It's a 20-minute walk to a bridge. What do you do?
a I walk across the ice.
b I cross the bridge.

READ THE ANALYSIS OF THE QUESTIONNAIRE AND CROSS OFF THE EXTREME SPORTS ON THE LIST THAT AREN'T RIGHT FOR YOU.

Choosing the right extreme sport is often a process of elimination. If you don't like heights, then don't choose base jumping or other sports that involve heights. If swimming isn't your cup of tea, then bodysurfing and free diving are not good choices.

It's important to know how much physical exercise you're prepared to do. If you usually run a mile from anything that involves exercise, don't try sports that involve physical effort such as free running. If you don't like using lifts because you don't feel safe, then a sport that relies on equipment such as rock climbing is a lost cause.

Other people are often required in extreme sports and you need to trust the people you're with. If you think working with other people can be a pain in the neck, choose sports like skateboarding or windsurfing that don't involve them.

Finally, there's the risk factor. All extreme sports involve an element of risk, but how much risk are you prepared to take? Remember – don't bite off more than you can chew.

Which extreme sports are left on your list? Choose the one you'd like to try. If you've crossed out all the sports, you can always try extreme ironing!

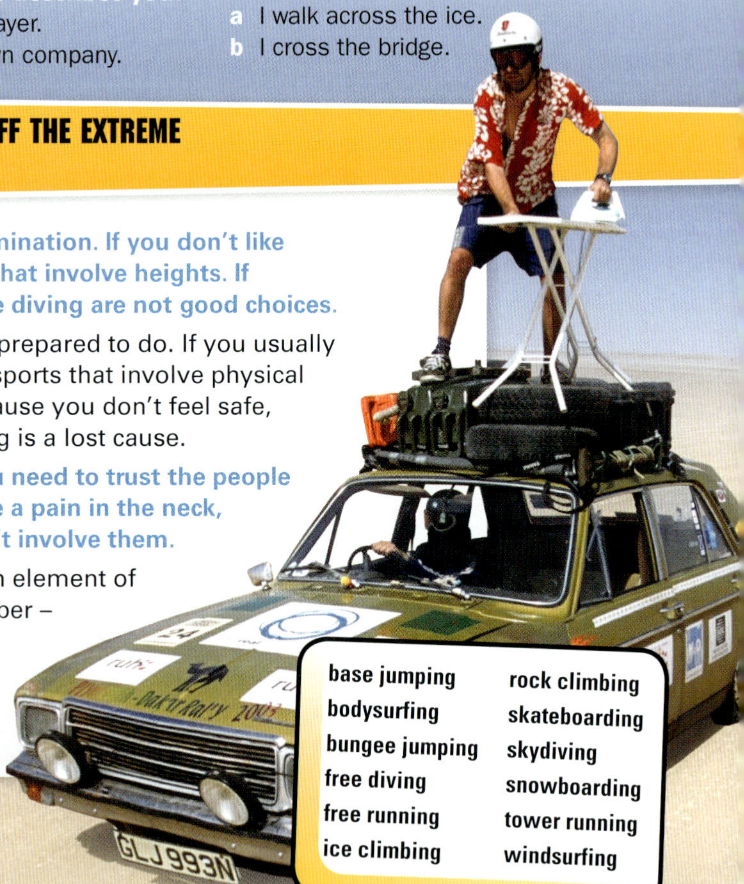

base jumping	rock climbing
bodysurfing	skateboarding
bungee jumping	skydiving
free diving	snowboarding
free running	tower running
ice climbing	windsurfing

3 a Read the tips in the HOW TO box.

b Match the idiom 'right up your street' from the introduction to the correct meaning.

a popular with other people like you
b exactly the type of thing that you are interested in or are good at

4 Find the idioms in the analysis that match the meanings (1–5).

1 something you don't like or don't find interesting (paragraph 1)
2 do everything you can to avoid (doing something) (paragraph 2)
3 something that will never succeed (paragraph 2)
4 very annoying (paragraph 3)
5 try to do something that is too hard for you (paragraph 4)

5 Which tips in the HOW TO box did you use for help with Exercises 3b and 4? Tick (✓) them.

HOW TO
recognise and understand idioms

- ☐ Look for expressions where the meaning isn't obvious.
- ☐ Look for clues before or after the idiom to help you understand.
- ☐ Think about how the image in the idiom relates to the text.

GO BEYOND

Write two more questions for the magazine feature in Exercise 2.

REACT

6 Work in pairs. Discuss the questions below with your partner.

Were you happy with the sports that were left on your list? Why?/Why not?

>>> Workbook, page 5

GRAMMAR Present tenses review

1

Talk about things happening now and things that are generally true

READ AND LISTEN

1 1.07 **Read and listen to the conversation. Who does Claire want to win and why?**

Jeff: Welcome to the final of the Wheelchair Basketball National Junior Championship at the Stoke Mandeville Stadium. Players from both teams are making final preparations and Claire Walden is sitting next to me. Wheelchair basketball is often described as a tough sport. Who do you think is the stronger team, Claire?

Claire: The Yorkshire team is playing exceptionally well these days. But the North West team always puts up a fight. My family's from Yorkshire so I want them to win.

STUDY

2 Complete the explanations with examples from Exercise 1.

Present tenses review

Present simple

Use: For habits, routines, things that are generally true.

____

Present continuous

Use (1): For things in progress now or around now

____

State verbs

Don't use the present continuous when verbs express mental states (*feel*, *know*), opinions (*believe*, ______________) and preferences (*like*, ______________).

Present simple passive

Use: When the action is more important than the person/thing that does the action.

Form: *am/is/are* + past participle

____

See GRAMMAR DATABASE, page 120.

PRACTISE

3 Choose the correct options.

These days, extreme sports (1) *become* / *are becoming* more and more popular among people with disabilities. In general, disabled athletes (2) *do* / *are doing* extreme sports for the same reasons as able-bodied people. They (3) *enjoy* / *'re enjoying* pushing the limits and they (4) *feel* / *are feeling* the same adrenaline rush. Many of the sports (5) *involve* / *are involving* the use of wheelchairs. The boy in the photo below (6) *takes* / *is taking* part in a wheelchair skateboarding event.

Workbook, pages 6–7

4 Complete the text with the present simple or present simple passive form of the verbs.

Extreme wheelchair sports (1) ___include___ (include) wheelchair basketball. The game (2) ______________ (play) on the same court as traditional basketball, the baskets (3) ______________ (place) at the same height, and players (4) ______________ (follow) the same general rules. At Paralympic™ level, a wheelchair (5) ______________ (make) for each individual player. Players (6) ______________ (strap) into the chairs which (7) ______________ (travel) at great speed and often (8) ______________ (crash) into each other.

5 1.08 **Complete the conversation with the correct form of the verbs. Then listen and check.**

Sally: (1) ___What's Jeff doing___ (what / Jeff / do)? (2) ______________ (he / play / still) basketball these days?

Layla: Yes. In fact, he's at the sports centre right now with the rest of the team. (3) ______________ (they / practise) for a match on Saturday.

Sally: (4) ______________ (he / play / usually) during the week?

Layla: No. (5) ______________ (they / only / train) on weekdays when there's a match.

Sally: (6) ______________ (he / talk / still) about the Paralympics™? (7) ______________ (I / know) that (8) ______________ (he / want / really) to go. When (9) ______________ (the teams / choose)?

Layla: The basketball team (10) ______________ (pick / normally) around now.

Sally: (11) ______________ (how / you / feel) about it?

Layla: (12) ______________ (I / think) it's exciting.

SPEAK

6 Work in pairs. Answer the questions in your own words.

1 Why do you think some Paralympic™ sports are often called extreme sports?
2 In what ways do you think wheelchair basketball is more exciting than traditional basketball?
3 What specific problems are faced by blind football players and how do you think they overcome them?
4 Do you know of any Paralympic athletes in your country? Who are they? What sports do they play?

LISTENING AND VOCABULARY I did it!

Take notes

SPEAK AND LISTEN

1 You're going to listen to a radio programme about the teenage boy in the photo. Work in pairs. Answer the questions.

1 Where do you think the photo was taken?
2 What information would you expect to hear in the programme?

2 a Read the tips in the HOW TO box.

b 1.09 Listen and take notes about Jordan Romero, the boy in the photo. Who is he? What was his dream?

c 1.09 Listen again and complete your notes. Then compare in pairs.

3 Which tips in the HOW TO box did you use for help with Exercises 2b and 2c? Tick (✓) them.

HOW TO

take notes

- ☐ Focus on the most important or interesting points.
- ☐ Write down key words or very short sentences.
- ☐ Use bullet points, abbreviations and symbols (*ie* = in other words, → = leads to, *eg* = for example).
- ☐ Leave space between lines to add more detail later.

REACT

4 Work in pairs. Answer the question from the radio programme.

How prepared is a teenager both physically and mentally to attempt to do something like Jordan did?

WORK WITH WORDS

5 1.10 Complete the achievements and challenges collocations with the verbs in the box. Then listen and check.

~~achieved~~ attempting encounter face fulfil overcome reached risk take up took

1 Jordan Romero *achieved* his dream while he was still a teenager.
2 He ______ the top of some of the world's highest mountains.
3 Some critics say it's wrong for young people to ______ their lives in this way.
4 But according to Jordan, he was successful because he never ______ risks.
5 It's normal to ______ problems when you're ______ a difficult task.
6 You might have to ______ your fears, but with the right people to help you, you'll be able to ______ obstacles blocking your way.
7 In recent years, Jordan's helped other young people ______ their potential.
8 He's encouraged them to ______ the challenge to find their own 'Everest'.

6 1.11 Complete the table with the words in the box. Then listen and check.

1 **achieve**	a dream	an ambition	
2 **attempt**	a difficult task		
3 **encounter**	a problem	difficulties	
4 **face**	your fears	a challenge	difficulties
5 **fulfil**	your potential		an ambition
6 **overcome**	obstacles	difficulties	
7 **reach**		the summit	your goal
8 **risk**	everything		
9 **take**		a chance	
10 **take up**	a challenge		an invitation

a dream
a risk
an offer
fame
problems
the top
to do something
your life

7 Work in pairs. Answer the questions.

1 What happens when someone fulfils all their dreams and ambitions by the age of 15?
2 What dream or ambition would you like to achieve?
3 Are you prepared to risk everything to reach your goal?

GO BEYOND

Do the Words & Beyond exercise on page 130.

Workbook, page 8–9

GRAMMAR Past tenses review

Talk about past achievements

READ

1 Read the report. Did Abby achieve her goal?

In 2009, Abby Sunderland was living a normal life in Thousand Oaks, California. Then, on February 6, 2010, at the age of 16, she left home and attempted to become the youngest person to sail solo around the world. Her brother, Zac, had already circumnavigated the globe the previous year. However, on June 10, while she was sailing in high winds about 3,200 kilometres west of Australia, she lost contact with the outside world. A rescue mission was launched and the following day she was found. Abby was alive and well when she was rescued, but her record-breaking attempt had ended.

STUDY

2 Read the explanations. Then underline an example of each tense in Exercise 1.

Past tenses review
Past simple
Use: For completed actions in the past.
Form: verb + *-ed*
Past continuous
Use: For actions in progress in the past.
Form: *was/were* + verb + *-ing*
Past perfect simple
Use: To show that an action happened before another action or time in the past. Use the past simple for the other action/time.
Form: *had/hadn't* + past participle
Past simple passive
Use: When the action is more important than the person/thing that did the action.
Form: *was/were* + past participle

See GRAMMAR DATABASE, page 120.

PRACTISE

3 a Write questions about the news report using the past simple, past continuous and past perfect simple.

1 What kind of life / Abby Sunderland / lead / in 2009?
What kind of life was Abby Sunderland leading in 2009?
2 How old / she / be / when she start / her voyage?
3 What / she / attempt / to do?
4 What / her brother / do / the previous year?
5 What happen / while / she / sail / 3,200 kilometres west of Australia?
6 How long / it / take / the rescue services / to find her?

b Work in pairs. Ask and answer the questions in Exercise 3a. Refer to Exercise 1 for the answers.

4 Complete the text with the correct form of the verbs.

Two months after Abby Sunderland (1) *had been rescued* (rescue), a 15-year-old Dutch girl called Laura Dekker (2) ______ (begin) her attempt to become the youngest person to circumnavigate the globe single-handedly. Laura was born on a yacht and (3) ______ (already / sail) solo by the time she was six years old. She (4) ______ (celebrate) her 16th birthday while she (5) ______ (make) her record-breaking trip, which she (6) ______ (complete) in January 2012. When she (7) ______ (arrive) on the Caribbean island of St Maarten, she (8) ______ (meet) by members of her family and fans. She (9) ______ (try) to break the record before, when she was just 14, but the Dutch authorities (10) ______ (prevent) her from sailing because she was too young.

SPEAK

5 a You're a journalist who is going to interview a teenager who has just sailed around the world. Write six questions to ask the sailor about their childhood, the trip and their opinion of young people going on dangerous journeys.

b Work in pairs. Complete the tasks.

- One of you is a journalist. The other is a teenager who has sailed around the world.
- Ask and answer the questions in Exercise 5a. The journalist should make notes of the sailor's answers.
- Swap roles.

c The journalists report to the class.

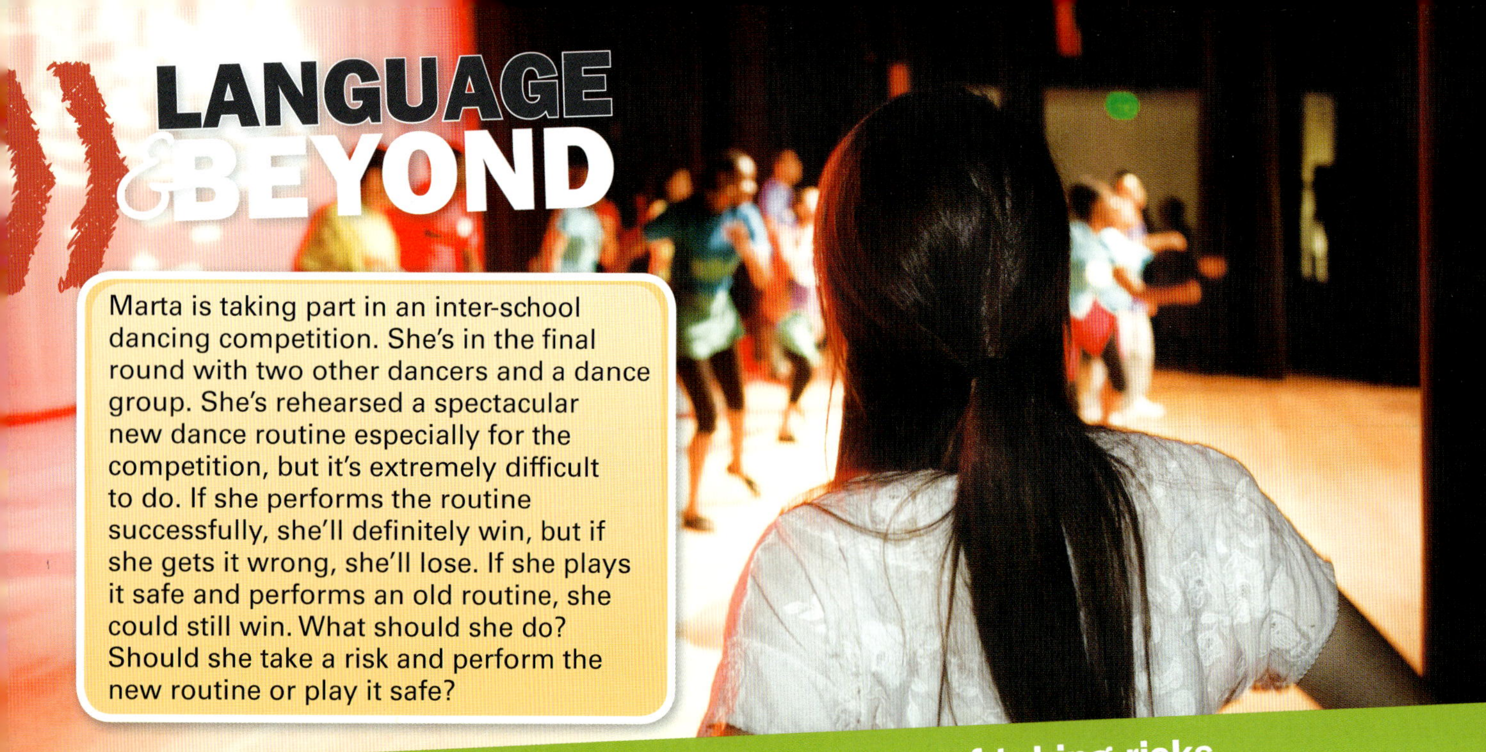

LANGUAGE & BEYOND

Marta is taking part in an inter-school dancing competition. She's in the final round with two other dancers and a dance group. She's rehearsed a spectacular new dance routine especially for the competition, but it's extremely difficult to do. If she performs the routine successfully, she'll definitely win, but if she gets it wrong, she'll lose. If she plays it safe and performs an old routine, she could still win. What should she do? Should she take a risk and perform the new routine or play it safe?

>>> Consider the positive and negative aspects of taking risks

KNOW YOURSELF

SPEAK AND READ

1 Work in pairs. Read about Marta and answer the questions.

1 What do you think Marta should do? Why?
2 Which of these quotes do you agree with? Explain why.
'If you don't take risks, you will never accomplish anything.'
'Taking risks is the quickest way to failure.'

DO

2 Work in groups. Look at the situations and discuss these questions.

- What are the risks in each one?
- Are the risks worth taking? Why?/Why not?

1 You want to walk home through a part of town that you don't know.
2 Your best friend asks to borrow some money.
3 Your teacher asks you to act in the school play.
4 You didn't do your homework, but a classmate says you can copy theirs.
5 A friend asks you to go bungee jumping with them.
6 You want to share a secret with a friend.
7 You have to visit a friend one night, but your bicycle lights aren't working.
8 You want to tell someone that you like them.

3 a People take risks for different reasons. Find an example for each of these reasons in Exercise 2.

a for a thrill
b because there's no alternative
c to achieve an ambition or improve their life
d to save time and effort

b Think of other situations for each of the reasons in Exercise 3a.

REFLECT

4 Discuss the questions with your class. Do you agree with the REFLECTION POINT?

1 In which situations can it be positive/negative to take risks?
2 Why do many people avoid taking risks?
3 Is it possible to achieve your ambitions without taking any risks?

> **REFLECTION POINT**
> Taking risks is necessary if you want to achieve things. However, before taking a risk, always think about the possible consequences to be sure that it's worth taking.

EXTEND

5 Work in groups. Write a short questionnaire about taking risks.

A friend asks you to go ballroom dancing with them. Do you …
a) take a risk and agree to go? *b) make an excuse?*

>>> Workbook, page 13

SPEAKING At the sports centre

1

Start and change topics in a conversation

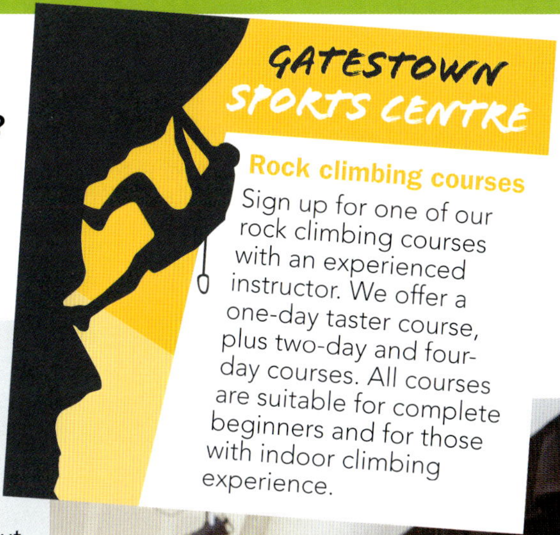

SPEAK

1 **Work in pairs. Read the notice. How many courses are there?**

WATCH OR LISTEN

2 1.12 **Watch or listen to the scene. Who's Nora and which course does Tom decide to do?**

Nora: Hi. (1) ______ rock climbing?
Tom: Yes. I mean, I'm thinking of doing a course.
Nora: (2) ______ members of the sports centre get a discount?
Tom: No, I didn't. But how do I decide which course to choose?
Nora: If you don't have any experience, you could try the one-day taster. You do some basic climbing and learn something about using ropes.
Tom: (3) ______ , do I need to buy any equipment?
Nora: No, the price includes all the climbing equipment and the instruction.
Tom: Right. (4) ______ , how much does it cost?
Nora: The one-day course is £90, but with the 20% discount it's £72.
Tom: OK. Sounds good. So what do I have to do?
Nora: Choose your dates and fill out a registration form. (5) ______ ! Is that the time? I'm sorry, but I have to go. Nice talking to you.
Tom: Thanks for your help. (6) ______ , what's the instructor like?
Nora: You're looking at her. See you on the course!

3 **Order the topics Tom and Nora talk about.**

___	equipment	*1*	rock climbing
___	member discounts	___	the instructor
___	prices	___	the time

4 a 1.12 **Watch or listen again and write phrases 1–6 in Exercise 2.**

b 1.13 **Listen and repeat the phrases, paying attention to intonation.**

5 **Write the phrases from the PHRASEBOOK in the sentences.**

1 ______ music?
2 ______ there's a concert on Saturday?
3 ______ I mustn't forget to buy tickets.
4 ______ tickets. Have you got your bus ticket?
5 ______ thanks for waiting for me. I'm sorry I was late.
6 ______ The bus is leaving. We've missed it!

6 **Write the phrases in the PHRASEBOOK that Tom and Nora use for ending the conversation.**

7 **Work in pairs. Practise saying the conversation.**

PHRASEBOOK 1.14

Starting a new topic
Are you interested in ... ?
Oh, look!
Did you know that ... ?

Changing the topic
That reminds me ...
Talking of ...
By the way, ...

Ending the conversation
______
______
______

ACT

8 **Work in pairs. Complete the tasks.**

- Write a notice for another extreme sport.
- Prepare a conversation between a student and an instructor. Use phrases from the lesson and information for your sport.
- Perform your conversation.

Workbook, page 11

WRITING History of a sport

Edit and proofread a text

SPEAK AND READ

1 Work in pairs. Look at the photos and answer the questions.

1 When do you think skateboarding started as a sport?
2 How do you think it started?
3 When do you think it first became popular?

2 Order the paragraphs in the article and check your answers to Exercise 1.

a Another famous name is Alan Gelfand who created the 'ollie', the first trick people learn when skateboarding. ☐

b The first skateboarding competition was held in 1963, but it wasn't until the 1970s that the sport became popular. ☐

c Today, skateboarding is extremely popular, but it can also be dangerous. At one point, the use and sale of skateboards were banned in Norway! ☐

d Most people say skateboarding started in California, USA, in the 1950s, when surfing was popular. The surfers wanted to find a way to surf on the pavement after they came out of the water. 1

e This popularity was largely due to the Z-Boys, a group of surfers from a poor area of Los Angeles. They used the sides of empty swimming pools to skateboard and the sport became faster and more exciting. ☐

STUDY

3 Tick (✓) the information that is included in the article.

1 When and where the sport started ☐
2 How it became popular ☐
3 Names associated with the sport ☐
4 An interesting or unusual fact ☐
5 Information about the sport today ☐

4 a Read the tips in the HOW TO box.

HOW TO

edit and proofread a text

- Check the length and structure of your work. Cut everything that isn't necessary.
- Check your spelling, punctuation and use of grammar especially.
- Then carefully read your work a final time to check that it makes sense. Or ask someone else to read it.

b Reduce the length of the article in Exercise 2 by removing one paragraph. Try not to affect the overall meaning of the article.

PRACTISE

5 Check and correct any spelling, punctuation or grammar mistakes in this paragraph.

The Z-Boys became the more successful and original skateboarders of all time and helped making skateboard popular around the world. They took their name from a shop called Jeff Ho Surfboards and Zephyr Productions who sold surfboards and skateboards. The story of the Z-Boys was said in the 2005 film *Lords of Dogtown*, which starred Heath Ledger.

6 Select the most important information from the paragraph in Exercise 5 and rewrite it using a maximum of 35 words.

PLAN, WRITE AND CHECK

7 You're going to write an article about the history of a sport using a maximum of 130 words. Do some research and choose a sport that has an interesting history. Use Exercise 3 to help you plan your article.

8 Write your article. Then check it using the checklist in the HOW TO box.

SHARE AND REVIEW

9 Swap your article with a partner. Read your partner's article and review it.

Workbook, page 12–13

VOCABULARY Extreme sports

1 Complete the names of the extreme sports with the words on the right.

TO THE EXTREME
The ultimate event for extreme sports fans
Coming soon to a city near you!

1 rock ....
2 free ....
3 snow ....
4 tower ....
5 bungee ....
6 wind ....
7 sky ....
8 ice ....
9 skate ....
10 free ....
11 base ....
12 body ....

DIVING
CLIMBING
BOARDING
JUMPING
RUNNING
SURFING

___ /12

Achievements and challenges

2 Complete Fred's introduction with the words in the box.

challenge fame invitation life obstacle potential problems risks something summit

'Hi! My name is Fearless Fred, and I want to help you fulfil your (1) .... At *To The Extreme* you don't just *watch* extreme sports, you *take part* in them. Of course, it's dangerous. But in life we all have to take (2) .... Every day, we encounter (3) .... and look for ways to overcome each new (4) .... that is put in our path. Here's your chance to attempt to do (5) .... challenging that's exciting at the same time. I'm not asking you to risk your (6) .... And if you face this (7) .... , then you could reach the (8) .... of the extreme sports mountain. I hope you'll take up this (9) .... and come to *To The Extreme*! Who knows – maybe you'll *even* achieve (10) ....'

___ /10

GRAMMAR Present tenses review

3 Complete the information with the present simple, present continuous or present simple passive.

HOW TO TAKE PART

(1) .... (you / think) about taking part in *To The Extreme*? If you're interested, you (2) .... (need) to complete the form on the website. If you're under the age of 18, make sure the form (3) .... (sign) by your parent or guardian. Please note that all the rides and equipment (4) .... (test) before each event. Trained doctors and nurses (5) .... (always / attend) the events in case of emergency. *To The Extreme* (6) .... (currently / tour) the world and places are limited. What (7) .... (you / wait) for? Contact us now!

___ /14

Past tenses review

4 Complete the facts with the past simple, past continuous, past simple passive or past perfect of the verbs in the box.

achieve have live organise skydive win work

TO THE EXTREME FACTS

1 The first *To The Extreme* event .... in Mexico in 2010.

2 Fearless Fred .... the idea for the event while he .... over New Zealand.

3 At the first event, Fred .... all the competitions and .... his goal of becoming Extreme Sportsperson of the Year.

4 Before becoming interested in extreme sports, Fred .... as a firefighter. In a recent interview he said that he .... with danger all his life.

___ /14

Your score: ___ /50

SKILLS CHECK

✓✓✓ Yes, I can. No problem!
✓✓ Yes, I can. But I need a bit of help.
✓ Yes, I can. But I need a lot of help.

I can recognise and understand idioms when I read. ....
I can take notes when I listen. ....
I can consider the positive and negative aspects of taking risks. ....
I can start and change topics in a conversation. ....
I can edit and proofread a text. ....

Workbook, page 14–15

UNIT 2

DIGITAL FOOTPRINTS!

IN THE PICTURE Digital devices

Talk about using digital devices

RECALL AND READ

1 **Work in pairs. Look at the photos and describe what you can see. What do you think is the connection between the photos?**

2 **Read the blog and check your prediction in Exercise 1. Why does the blogger say that we're 'never anonymous'?**

THE DIGITAL LONDON BLOG HOME BLOG

New post Comments (2)

When you connect to the virtual world to browse websites or upload personal information, you feel anonymous. But your computer or mobile device has a unique identity number that makes you visible wherever you go online.

In the real world, you're never anonymous either. Your phone and apps such as maps are constantly tracking where you are and giving away your location. The same is true when you swipe your travel card to take the Underground, or use your bank card at a cashpoint.

But even if you turn off your mobile device, you're still visible. Modern HD CCTV cameras can make out your face in the crowd from close to a kilometre away. If face recognition software is used to identify you, searching the Net will then reveal your personal information.

Cameras link the real and virtual worlds. As a result, we're never out of sight.

3 **THE MOVING PICTURE** **Watch the video. Who's Big Brother, and why does the speaker think Big Brother is here?**

4 **Work in pairs. Add words from the blog in Exercise 2 to the network. Then add more words you know.**

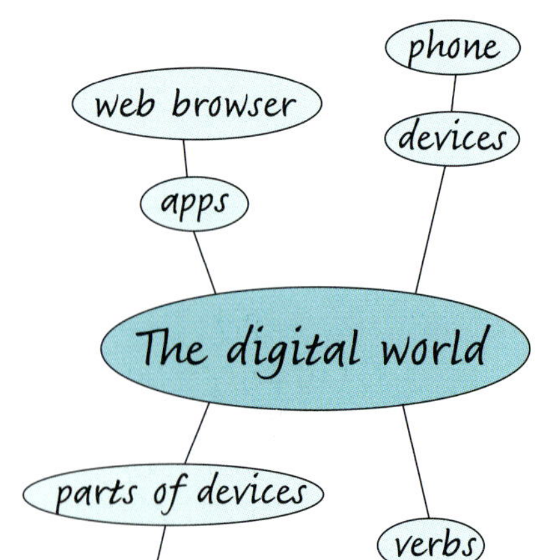

WORK WITH WORDS

5 **Match the verbs and their opposites in the box to the definitions.**

back up download/upload log on/out
swipe ~~turn on/off~~ turn up/down

1 *turn on* : press a button to make a device start working
Opposite: *turn off*
2 .... : move information from the internet to a digital device
Opposite: ....
3 .... : increase the volume of a device
Opposite: ....
4 .... : access a computer system using a username and password
Opposite: ....
5 .... : make a copy of information on a digital device
6 .... : pass a card over an electronic reader, or move your finger across a touch screen

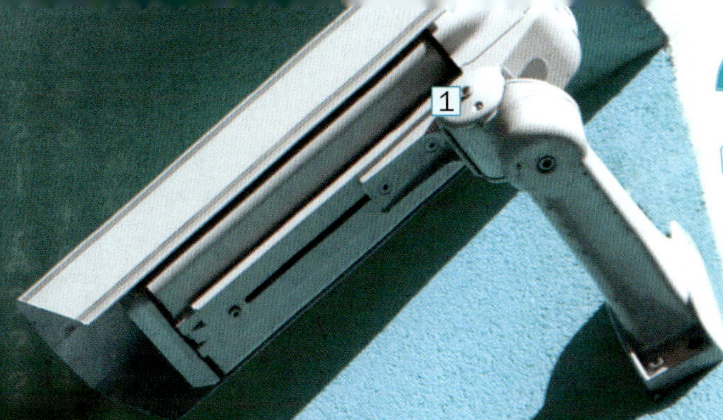

6 Complete the tips in *How to avoid digital dangers* with the verbs.

click enter scan set up tap update

7 a 1.15 PRONOUNCE **Listen and repeat the words, paying attention to the /k/ and /g/ sounds.**

back /bæk/ log /lɒg/

b 1.16 **Listen and circle the words you hear. Then listen and repeat the words.**

1 log / lock
2 bag / back
3 cap / gap
4 could / good
5 block / blog
6 class / glass

8 1.17 **Listen and repeat all the verbs in Exercises 5 and 6.**

EXTEND

9 Complete the answer with verbs from Exercise 6.

What's a phrasal verb?
It's a verb + an adverb or preposition.
If it needs an object, it's 'transitive': *turn on/off* ***a computer****, turn up/down* ***the volume****, ______ your information, ______* ***an account***
If it doesn't need an object, it's 'intransitive': ______ *when you start/finish*
Use a dictionary to check if a phrasal verb is transitive (T) or intransitive (I).

SPEAK

10 Work in pairs. Do one or both of the tasks.

A Take it in turns to explain how to use a digital device to send a message or update your profile page. Your partner should ask questions.
B Discuss the blog post in Exercise 2. Are you worried about the way that digital devices, cameras, etc can track your movements? Why?/Why not?

How to avoid digital dangers

- Install antivirus software on your digital devices. (1) ______ the program regularly to have the latest version, and (2) ______ your device regularly to check for viruses and spyware.
- When you (3) ______ an online account, use a password that other people can't guess. Don't use the 'save password' option when you (4) ______ your password to **log on** at the start of an online session, and always **log out** when you finish.
- If you see a link in an email to an attachment or website, never (5) ______ on it (if you have a touch screen) or (6) ______ on it (with a mouse) unless you are sure the other person really sent it to you.
- Regularly **back up** all the information on your devices in case you lose it.

GO BEYOND

Do the Words & Beyond exercise on page 131.

»» Recognise main ideas and supporting points

SPEAK AND READ

1 Work in pairs. Look at the title of the magazine article and answer the questions. (You will look at your answers again in Exercise 6.)

1. Are you for or against internet privacy? (You don't need to agree.)
2. What arguments are there for and against internet privacy? Make a list.

2 (1.18) **Quickly read the article to find out who's for and who's against internet privacy.**

THE DIGITAL DEBATE INTERNET PRIVACY: ARE YOU FOR OR AGAINST?

The case, by Jirka M

If you're reading this, you're probably worried about online privacy. After all, many of the things you've heard are scary. Your favourite sites *do* track your browsing habits, even when you log out. And some have sold information about you to companies that want to sell their products to you.

But I would argue that makes browsing a better experience. Because your web browser knows your habits, it can show the search results that you really want to see. And while you're online, you only see ads for products that really interest you.

More importantly, perhaps, it also explains why the internet has remained free. If internet companies couldn't sell information and advertising space, they would have to charge for using their sites. If they did that, fewer people would use them, and your social network would suddenly be much smaller. Isn't losing some of your privacy a small price to pay for a free internet?

The case, by Maria B

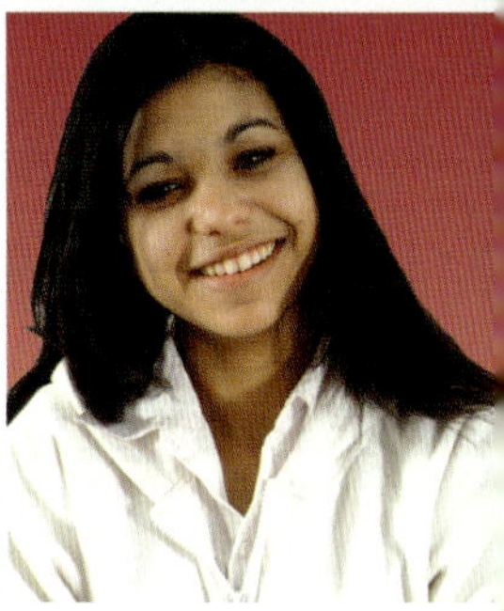

Before I make my case, let me say that I'm not against the internet. On the contrary, I love using the Net and think it's probably the greatest gift that technology has ever given us. But I think the issue of privacy gives it a dark side too.

For example, somewhere on the Net there's a record of every site you've ever visited, and of every email or message you've sent since you first went online. And the sites you use to search for information and stay in touch with your friends collect and keep information about your online habits. All this information is collected and stored without our permission, and that's unacceptable.

It's also unacceptable that we have no way to erase the personal information that exists about us on the Net. And that's scary, because if the information gets into the wrong hands, it could be used to rob us. Somebody could also use it to commit a crime in our name.

3 a Read the tips in the HOW TO box.

b Work in pairs. Each choose a different opinion in the article and make notes under the headings below.

Topic & writer's opinion
First main idea & supporting points
Second main idea & supporting points

c Tell your partner what the main ideas and supporting points are in the opinion you read.

4 Read the other opinion in the article. Are there any points your partner didn't mention?

5 Which tips in the HOW TO box did you use for help with Exercises 3b and 4? Tick (✓) them.

HOW TO

recognise main ideas and supporting points

- ☐ Identify the writer's opinion. Look in the introduction or next paragraph.
- ☐ Look for one main idea in each paragraph. This is usually in the first or last sentence.
- ☐ Look for supporting points (examples, statistics, etc) that show why a main idea is correct.

GO BEYOND

Think of another argument for or against internet privacy. Write a short paragraph with a sentence that summarises your argument plus one or more supporting points.

REACT

6 Work in pairs. Answer the questions.

1. Which arguments on your list from Exercise 1 are mentioned in the article? Which ones aren't on your list?
2. Has your opinion about internet privacy changed after reading the magazine article? Why?/Why not?

»» Workbook, page 17

GRAMMAR Present perfect simple

››› Connect past actions with the present

READAS

1 Read the messages. Who feels more positive about the video, Gerry or Simone?

STUDY

2 Complete the explanations with examples from Exercise 1.

Present perfect simple

Form:
have/has + past participle

Use: (1)
For past actions when we don't know the exact time or it isn't important:
Have you seen the video Dom's uploaded?

Use: (2): with *ever* and *never*
For experiences in your life:
……………………………

Use *ever* with a superlative adjective and to emphasise how good or bad something is:
……………………………

Use: (3): with *just*, *yet* and *already*
For recent actions: ……………………………

Use: (4): with *for* and *since*
For actions that started in the past and continue to now: ……………………………
for + periods of time
since + dates, points in time

See GRAMMAR DATABASE, page 121.

PRACTISE

3 1.19 Choose the correct options to complete the conversation. Then listen and check.

Kim: I (1) *haven't seen* / *didn't see* that phone before. How long (2) *do you have* / *have you had* it?
Carol: (3) *For* / *Since* about a month now. (4) *I've got* / *I got* it for my birthday.
Kim: Is your internet connection working?
Carol: I don't know. I (5) *haven't been* / *didn't go* online yet. Why do you ask?
Kim: Well, apparently (6) *Dom's posted* / *Dom posted* a really funny video on his page at the weekend. Everyone else (7) *has already watched* / *already watched* it, but I can't get online. So I was wondering if I could try with your phone.
Carol: OK, let's look together. I (8) *'ve never seen* / *never saw* Dom's page.

4 Write complete sentences using the present perfect simple and *for* or *since* if necessary.

1 I / never / write / a letter
I've never written a letter.
2 My house / have / an internet connection / I was born
3 I / already / update / my profile page today
4 Someone / just / send / me a message
5 I / not download / many videos from the Net
6 I / have / my phone / more than a year
7 Our computer at home / never / have / a virus
8 I / not use / a mouse many times

5 Complete the questions for the sentences in Exercise 4.

1 Have *you ever written a letter*?
2 How long … ?
3 Have … ?
4 Has … ?
5 How many … ?
6 How long … ?
7 Has … ?
8 How many … ?

SPEAK

6 Work in pairs. Ask and answer the questions in Exercise 5. For each question, ask at least one other question to get more information. (Remember to use the past simple if you ask for or give details about something in the past.)

Have you ever written a letter?
Yes, I have.
When?
About three months ago.
Who did you write to?
My grandmother. I wanted to say thank you for my birthday present.

››› Workbook, pages 18–19

LISTENING AND VOCABULARY Record. Stop. Play.

»» Use the audio type, grammar and pronunciation to help you understand

SPEAK AND LISTEN

1 Work in pairs. Make a list of the different types of talking you hear during a typical day.

A teacher talking to a class.
A TV presenter reading the news.

2 a Read the tips in the HOW TO box.

b 1.20 Listen to the recording and answer the questions.

1 What type or types of audio do you hear?
2 Where are the people? Make a list.
3 Who made the recording? How?

3 1.21 Listen to the eight conversations and choose the best answer (A or B) for each conversation.

1 Matt's late for breakfast because he was ...
A doing homework. **B** playing with his phone.
2 Matt's ... late.
A always **B** sometimes
3 Lucy's annoyed about the ... of the maths homework.
A quantity **B** difficulty
4 The people on the Underground ...
A have missed a meeting. **B** think it's too expensive.
5 The man's annoyed because ...
A he's lost. **B** his train's late.
6 Lucy ... that the teacher doesn't believe Matt's excuses.
A is surprised **B** isn't surprised
7 Matt ... the Underground as an excuse for being late before.
A has used **B** hasn't used
8 Lucy's angry because what Matt did ...
A didn't respect her privacy. **B** was illegal.

HOW TO

use the audio type, grammar and pronunciation to help you understand

- ☐ Identify the type of audio (a conversation, a talk, the news, etc).
- ☐ Listen for verbs. Are people talking about the past, present or future?
- ☐ Listen for stressed words. They communicate the meaning.
- ☐ Listen for big changes in intonation. They show strong feelings.

4 Which tips in the HOW TO box helped you with Exercises 2b and 3? Tick (✓) them.

REACT

5 Work in pairs. Has Matt done something wrong? Discuss why/why not.

WORK WITH WORDS

6 Look at the negative adjectives in the box and complete the explanation.

To form negative adjectives, the most common prefixes are ____ and ***in-***. The prefix ***in-*** changes to:

- ***im-*** before words beginning with *m* or ____ .
- ***il-*** before words beginning with ____ .
- ***ir-*** before words beginning with ____ .

illegal	illogical	immoral	impatient
incapable	irrelevant	irresponsible	unaware
unfair	unlikely	unusual	unwell

7 1.21 Complete the sentences with adjectives from the box in Exercise 6. Listen to Matt's recording again if necessary.

1 Matt's mum thinks he looks ________ , but really he's just tired.
2 Lucy thinks Matt's ________ of being on time.
3 Lucy doesn't get angry with Matt because she isn't ________ .
4 The passenger says she's ________ to get to her meeting on time.
5 Matt thinks his teacher's ________ for never believing him.
6 The teacher thinks Matt's ________ because he's always late.
7 When Matt records people they're ________ that he's doing it.
8 Lucy thinks it's ________ to record people without permission.

8 Write true sentences using five adjectives from Exercise 6. Then compare your sentences in pairs. Are any the same or similar?

It's been illegal to smoke in public places in my country since 2011.

GO BEYOND

Do the Words & Beyond exercise on page 131.

»» Workbook, pages 20–21

GRAMMAR Present perfect continuous

Talk about activities in progress before or until now

READ AND LISTEN

1 (1.22) **Read and listen to the conversation. Where's Jason? What does Talia help him to do?**

Talia: I've been waiting at the gate for 20 minutes.
Jason: I'm really sorry. I've been doing the geography project all afternoon.
Talia: I've known you for years, and I've never seen you spend so long in the library!
Jason: It's a lot of work.
Talia: I've done my project. Do you need some help?
Jason: Yes and no. I've found a lot of information, but I've lost it all.
Talia: Hang on, I'm coming. … Let me have a look. … You've been saving it in somebody else's folder. That's why you can't find it.

STUDY

2 Read the explanations. Then underline examples of the different uses of the present perfect continuous in Exercise 1.

Present perfect continuous
Use (1): With *for/since* for actions that started in the past and continue to now.
Use (2): For actions in progress recently.
Time expressions: *all afternoon/week*, *recently*, *lately*, etc
Form: *have/has* + *been* + verb + *-ing*

3 Choose the correct options to complete the explanations.

Present perfect simple or continuous?
Use the ***simple*** / ***continuous*** form to emphasise how long or difficult an action has been: *I've been doing the geography project all afternoon.*
Use the ***simple*** / ***continuous*** form to emphasise the result of an action, especially to say *how much* or *how many* (times): *I've done the geography project.* *I've found enough information.*
The simple and continuous forms with *for* and *since* often have a similar meaning: *I've been living here for about five years.* *I've lived here for about five years.* See GRAMMAR DATABASE, page 121.

PRACTISE

4 (1.23) **Complete the conversations with the present perfect continuous form of the verbs and/or *for* or *since*. Then listen and check.**

1 **Pepe:** Hey Jules. I (1) *'ve been trying out* (try out) that new app you created. It's amazing!
Jules: I'm glad you like it. (2) __________ (it / work) OK?

2 **Cole:** You see that man over there? He (3) __________ (stand) there (4) __________ over an hour.
Sheila: I know. And he (5) __________ (take) photos of the house. Who do you think he is?

3 **Dad:** The computer's got a virus. (6) __________ (you two / download) games again?
Liam: No, we haven't. In fact, we (7) __________ (not use) it at all recently.

4 **Helen:** How long (8) __________ (you / learn) to play the guitar?
Joe: Only (9) __________ my birthday. So I (10) __________ (not play) very long.

5 (1.24) **Choose the correct options to complete the conversation. Choose the continuous form if possible. Then listen and check.**

Henk: Trisha! I haven't (1) *seen* / *been seeing* you for ages!
Trisha: I've (2) *studied* / *been studying* a lot. I've got some important exams this week.
Henk: Have they (3) *gone* / *been going* well?
Trisha: I've (4) *done* / *been doing* three already, and I think they went well. But, obviously, I haven't (5) *had* / *been having* any results yet.
Henk: Well, you're looking very well.
Trisha: Thanks. I've (6) *slept* / *been sleeping* well because I haven't (7) *left* / *been leaving* all my revision to the last minute this year. What have you (8) *done* / *been doing* since I last saw you?
Henk: Not much really. The usual – studying, playing basketball, going out.
Trisha: Well, let's try and meet up soon to catch up.

SPEAK

6 a Complete the notes with information about you.

- Recent activities:
- Recent schoolwork:
- Your favourite hobby:
- When you moved into your house:
- When you started learning English:

b Work in pairs. Ask each other questions in the present perfect continuous about the information in Exercise 6a.

What have you been doing recently?

How long have you been … ?

LANGUAGE & BEYOND

››› Deal with peer pressure

GET THINKING

SPEAK AND READ

1 Work in pairs. Read the definitions of *peer group* and *peer pressure*. Then answer the questions about you and your peer group.

1 What fashions do you follow (clothes, haircut, bags, etc)?
2 What do you do when you're together? What do you talk about?
3 Which famous people influence your appearance and behaviour?

peer group
NOUN [COUNTABLE]
a group of people of about the same age
peer pressure
NOUN [UNCOUNTABLE]
the influence that other people of your own age have on the way you behave or dress

2 Read the comments (A–H). Then write the letters in the table to show what they're about and who would say them – a parent, a peer or both.

Topic	Appearance	Social networking	Studying
Parent			
Peer			

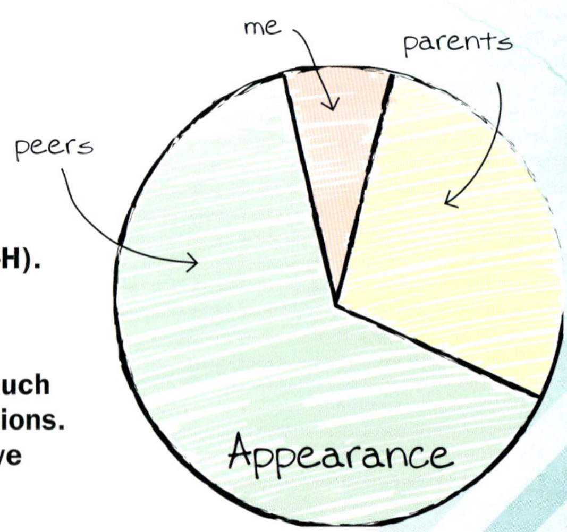

DO

3 Work in pairs. Answer the questions about the comments (A–H).

1 Do *your* parents and friends say these things? Give examples.
2 What would happen if you followed the idea in each comment?

4 For the topics in Exercise 2, make a pie chart to show how much influence you, your peers and your parents have on your decisions. Then work in pairs. Discuss which areas *you* would like to have more influence over, and why.

REFLECT

5 Discuss the questions with your class. Do you agree with the REFLECTION POINT?

1 Who has the biggest influence on your decisions?
2 Who best understands the consequences of your decisions? Why?
3 Why can it be so difficult to ignore peer pressure?

REFLECTION POINT
It's important to understand the influence of peer pressure on your decisions. Being aware of peer pressure and its consequences will help you make decisions that are right for you.

EXTEND

6 Work in pairs. Discuss what your peers and parents think about the music you listen to, your free-time activities and your behaviour. What do *you* think about these things?

››› Workbook, page 25

SPEAKING Be very careful

Give warnings and prohibitions

SPEAK

1 Work in pairs. Look at the signs (1–6) and answer the questions.

1 Which are warnings (things you shouldn't do because of possible danger), and which are prohibitions (things you mustn't do)?
2 Where would you see them and what do they mean?

1

2

3

4

5

6

WATCH OR LISTEN

2 1.25 Watch or listen to four scenes and answer the question about each one.

What's the situation and what warnings/prohibitions are expressed?

3 1.25 Watch or listen again and write one word in each gap.

1 **Luis:** Are you sure you trust that site? I'd (1) ______ out if I were you.
Ava: Why? I'm only downloading a game.
Luis: You might download a virus too if you're not (2) ______ .
Ava: Do you really think so?

2 **Guard:** I'm sorry, you can't go in there.
Ellie: I just want an autograph.
Guard: I'm sorry, you're not (3) ______ to go backstage.
Ellie: Can I stay here and take a photo?
Guard: No, it's (4) ______ .
Ellie: Says who?
Guard: Says me.

3 **Gran:** (5) ______ the step. You could fall and hurt yourself.
Dan: Don't worry, Gran, I'll be careful. Let's cross the road here.
Gran: (6) ______ out! There's a car coming.
Dan: It's OK, we're on a zebra crossing, it has to stop.
Gran: Better safe than sorry.

4 **Warden:** Excuse me, you mustn't sit on the grass. It's (7) ______ .
Luis: Can I just finish my sandwich?
Warden: There's also a (8) ______ on eating picnics in the park.
Luis: I've nearly finished.
Warden: If you don't get off the grass now I'll have to call the police.
Luis: OK, OK, I'm going.

4 1.26 Listen and repeat the warnings and prohibitions.

5 1.27 Match the sentence halves. Listen and check your answers. Then listen and repeat.

1	Are you sure	a	to cycle here.
2	I'd be careful	b	you could hurt someone.
3	You might fall	c	that's a good idea?
4	If you don't watch out,	d	if you're not careful.
5	You're not allowed	e	cycling in the centre.
6	There's a ban on	f	if I were you.

ACT

6 Work in pairs. Think of two situations, one in which you would hear or give a warning, the other a prohibition.

- Prepare and practise a short conversation for each situation. Include language from the PHRASEBOOK.
- Present your conversations to other students without reading them. Can they identify the situations?

PHRASEBOOK 1.28

Give prohibitions

You can't go/take ...
You're not allowed to wait/ask ...
It's prohibited/forbidden.
There's also a ban on eating/walking ...

Give warnings

Watch out! / Look out! / Be careful!
Mind the steps/gap.
Are you sure you trust that site / that's a good idea?
I'd watch out / be careful if I were you.
You might download/have ... if you're not careful.
You could fall / hurt yourself ...

Workbook, page 23

WRITING Keep in touch

Organise information in informal emails and letters

SPEAK AND READ

1 Work in pairs. Answer the questions.

1 How often do you write emails?
2 Who do you write emails to, and why do you write them?

New mail | Reply | Forward

Hi Harry,

1 How's it going? It was great to see you last weekend. We haven't been in touch much since you moved away, so it was good to catch up. I've uploaded some photos to my page, by the way.

2 The main reason I'm writing now is to ask a favour. Do you remember I told you about a game I've been developing? Well, I've finally finished it, but it needs testing. Could you try it out for me? If so, I'll tell you how to download it.

3 Apart from that, I wanted to ask about your basketball team. You said you've been training a lot lately. Have you been getting good results?

4 One last thing. I'll be in Liverpool on Saturday 28th. Would you be able to meet up that day?

5 Anyway, I must go. I've got a long day tomorrow.

Take care,

Kevin

2 Read the email and find:

1 four pieces of new information.
2 two questions that ask if Harry can do something.
3 two questions about Harry's life.

Get it right

*I told **you** about ...*
*I told **you** (that) ...*
I said ~~you~~ (that) ...

STUDY

3 Read the email again and match the paragraphs to their contents.

1	a the most important news
2	b saying goodbye
3 & 4	c your recent contact
5	d other news

4 a Read the tips in the HOW TO box.

HOW TO
organise information in informal emails and letters

- Start with an expression like *How are you?* and mention your last contact.
- Continue with expressions like *I'm writing to ...* , *Apart from that, ... One other/last thing ...* .
- Use *by the way* to introduce new information.
- Use expressions like *Do you remember ... ?* to refer back to something.
- Use *Anyway, ...* or *Well, ...* to start saying goodbye.
- End with *Best wishes*, *All the best*, etc. Use *Love* with family and close friends.

b Underline the expressions from the HOW TO box, or similar expressions, in the email.

PRACTISE

5 Put the words in order to make new expressions. Then match them to expressions or points in the HOW TO box.

1 good / It / to / from / was / you / hear .
2 long time / I / for / haven't / written / Sorry / such / a .
3 just / know / This / to / is / my new email address / you / let .
4 a blog / you / I / writing / remember / was / Do ?
5 to / you / hear / again / hope / soon / I / from .
6 soon / touch / be / I'll / in .

PLAN, WRITE AND CHECK

6 You're going to write an email to a friend in New York who you haven't written to for a long time. Look at Exercise 3 and make notes for each paragraph. You can use real or invented news.

7 Write your email. Use expressions from the HOW TO box and Exercise 5 to help you organise it. Then check it.

SHARE AND REVIEW

8 Swap your email with a partner. Read your partner's email and review it.

Workbook, pages 24–25

VOCABULARY Digital devices

1 Alan's teaching his three-year-old sister, Jess, to use a tablet. Complete his explanations with the verbs.

back up click enter log on scan set up swipe tap turn on turn up update upload

First, we need to (1) ______ the tablet, Jess. It's off now. These are icons. On a computer you (2) ______ on them with the mouse, but here, you (3) ______ on the screen and they open. Let's look at some photos. If you (4) ______ the screen with your finger, you go to the next photo. Don't worry if you delete one – I regularly (5) ______ the photos onto my computer. Now let's look at my social networking page. First, I need to (6) ______. To do that I (7) ______ a secret password. I (8) ______ my page every day with my news and I also (9) ______ photos and videos. This video's really funny. It's quiet, so let's (10) ______ the volume. Every now and then I (11) ______ the tablet for viruses. No, I can't (12) ______ a page for you, you're too young!

___ /12

Negative prefixes

2 It's ten years later. Make the adjectives negative with the prefixes *un-*, *in-*, *im-*, *ir-* and *il-*.

Alan: Are you still online? You'll make yourself (1) ___well.
Jess: I'm fine, don't worry.
Alan: That's an (2) ___usual website. Can I see? Jess, that's a government website! Get out of there now!
Jess: Don't be so (3) ___patient. I know what I'm doing. But they're (4) ___capable of protecting their sites.
Alan: That's (5) ___relevant. It's (6) ___legal to hack into a government website. Are you completely (7) ___aware of the risks? It's (8) ___responsible. It's (9) ___fair for us too. What if they catch you?
Jess: That's (10) ___likely. And you're being (11) ___logical. And I'm not doing anything (12) ___moral. Thanks to me they know how bad their online security is.

___ /12

GRAMMAR Present perfect simple

3 Complete with the present perfect simple or past simple of the verbs.

Mystery hacker strikes again

A hacker (1) ______ (**break**) into the government's website and replaced all the photos with cartoon characters. The attack (2) ______ (**happen**) on Saturday night, and investigators believe that the same person (3) ______ (**already** / **hack**) into three other official networks. During Saturday night's attack the hacker (4) ______ (**leave**) a message to say that even a child could access the website. Investigators (5) ______ (**not discover**) anything about the hacker's identity since the attacks (6) ______ (**begin**).

___ /12

Present perfect continuous

4 Complete with the present perfect continuous form of the verbs if possible. If not, use the present perfect simple.

Presenter: I understand you (1) ______ (**be**) a hacker since you were 13.
Jess: I was a hacker, but for the last two years I (2) ______ (**work**) as an ethical hacker.
Presenter: What does an ethical hacker do?
Jess: Well, it's someone who's paid to attack an organisation's computer system to reveal security problems. This week, I (3) ______ (**try**) to hack into a big bank's website, and I (4) ______ (**already** / **find**) more than 10 things they need to fix.
Presenter: How do you become an ethical hacker?
Jess: You have to take a course. I (5) ______ (**finish**) my training so I'm a qualified ethical hacker now, and I (6) ______ (**do**) some part-time teaching on the course recently.
Presenter: And is there a lot of work for ethical hackers?
Jess: Oh, yes, I (7) ______ (**not stop**) working since I qualified. I'm always busy.

___ /14

Your score: ___ /50

SKILLS CHECK

✓✓✓ Yes, I can. No problem!
✓✓ Yes, I can. But I need a bit of help.
✓ Yes, I can. But I need a lot of help.

I can recognise main ideas and supporting points when I read. ______
I can use the audio type, grammar and pronunciation to help me understand. ______
I can deal with peer pressure. ______
I can give warnings and prohibitions. ______
I can organise information in informal emails and letters. ______

Workbook, pages 26–27

READ AND COMPLETE

1 Read the website comment. Use the word in brackets to form a word that fits in each gap.

Extreme Olympic Sports

In my opinion, it's time to include more extreme sports in the summer Olympics. Extreme sports are taken more (1) __________ (SERIOUS) these days. There's the annual X Games (2) __________ (COMPETE) in the United States which includes skateboarding and surfing. And snowboarding became a winter Olympic sport in 1998. But when will the summer Olympics include base jumping, bodysurfing and rock climbing? These are (3) __________ (EXCITE) sports and they're popular with young people like me.
I understand that it's impossible to include every sport in the Olympics but I think it's (4) __________ (LOGIC) that sports such as sailing and synchronised swimming are included in the Olympics but extreme sports aren't. In my view, the time has come to give extreme sports as much (5) __________ (IMPORTANT) as traditional sports.

Reading and completing: ______ /5

EXAM TIPS

do a word formation exercise

- Read the title and first paragraph to find out what the text is about.
- Read each sentence carefully and decide what type of word is missing.
- Don't forget that the missing word might be negative, plural etc.
- Read the sentence again with your word in it. Does it make sense?

2 For questions 1–5, complete the second sentence so that it has a similar meaning to the first sentence. You must use between two and five words, including the word given. Do not change the word given.

1 I did my first parachute jump and then couldn't wait to do another.
AFTER
I couldn't wait to do another parachute jump __________ my first one.

2 You're not allowed to ski on this part of the mountain.
BAN
There's __________ skiing on this part of the mountain.

3 CCTV cameras constantly record our movements in public places.
ARE
Our movements __________ in public places by CCTV cameras.

4 I started to download this app 20 minutes ago and it still hasn't finished downloading.
HAVE
I __________ this app for 20 minutes.

5 A few minutes ago, I found out that it's illegal to post photos of people without their permission.
JUST
I __________ that it's illegal to post photos of people without their permission.

Reading and completing: ______ /5

EXAM TIPS

do sentence transformations

- Read the instructions. How many words can you use?
- Read both sentences carefully.
  - Decide what structure you need in order to use the given word.
  - Remember that you can't change the form of the given word.
- Check that the meaning is similar and your spelling is correct.
- Check that you haven't used more words than allowed. Note that contracted forms are counted in full (eg *isn't* = *is not* = two words).

recognise and understand idioms
See page 8.

recognise main ideas and supporting points
See page 18.

LISTEN

3 1.29 **You will hear five different people talking about smartphones and the internet. Choose each person's attitude from the list (A–H). There are three extra letters which you do not need to use.**

A is worried about online security issues
B doesn't feel safe without a smartphone
C is the victim of peer pressure
D often receives unwanted messages
E doesn't want to own a smartphone
F feels safe using the internet
G never clicks on links in emails
H doesn't regularly use any digital devices

Speaker 1 ......
Speaker 2 ......
Speaker 3 ......
Speaker 4 ......
Speaker 5 ......

Listening: ______ /10

WRITE

4 **You have received an email from your English-speaking friend, Sam. Read Sam's email, and then write your reply (140–190 words).**

From: Sam Wallis
Subject: Birthday plans

Hi!

How are things? What have you been doing?

I'm writing because it's my birthday next month and I've decided to go skydiving! Would you like to come? I need to know soon, so please ask if you have any questions.

I look forward to hearing your news – and your answer!

All the best,

Sam

Writing: ______ /10

Progress check score ______ /30

EXAM TIPS

do a multiple-matching exercise

- Read the task and all the options carefully.
- Concentrate on the general message when you listen the first time.
- When matching options to speakers, remember that
  - speakers won't use exactly the same words as in the options.
  - there are options that don't match to any speaker.
  - you will listen again, so make notes if you're unsure of any answers.
- Check/complete your answers when you listen again.

use the audio type, grammar and pronunciation to help you understand
See page 20.

EXAM TIPS

write an email

- Read the task. Who are you writing to? Is it a formal or informal email?
- Read the task again. Underline any questions, requests or instructions.
- Decide how to react to news or information in the task.
- Plan your email before you write.
  - Decide how many paragraphs to use.
  - Make sure your email covers all the points in the task.
- Check your work. Is it the right length?

edit and proofread a text
See page 14.

organise information in informal emails and letters
See page 24.

UNIT 3 EYEWITNESS

IN THE PICTURE Our environment

>>> Talk about natural disasters in films

RECALL AND READ

1 a Make a network about landscapes. You have three minutes. Include natural features and climate, as well as your own opinions.

b Work in pairs. Compare your networks. Tell your partner about your favourite landscape.

2 a Read Matt's list below and look at the film posters. Complete the titles of the first four films.

b Which films sound most and least interesting? Tell a partner, explaining your reasons.

Best ever disaster films: A list by Matt Weston

FILM	SUMMARY
1 .... (USA 1996)	Two teams of storm chasers are in a race to test a scientific gadget on a **tornado**.
2 .... (USA 2000)	The true story of a fishing boat crew who get caught at sea in a **hurricane**.
3 .... (China 2010)	An emotional family story about the real-life 1976 **earthquake** which destroyed Tangshan and buried thousands of people.
4 .... (USA 1997)	A **volcanic eruption** sends lava into the streets of Los Angeles.
5 *The Kid Who Lies* (Venezuela 2011)	A boy sets out to find his family ten years after heavy rain caused terrible **floods** and **landslides** in Vargas, Venezuela.
6 *Avalanche* (Canada 2004)	In the Russian mountains, two brothers try to rescue the survivors of an **avalanche** from under the snow.
7 *Firestorm: Last Stand at Yellowstone* (USA 2006)	A **drought** causes a **wildfire** to spread one hot summer in the forests of Yellowstone National Park.
8 *Haeundae* (South Korea 2009)	A huge **tsunami** is about to strike the beach of Haeundae.

3 THE MOVING PICTURE Watch Matt and Emmie's review of three films in Exercise 2. How many stars (1–5) do you think they would give each film?

3

AFTERSHOCK

WORK WITH WORDS

4 1.30 **Write the correct natural disasters from Exercise 2. Then listen and check.**

1 A .... is a large wave. (The word comes from Japanese.)
2 A .... is a fire that starts in the countryside or a forest and spreads very quickly.
3 A .... is when a volcano sends hot gas, ash and melted rock (or lava) into the air.
4 A .... is a heavy fall of earth, rocks or mud down a hill.
5 An .... is a shaking movement of the Earth.
6 An .... is a large amount of snow and ice that falls down a mountain.
7 A .... is a violent storm with strong winds and heavy rain that starts over the sea.
8 A .... is a strong wind that goes round in a circle over land.
9 A .... is a long period without rain.
10 A .... is a large amount of water that covers an area that is usually dry.

EXTEND

5 **Look at the words in the box. Decide if they are causes of natural disasters or consequences or possibly both.**

death   disease   global warming   homelessness   nuclear explosion   war

SPEAK

6 **Work in pairs. Do one or both of the tasks.**

A Tell your partner about a disaster film that you have seen.
B Discuss why people are fascinated by disaster films.

GO BEYOND

Do the Words & Beyond exercise on page 132.

Workbook, page 28

READING A new world

Recognise and understand similes

SPEAK AND READ

1 Work in pairs. Read the dictionary entry for 'dystopia' and answer the questions.

1 What's a 'utopia'? What would be 'utopia' for you?
2 What examples of dystopias and utopias do you know from novels or films? Do you enjoy reading or watching stories like this?

dystopia /dɪs'təʊpiə/
NOUN [UNCOUNTABLE]
an imaginary place or situation in which everything in society is extremely bad ≠ UTOPIA

2 1.31 Read the introduction and a short extract from the story, and answer the questions.

1 Why was Lucy alone?
2 Why did she have to camp in Central Park?
3 What was she trying to do in this extract?

3 Read the extract again. Complete the sentences in your own words. Underline the places in the text that support your answers.

1 Lucy doesn't really know where she is because …
2 Lucy encounters several problems: …
3 When Lucy is on the bridge, she feels …
4 If I had to describe Lucy's personality, I'd say …

GLOSSARY

PLAGUE: a serious disease
GORGE/RAVINE: a deep, narrow valley with high sides
CANYON: a deep valley with steep sides
PLATEAU: a flat area of land which is higher than the land around it
SPEARHEAD: the hard pointed end of a spear (a long weapon)

Ashes, Ashes by Jo Treggiari

Sixteen-year-old Lucy Holloway had been living a normal life near New York until rising sea levels and floods, hurricanes and earthquakes devastated the city. Only a few islands of land remained and some could only be reached during periods of drought. Then the plague killed 99% of the population, including Lucy's family. 'Sweepers' had started to hunt survivors, so Lucy escaped and hid in the wilds of Central Park. She had been surviving off wild animals and plants when a tsunami forced her to leave her camp and run …

Lucy estimated that she was around Second Avenue and 92nd Street, although acres of road and earth had been moved in the big earthquake; the landscape had been completely changed. It looked as if a toddler had built a city out of blocks and then knocked them all down.

She had reached a gorge that was as big as a canyon. There was no way round it. When she finally pulled herself up the last slope, she found herself on top of a plateau. Straight ahead was a deep, wide ravine and a suspension bridge. Sweat trickled down Lucy's back. It was so high. The bridge was attached to an outcrop of rock by a rope. Lucy pulled on it and then stepped onto the bridge, which moved with her weight. She crept forward, holding on to the rope with both hands. Her eyes were drawn to the ground far below. The canal was almost completely dry and sharp rocks lay on the bottom along with mounds of garbage.

Part of the bridge snapped with a sharp crack. Lucy's ankle twisted. Her foot went through the hole and the bridge swung crazily from side to side. Lucy grabbed at the ropes, burning red stripes across her hands. She closed her eyes, trying to erase the image of the rocks sticking up like spearheads at the bottom of the canal.

HOW TO recognise and understand similes

- Look for sentences which compare two things or people.
- Look for comparisons with *as … as*, *like …* and (*looked/felt/sounded*) *as if …* .
- Think about what qualities the two things share. Try and build a picture in your mind.

4 a Read the tips in the HOW TO box.

b Underline three similes in the extract. What two things are compared and what picture or message do they communicate?

c Write two or more similes of your own to describe your country's landscape, your home area or climate.

GO BEYOND

How would you feel if you were in a situation like Lucy's? Write a list of adjectives.

REACT

5 Discuss with a partner.

1 How do you think Lucy felt about surviving the plague?
2 What do you think happens to Lucy next?

Workbook, page 29

GRAMMAR Past perfect simple and past perfect continuous

»» Talk about actions before another time in the past

READ

1 Read about another dystopian novel. Complete the details about the characters.

Name	Boy/Girl	Ugly/New Pretty	Lives in
Tally	*Girl*	*Ugly*	*Uglyville*
Peris			
Shay			

My favourite book: UGLIES

Tally **had been waiting** impatiently for her 16th birthday and the government operation to make her pretty. Her best friend Peris **had already become** a New Pretty and Tally **had** only **seen** him once since he **had moved** to New Pretty Town. But then Tally met Shay, another Ugly. Shay **had heard** about an illegal community called The Smoke for people who didn't want to be pretty. She **had been trying** to decide for a long time if she should join them, and she **had just decided** to run away from Uglyville.

STUDY

2 Complete the explanations. Use the examples in bold in Exercise 1 to help you.

Past perfect simple and past perfect continuous

Use: To show that an action happened before another action or time in the past.

Form: simple
had/hadn't + past participle

Form: continuous
had/hadn't + ____________ + verb + ____________

3 Choose the correct options to complete the explanations. Use Exercise 1 to help you.

Past perfect simple or past perfect continuous?

Use the ***simple*** / ***continuous*** form for an action in progress up to a time in the past.

Use the ***simple*** / ***continuous*** form for a finished action before another past action or time.

You often use the ***simple*** / ***continuous*** form with *before*, *after*, *just*, *yet* and *already* and verbs like *thought* and *realised*.

Use the simple and the continuous forms with *for* and *since*.

See GRAMMAR DATABASE, page 122.

PRACTISE

4 Read more about *Uglies*. Decide if the verbs in bold are correct. Correct the ones that are wrong.

Tally flew to The Smoke on her hoverboard. Shay (1) **had already been going** there but the government (2) **had forced** Tally to go as a spy. The government (3) **had looked** for the illegal community for a long time. Tally (4) **hadn't been wanting** to go. But she (5) **had agreed** to find The Smoke so that she could have the operation to become pretty.

5 Complete the text about *Uglies* with the past perfect simple or the past perfect continuous.

Tally (1) ____________ (travel) for five days when she arrived in The Smoke. She (2) ____________ (plan) to send a message to the government when she got there. But then she met David, and she realised that she (3) ____________ (nearly / make) a big mistake. David's parents were doctors and they (4) ____________ (study) the effects of the operation on the brain for years. They (5) ____________ (discover) that the operation didn't only make Uglies pretty. After they (6) ____________ (have) the operation, New Pretties not only looked the same, they thought the same …

LISTEN AND WRITE

6 1.32 Listen to the dictation and find out the ending to the story. Write down everything you hear and compare your dictation with a partner. Then listen again and complete the dictation.

LISTENING AND VOCABULARY Survival stories

>>> Focus on important information

SPEAK AND LISTEN

1 a Read the headlines. What do you think the news stories are about?

OUR FIGHT IN FACE OF FLOOD

TEARS AND CHEERS AFTER AVALANCHE

HURRICANE DESTROYS HOMES BUT NOT HOPE

b In the headlines above, find examples of rhyme and 'alliteration' (the use of the same letter or sound at the beginning of words).

2 1.33 Listen to two interviews with eyewitnesses. Work in pairs. Write a headline for each one. Compare them with another pair.

3 a Read the tips in the HOW TO box.

b 1.33 You're going to write three or four sentences about each eyewitness's statement for two newspaper articles. Listen again and take notes (see page 10) on the most important information. Include one quote.

4 Which tips in the HOW TO box did you use for help with Exercise 3b? Tick (✓) them.

5 Write the information for your newspaper articles. Include your headline from Exercise 2 and your quote.

HOW TO

focus on important information

- ☐ Identify the main topic. Focus only on information that relates to it.
- ☐ Listen for information which is repeated or emphasised.
- ☐ Ignore small details and examples.
- ☐ If you quote somebody (write what somebody says), write their exact words.

REACT

6 Discuss this statement. Explain your opinions.

I think it's unacceptable that the press interview people when they have just gone through a terrible experience.

WORK WITH WORDS

7 1.34 Listen to the sounds for the noise verbs 1–12. Then listen and repeat the words.

1 **scr**eam	3 whi**sp**er	5 **gr**oan	7 **cr**ash	9 **sl**am	11 bang
2 sigh	4 yell	6 roar	8 **sm**ash	10 bur**st**	12 e**xpl**ode

8 a PRONOUNCE Look at the consonants in bold in Exercise 7. Do you find any of the consonant combinations difficult? Which ones? If so, practise saying the consonants slowly.

sssscccrrrrream

b If you leave out consonants, the meaning of the word could change. What does *crash* mean without 'r' or without 'c'?

9 a 1.35 Listen to the four situations. Match two of them to the correct scripts below.

a A bomb explodes. Windows smash and people scream.

b A car tyre bursts loudly. Then a car crashes into a tree. There's a short silence, then somebody sighs in relief.

b 1.36 Listen to the other two scenes again and write the scripts. Explain what you think happened.

GO BEYOND

Do the Words & Beyond exercise on page 132.

Workbook, pages 32–33

GRAMMAR Sense verbs + *-ing* or infinitive

>>> Talk about things that you see, hear, feel and smell

READ

1 Read the speech bubbles. Did the boy in the pictures see the accident? How did he know what had happened?

It was a normal day. I was sitting on my bed and thinking. I was watching a spider crawling across the ceiling and listening to my parents arguing about housework. I could smell something delicious cooking for dinner.

Suddenly, I heard something crash and I felt the building move a little. I looked out the window. A lorry had driven into our building! I saw the driver lying in a funny position and heard people shouting and running to help him.

STUDY

2 Read the explanations. Then underline examples of each form in Exercise 1.

Sense verbs + *-ing* or infinitive

Use: To talk about actions we see, hear, feel and smell.

Form:
For actions in progress, use:
see/watch/hear/listen to/feel/smell + object + verb + *-ing*

For completed actions, use:
see/watch/hear/listen to/feel/smell + object + infinitive without *to*

See GRAMMAR DATABASE, page 122.

>>> Workbook, page 34

PRACTISE

3 Complete the conversations with the verbs in the box.

burning	crossing	drive	fall	hit	turning

Zeynep: A lorry crashed into your building?
Dan: Yes, I didn't see it (1) ________ into the wall, but I heard it (2) ________ the building.
Zeynep: But is the driver OK? What happened?
Dan: He's in hospital, but he's fine. He hadn't seen a little boy (3) ________ the road in front of him. He was trying to avoid hitting him.

Dev: I just saw a cyclist (4) ________ off her bike.
Luna: Oh, no. What happened?
Dev: The driver didn't see her (5) ________ right. He braked really hard – I could smell the rubber on his tyres (6) ________ . Luckily, she wasn't hurt.

4 a Complete the sentences with the *-ing* or infinitive form of the verbs.

1 **Maria:** I heard the people behind me ________ (eat) crisps and ________ (whisper), so I looked at them angrily.
2 **Siji:** I closed my eyes. I heard the little train ________ (set off) down the track and then I felt my stomach ________ (turn over).
3 **Britt:** I smelled the bread ________ (bake) in the oven and felt my mouth ________ (start) to water.
4 **Jed:** I saw the orange light ________ (shine) on the water and then I saw the sun ________ (disappear).

b Where do you think the speakers are? What's happening or what are they doing?

SPEAK

5 Choose a photo. You were in one of these places yesterday – what did you hear and see happening? What did you smell and feel? What happened next?

LANGUAGE & BEYOND

a 'I bet you'll change your mind when you're older. Everybody wants kids!'

b 'Rubbish! If everybody thought that way, we wouldn't have a future at all!'

c 'I totally understand why you say that. It's frightening how many people our world has to support. But don't you think …'

d 'Really? I want lots of children, myself.'

e 'Oh, come on, they can't hurt you. They're much more frightened of you.'

f 'Yes, they are a bit creepy. Most people have a fear of something. It's important to …'

g 'Did I tell you I had a tarantula as a pet when I was small? It was huge and really hairy.'

h 'There's one. I'll kill it for you. … There, got it! No worries, now!'

Luke worries about the future of the planet when there are so many people. He says he never wants children because he doesn't know what sort of a world they'll grow up in.

Livia panics when she sees spiders, even small ones. But she never kills them because she thinks it's important to protect any form of life.

››› Understand another person's feelings

RESPECT OTHERS

READ AND SPEAK

1 Think of something that you worry about or fear.

- Close your eyes and try to visualise it in your mind. Think how you feel.
- Write down your feelings (privately – you don't need to show anyone).
- Remember these feelings when you do the next exercise.

2 a Read the descriptions of two students' fears and some reactions above. Which do you think is the most appropriate reaction?

b Finish the incomplete reactions (c and f). Compare with a partner.

DO

3 Look at the tips on the right. Find examples of the *DON'T*s above, in a-h.

4 Role-play the two situations about Luke and Livia.

- Explain your fear: your partner tries to put him/herself in your shoes and support you. Swap roles and role-play the other situation.

REFLECT

5 Discuss the questions with your class. Do you agree with the REFLECTION POINT?

1 Why do we find it hard to understand other people's worries?
2 Think of a situation when you felt a friend or relative didn't take a worry that you had seriously. How did they react and how did you feel?
3 In Exercise 4, what did you notice about your partner's body language?

EXTEND

6 Work in pairs. Discuss your worry from Exercise 1. Or talk about a worry in the future (a school test, etc).

PUT YOURSELF IN THEIR SHOES

1 Really listen to what the other person says.
2 Don't act as if their fears are something stupid or not important.
3 Try to understand what they're feeling.
4 Repeat and clarify the other person's words if necessary.
5 Don't use what the person's saying to talk about yourself.
6 Sympathise and comfort.

REFLECTION POINT

Everybody is different and has different worries and fears. We can make other people feel better by really listening to them and trying to help them.

››› Workbook, page 37

SPEAKING That's not true

Contradict facts and opinions

SPEAK

1 Do the quiz.

WHAT DO YOU KNOW ABOUT GLOBAL WARMING?

Take our mini-quiz!

1. Since 1880, average global temperatures have climbed …
   A 0.08°C. B 0.8°C. C 2.8°C.
2. The Arctic may have its first summer without ice by …
   A 2040. B 3000. C 3040.
3. If we cut emissions of all dangerous gases to zero, global warming …
   A would get worse. B would stop immediately.
   C wouldn't stop immediately.

WATCH OR LISTEN

2 1.37 Lily and Josh are checking the quiz answers. Watch or listen to the scene.

1 Check your answers from Exercise 1.
2 Do you agree with Josh's opinion about the future of our planet or with Lily's?

Lily: I have 0.08 degrees.
Josh: You're (1) ________ there. It's 0.8 degrees.
Lily: Really? That much? … What about no ice in the Arctic? I have 3000.
Josh: Well, as a (2) ________ of fact it's 2040.
Lily: Oh, but that isn't very far away! I thought the ice was melting slowly.
Josh: That's not (3) ________ at all! Temperatures in the Arctic have increased much more than anywhere else.
Lily: OK, but if we stopped putting gases into the air now, global warming would stop immediately, right?
Josh: Well, it's very (4) ________ that we could just cut all emissions. And in (5) ________ of fact, if we did do it, global warming wouldn't stop immediately. We've destroyed the planet; it's too late.
Lily: I take your (6) ________ , but there must be something we can do.

3 1.37 Watch or listen again and complete the phrases (1–6) Josh and Lily use to contradict each other (say somebody is wrong or disagree).

4 a Look at the phrases for contradicting facts.

1 Which are direct? Which are more indirect or more polite?
2 Which words make the polite phrases less direct?

b 1.38 Listen and repeat the phrases, paying attention to intonation and tone of voice.

PHRASEBOOK 1.39

Contradicting facts

That's not true (at all)
You're wrong there.
I don't think so.
I'm afraid that's not quite true.
It's very unlikely.
I'm not sure how true that is, actually.
Well, actually / as a matter of fact / in point of fact …
That's true, but …
I take your point, but …

ACT

5 a Individually, invent and write down three nonsense facts or opinions (for example, about your school, your town, your favourite team, etc).

b Work in pairs. Take it in turns to read out a fact or an opinion and to contradict your partner. Use a phrase from the PHRASEBOOK and add an explanation if possible.

Our school football team has won all its games this season.

I'm afraid that's not quite true. It's lost all its games!

I think the food in our school canteen is very healthy.

Well, actually, chips and pizza every day isn't good for you.

Workbook, page 35

WRITING It happened to me

Link ideas in a story

SPEAK AND READ

1 a Work in pairs. Look at the title of Rosie's story. This is a common English saying. What do you think it means?

b Do you have a saying with a similar meaning in your language?

2 Read Rosie's story. What bad experience did she have? How did it have 'a silver lining'?

Rosie

Every cloud has a silver lining

I was sitting in the dentist's chair and I wasn't feeling too happy. I really hate going to the dentist, but my tooth had been hurting all week. It felt as if somebody was hitting it with a little hammer.

While I was waiting for the dentist, the fire alarm went off. 'Oh, no, fire practice,' I thought. But it wasn't. All at once, I saw smoke coming under the door and I knew it was for real.

As soon as they realised there was a fire, everyone started running and pushing. Meanwhile, the smoke was getting thicker. I lost my jacket during the rush to get to the stairs, but I managed to get out of there safely.

Strangely enough, my tooth just stopped hurting after that. To my relief, I didn't even have to go back to the dentist. My cloud definitely had a silver lining!

Get it right

while + verb, *during* + noun

STUDY

3 Look at Rosie's story again. Write the descriptions in the box next to the correct paragraphs.

ending   further development of the story
setting the scene   what happened first

WRITING PLAN a story

1 ....
2 ....
3 ....
4 ....

4 In Rosie's story, find one example of:

- a simile.
- a reference to the senses.
- three different tenses.

5 a Read the tips in the HOW TO box.

HOW TO

link ideas in a story

- Show the order of events:
  - Between sentences: *Beforehand, … Meanwhile / In the meantime, … Afterwards, … Finally / In the end, …*
  - Within sentences: *before, while, when, after, as soon as …*
- Say if something happened quickly or unexpectedly: *Suddenly, … All at once, … Out of the blue, …*
- Show your attitude: *Luckily / Fortunately, … Unfortunately, … Strangely enough … , To my surprise/disappointment / relief …*

b Underline six of these linking words or phrases in the story.

PRACTISE

6 Replace the underlined words with one of the linking phrases from the HOW TO box.

1 <u>Due to good luck</u>, I was unhurt.
2 <u>Totally unexpectedly</u>, I got an exciting phone call.
3 <u>Immediately after</u> I heard the explosion, I knew what had happened.
4 <u>Before the event</u>, I had remembered to check my messages.
5 <u>Sadly</u>, it wasn't good news.

PLAN, WRITE AND CHECK

7 You're going to write a story about a personal experience with the same title as Rosie's. It can be real or you can invent it. Use the plan in Exercise 3 and make notes.

8 Write your story. Try and include the things in Exercise 4. Then check it.

SHARE AND REVIEW

9 Swap your story with a partner. Read your partner's story and review it.

Workbook, pages 36–37

UNIT REVIEW

3

VOCABULARY Our environment

1 Read the similes and write the natural disasters.

http://www.disasterfiction.com

Competition time!

Our favourite similes from your stories

1 The Earth shook as if a huge dinosaur was walking on it. e ______
2 The water was as high as my waist. f ______
3 The wind went round in circles like a ballet dancer. t ______
4 The town was covered in mud like a big chocolate biscuit. l ______
5 The sea looked as if it was one giant wave. t ______
6 The once-green fields looked like a desert. d ______
7 It took the roofs off the houses as if they were toys. h ______
8 The forests were burning like paper. w ______
9 Snow covered everything as far as we could see. a ______
10 It looked just like an enormous firework. v ______ e ______

___ /10

Noise verbs

2 Complete the descriptions with the verbs in the box.

banged burst exploded groaning smashed yelled

Our favourite story beginnings

There was a sound like a huge balloon had (1) ______ . Then our neighbour (2) ______ on the door and (3) ______ that a house in our street had (4) ______ . We ran there. The windows had (5) ______ and a man inside was (6) ______ .

crashed roared screamed sighed slammed whispered

The water (7) ______ into the street like an angry lion. 'The river has flooded,' (8) ______ my mother anxiously in a low voice. We (9) ______ the doors and windows shut and waited. Suddenly, the water (10) ______ through the windows into the house. My mother (11) ______ loudly in fear and then (12) ______ sadly, 'We knew it would happen.'

___ /12

GRAMMAR Past perfect simple and past perfect continuous

3 Complete the sentences with the correct form of the past perfect simple or continuous.

Our favourite story ending

Dan (1) ______ (wait) for hours and hours. He (2) ______ (think) of her every minute. Where was she? (3) ______ (she / die) or (4) ______ (she / survive)? Perhaps she (5) ______ (not understood) when he yelled the meeting place. Perhaps she (6) ______ (look) for him all this time. Or perhaps she (7) ______ (already / leave) town. He looked up. She was there. She (8) ______ (make) it.

___ /16

Sense verbs + *-ing* or infinitive

4 Choose the correct form.

Our favourite poem

I heard the wild dog (1) *bark* / *barking* once.
I saw it (2) *stop* / *stopping* beneath the tree.
I watched it (3) *jump* / *jumping* up at me again and again.
I heard it (4) *breathe* / *breathing*.
I saw it (5) *walk* / *walking* away.
I felt my heart (6) *beat* / *beating*.

___ /12

Your score: ___ /50

SKILLS CHECK

✓✓✓ Yes, I can. No problem!
✓✓ Yes, I can. But I need a bit of help.
✓ Yes, I can. But I need a lot of help.

I can recognise and understand similes when I read. ______
I can focus on important information when I listen. ______
I can understand another person's feelings. ______
I can contradict facts and opinions. ______
I can link ideas in a story. ______

Workbook, pages 38–39

UNIT 4 THINKING AHEAD!

IN THE PICTURE Jobs

Talk about jobs and apprenticeships

RECALL AND READ

1 Work in pairs. Do the tasks. You have three minutes.

a Match the pictures (a–h) to the job categories (1–8).

1 Agriculture, Gardening and Animal Care ____
2 Arts, Media and Publishing ____
3 Business, Administration and Law ____
4 Construction ____
5 Health, Education and Public Services ____
6 Information and Communication Technology ____
7 Leisure, Travel and Tourism ____
8 Retail, Manufacturing and Services ____

b Write the names of at least two jobs for each category.

2 Read the advertisement on page 39 and answer the questions.

1 What is an apprenticeship?
2 What are the benefits of doing an apprenticeship?
3 How old do you need to be to become an apprentice in England?

WORK WITH WORDS

3 2.01 Match each job in the box to a category in Exercise 1. Listen and check.

accountant	app/software/web developer	beauty therapist	carpenter
electrician	firefighter	flight attendant	gardener
healthcare assistant	lighting/sound technician	plumber	veterinary nurse

4 2.02 Listen and repeat the jobs from Exercise 3.

5 Complete the descriptions with the apprenticeship jobs from Exercise 3.

1 'I love making things so being a(n) ____ is perfect for me. Maths is really important when you work with wood.'
2 'It's fantastic to be an apprentice ____ and follow the process of creating a new program from the initial concept through to the end.'
3 'I like looking after people and the ____ apprenticeship programme has really helped me pick up nursing skills.'
4 'Being a(n) ____ involves applying make-up, giving customers advice and doing manicures and pedicures.'
5 'I wanted to do the ____ apprenticeship because I've always been good with numbers. Recently I've been learning about spreadsheets.'
6 'Sometimes people ask me – why do you want to be a(n) ____? I think it's like being a doctor. People will always need someone to fix their kitchens and bathrooms.'

6 2.03 Listen to six teenagers talk about their apprenticeships. Listen and write the correct job from Exercise 3.

1 Jeff ____ 3 Tom ____ 5 Arjun ____
2 Sanjana ____ 4 Iona ____ 6 Harry ____

LEARN WHILE YOU EARN

Finding your first job in today's changing world can be difficult. One option is to do an apprenticeship.

An apprenticeship is a job that includes training. As an apprentice you can learn specific skills, get some qualifications and earn a salary at the same time.

Apprenticeship schemes exist in most countries. In England, there are more than 200 different types of apprenticeships in areas such as engineering, veterinary nursing and accountancy. They take between one and four years to complete and are available to young people aged 16 and over.

Choosing the right apprenticeship will depend on your interests and the opportunities in your area. For more information, please visit our website and find out how an apprenticeship could change your life.

7 a 2.04 PRONOUNCE **A diphthong is two vowel sounds said one after the other. Listen to the diphthongs in these words.**

/ɪə/ engineer
/aʊ/ accountant, sound engineer
/aɪ/ firefighter, flight attendant, lighting assistant
/eə/ software, healthcare

b 2.05 **Listen and repeat the words, noticing the way your mouth moves.**

EXTEND

8 Write definitions for these jobs. Use a dictionary to help you.

architect estate agent florist ~~park ranger~~ tailor

A park ranger is someone who takes care of a national park.

9 THE MOVING PICTURE **Watch the video. What apprenticeship are Joe and Alister doing? How long have they been apprentices?**

SPEAK

10 Work in pairs. Read the instructions on page 141 and play The Apprenticeship Game.

PHRASE BYTES

I think it would be good to do an apprenticeship in … because …

It's an opportunity to learn (how to) …

This job can help people develop their … skills.

An apprentice … is able to …

GO BEYOND

Do the Words & Beyond exercise on page 133.

Workbook, page 40

READING Job advice

Recognise formal and informal writing

SPEAK AND READ

1 Work in pairs. Answer the questions about your country.

1 How old do you have to be to work full time?
2 Which jobs are traditionally done by young people?

2 a Read the tips in the HOW TO box.

b 2.06 Read the work advice page and order the people from the most (*1*) to the least (*4*) formal.

___ Sylvia ___ Maurice ___ Raj ___ F.S.

HOW TO

recognise formal and informal writing

Formal writing: look for ...

- ☐ formal greetings and vocabulary (*Dear Mr/Ms ...*).
- ☐ longer, more complex sentences with full verbs.
- ☐ correct spelling and punctuation.

Informal writing: look for ...

- ☐ informal greetings and vocabulary (*Hi Dad*).
- ☐ shorter, simpler sentences with contractions (*I'll, don't*).
- ☐ abbreviations, exclamation marks and emoticons.

YPW (YOUNG PEOPLE & WORK)

Maurice Clarke

Hi Maurice. I'm 15 and want to get a job to start saving money. My mates at school tell me I'm too young to work. Are they right? Sylvia (Liverpool, England)

Thank you for your question, Sylvia. In the UK, you cannot work full time until you are 16. However, the Children and Young Persons Act of 1933 sets 13 as the minimum age at which children are allowed to do part-time work. The law only allows you to do 'work which is not likely to be harmful to the safety, health or development of children'. And you cannot let your job affect your schoolwork. During the school term you can work a maximum of 12 hours per week which increases to 35 hours during holidays.

Dear Mr Clarke,

Our family has a shop and I often help Mum and Dad when I come home from school. Sometimes Dad makes me work on Saturdays because he wants me to join the business when I leave school. I don't want to join the business. What can I do? Raj, age 16 (Birmingham, England)

The first thing to remember, Raj, is that your father has probably spent years building the business and he wants it to continue. Having said that, he cannot make you join the business if you do not want to. Help him see that working outside the family for a while will benefit everyone. You will learn a lot by working in other situations and you can bring that experience to the family business if you decide to join it in the future.

I wanna be rich + famuos. :-) Can u help me get an actor or model job! F.S.

The employment laws in the UK and the USA let children work in television, film, theatre and modelling. However, these types of job are strictly controlled. I should add that making a good impression is essential when trying to get any job so I suggest you improve your writing skills before applying for a job. Apart from your bad spelling and grammar, you do not give your full name, age, or say where you are writing from.

3 a Find examples of these things in the message from F.S.

1 A spelling or grammar mistake
2 Incorrect punctuation
3 Words that have been shortened or changed
4 A word replaced by symbols

b Rewrite the message, correcting the mistakes and making it more formal.

4 Which tips in the HOW TO box did you use for help with Exercises 2b and 3? Tick (✓) them.

5 Read the sentences and decide if they are true (*T*) or false (*F*). Correct the false sentences.

1 In the UK, you can work full time when you're 16. T/F
2 When you're 13 you can do any type of part-time work. T/F
3 Raj's family is in the retail business. T/F
4 Maurice thinks Raj should start his career in the family business. T/F
5 The work conditions for child actors are very relaxed. T/F
6 Maurice thinks F.S. might have problems finding work. T/F

REACT

6 Work in pairs. What do you think? Tell your partner.

1 How much of the information in Maurice's answers is relevant to young people in your country?
2 Do you think it's right for young people to work while they're still at school? Why?/Why not?

GO BEYOND

Write a question that you would like to ask Maurice about work. Give your question to another student. Can he/she answer it?

Workbook, page 41

GRAMMAR *Make*, *let* and *allow*

>>> Talk about obligation and permission

READ

1 Read Olga's description of work experience. What has she learned from the experience?

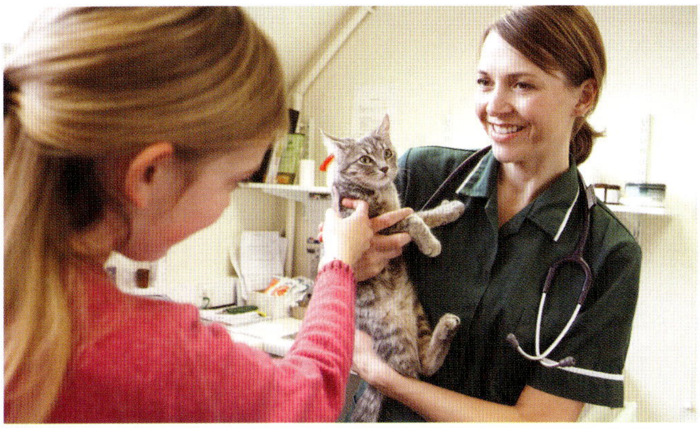

Our school lets students do some work experience in their final years. Nobody makes us do it, but personally I think it's a really good idea. The school allows us to choose the type of job we'd like to do. I chose to work at a local veterinary practice because I'd like to be a veterinary nurse one day. I'm not allowed to give injections or anything like that, but they let me exercise the animals and work in reception. Sometimes they make me work hard, but I don't mind because I want to achieve my ambition.

STUDY

2 Complete the explanations with examples from Exercise 1.

Make, let and allow

make

Use: For obligation that comes from another person.

Form:
make + object + infinitive without *to*
Nobody makes us do it.

....

Let and allow

Use: For giving or not giving permission.
Allow is more formal than *let*.

Form:
(not) let + object + infinitive without *to*
Our school lets students do work experience.

....

(not) allow + object + infinitive with *to*
The school allows us to choose the type of job we'd like to do.

be allowed

Use: To say you have or don't have permission.

Form:
(not) be allowed + infinitive with *to*

....

See GRAMMAR DATABASE, page 123.

PRACTISE

3 Choose the correct options in the conversation between Helen and her older brother, Jake.

Jake: Hi. How's your work experience going?
Helen: It's OK, but they don't (1) *allow* / *let* me do a lot of the interesting work. I want to be an electrician, but I'm not (2) *allowed* / *let* to do any repairs. They (3) *allow* / *make* me do a lot of paperwork instead.
Jake: They'll probably (4) *allow* / *let* you to do more interesting work when they know you better. When I did work experience at the restaurant, they (5) *allowed* / *made* me talk to the customers most of the time. They didn't (6) *allow* / *let* me do any kitchen work until I realised how important social skills are for the job.
Helen: I guess you're right.

4 a Write the complete sentences.

1 You / not / allow / use / the toilets when the seat belt sign is on.
You aren't allowed to use the toilets when the seat belt sign is on.
2 I / can't / let / you / go into the building because there's too much smoke.
....
3 Some animals / not let / me / give them an injection because they're too nervous.
....
4 According to the park rules / you / not / allow / pick flowers.
....

b Who's speaking in each sentence in Exercise 4a?

1 *a flight attendant*

5 Complete the sentences about you.

Home, School, Work

1 At home, I'm allowed to ...
2 At school, we aren't allowed to ...
3 Doing an apprenticeship lets you ...
4 In some jobs, employers make their employees ...
5 Teachers sometimes make us ...
6 At home, my ... doesn't let me ...

SPEAK

6 Work in pairs. Compare your answers to Exercise 5. Discuss the advantages and disadvantages of being at school or having a job. Which do you think is better and why?

The main advantage of having a job is ...

But on the other hand, being at school lets you ...

Workbook, pages 42–43

Infer meaning when you listen

SPEAK AND LISTEN

1 Work in pairs. Answer the questions.

1. What was the last film you saw? Who starred in it?
2. Do you watch the credits at the end of a film? Why?/Why not?

2 2.07 Listen to Jennifer on the location of her new film. In which order does she speak to/about the people in the photos?

a Sally (stunt double)

b Martin (make-up artist)

c Mario (caterer)

d Jack (gaffer) & Derek (best boy)

e Pamela (dialogue coach)

3 2.07 Listen again and choose the correct answer.

1 What kind of film is Jennifer making?
A a horror film B a musical C a thriller D a western
2 What's the best boy doing?
A working B talking C eating D acting
3 What does Jennifer spend a lot of time doing with Pamela?
A learning her part
B practising her pronunciation and accent
C talking about everyone
D choosing outfits to wear for the film
4 What do most people call the make-up artist?
A Martin B Matt C Magic D Marty
5 Who's jumping out of a moving car in the afternoon?
A an extra B Jennifer C Sally D Jack

4 a Read the tips in the HOW TO box.

b 2.08 Listen to the extracts. In which sentences do you think Jennifer doesn't mean exactly what she says? Why?

1 It's good to see you working so hard!
2 So that's very clear then!
3 He's the person responsible for making me look 'beautiful'.
4 I have to sit here for hours while Martin works his magic.
5 Mario, who's the most important person here, …

5 Which tips in the HOW TO box did you use to help with Exercise 4b? Tick (✓) them.

REACT

6 Work in pairs. Answer the questions.

- What are the advantages/disadvantages of working in the film industry?
- Would you like to work in the film industry? Why?/Why not?

WORK WITH WORDS

7 a 2.09 Complete the director's orders with the film jobs in the box. Listen and check.

cinematographer costume designer dialogue coach director editor extra producer

1 Listen to me! I'm the __________ !
2 Tell that __________ to walk up and down the street like a normal person in a crowd.
3 Send a note to the __________ telling her to cut ten seconds from the scene.
4 I can't understand what the actor's saying. Call the __________ .
5 Where's the __________ ? We can't start until he's behind the camera.
6 Call the __________ and tell him we need more time and more money.
7 Your outfit looks terrible. Go and see the __________ and find something else to wear.

b 2.10 Listen and repeat the job titles.

HOW TO
infer meaning when you listen

If you infer meaning, you understand what people don't say directly.

☐ Listen to *how* people talk. Their voice often tells you what they really think.

☐ Identify the *relationship* between speakers:
- People are more careful with their words when they don't know or don't trust someone.
- Friends are likely to use humour and sometimes mean the opposite of what they say.

GO BEYOND
Do the Words & Beyond exercise on page 133.

Workbook, pages 44–45

GRAMMAR Defining and non-defining relative clauses

»» Add extra information to a sentence

READ

1 Read the article. What's special about the film director Allen Smithee?

Allen Smithee is the name of a film director who made his first film in 1969. Since then the director, whose first name is sometimes spelt A-l-a-n, has made a lot of films. His films, which are usually bad, include westerns and science fiction fantasies. But Allen Smithee isn't a real person – the name's a pseudonym, which is a name that someone uses instead of their real name. In Hollywood, where directors often argue with producers and studios, the name is used by film directors that don't want their real name to be associated with a film they've made. The popular films we watch on daytime TV are often heavily edited, which explains why Allen Smithee's name sometimes appears as the director.

STUDY

2 Complete the explanations with *where*, *which* and *who*. Use Exercise 1 to help you.

Defining relative clauses

A film director is somebody who directs films.

Use: To identify and describe people, things and places.

Form: Use .... /*that* for **people.**
Use .... /*that* for **things.**
Use .... for **places.**
Use *whose* for **possessions.**

You can leave out the relative pronoun (that, etc) if *it's* the object of the next verb:

object subject verb
films (that) you sometimes watch on daytime TV

3 Read the explanations. Then underline four non-defining relative clauses in Exercise 1.

Non-defining relative clauses

*His films, **which are usually bad**, include westerns and science fiction fantasies.*

Use: To give extra information.

Form:
Don't start with *that*.
Use a comma at the start of the clause and a comma or full stop at the end.
You can't leave out the relative pronoun.

See GRAMMAR DATABASE, page 123.

PRACTISE

4 a Choose the correct pronouns.

1 The location is the place *which* / *where* a film is made.
2 A set is a place *that* / *where* is built for a film.
3 Extras are people *who* / *which* appear in crowd scenes.
4 The screenwriter is the person *who* / *whose* words are filmed.
5 A clapper is a board *that* / *who* somebody shows at the start of a shot.

b In which sentences in Exercise 4a can you leave out the relative pronoun?

5 Combine the sentences. Use non-defining relative clauses with *who* or *which*.

1 *The Shining* is a famous horror film. It was directed by Stanley Kubrick.
The Shining, which was directed by Stanley Kubrick, is a famous horror film.
2 The film is based on a story by Stephen King. It was released in 1977.
....
3 The main character was called Jack Torrance. He was played by Jack Nicholson.
....
4 The location was a real hotel in Oregon USA. It was called Overlook Hotel in the story.
....

6 Complete the text with the pronouns in the box. One gap doesn't need a pronoun.

that	where	which	who	whose

Pseudonyms are often used by authors (1) .... want to write in another style. The author Stephen King, (2) .... novels include *The Shining* and *The Shawshank Redemption*, used the pseudonym Richard Bachman in the 1970s. His secret was discovered in Washington DC (3) .... a bookseller noticed a similarity in the writing style. The book (4) .... King was writing at the time was a new Richard Bachman story, but it was King's name (5) .... appeared on the cover when it was published. The book, (6) .... was later turned into a film, was called *Misery*.

7 Write five sentences with defining or non-defining relative clauses about a film, TV series or book. Don't include its title.

The film is based on a book that was written by Suzanne Collins.

SPEAK

8 Work in pairs. Read out the sentences you wrote in Exercise 7. Can your partner identify the film, TV series or book?

»» Workbook, page 46

LANGUAGE & BEYOND

PART 1

Meet Jake. He's going to visit his cousin who lives in a village somewhere over the hills, across the valley, on the other side of the lake. Jake, who has never been to the village before and doesn't know how to get there, has to make the journey on foot. How should he prepare for his journey?

PART 2

***Jake stands at the crossroads.** After walking a few miles, he comes to a crossroads. There are three roads (a, b and c) that lead to his cousin's village. The first road (a) is the quickest and most popular route to the village. The second road (b) takes longer but passes through some interesting places. The third road (c) is quite rough and isn't used much. Which road do you think Jake should choose and why?*

»» Think ahead and make plans

SPEAK AND READ

1 **Work in pairs. Read part 1 of Jake's story and answer the question at the end.**

2 **Make a list for Jake of the things he needs to do and take with him. Compare your list with another pair.**

PHRASE BYTES

He should buy … so that he can / in order to …

He'd better take a/some …

He ought to find out …

DO

3 **Work in groups. Read part 2 of the story and answer the question.**

4 **Answer the questions below, giving reasons for your choices.**

1 Did you all agree on which road Jake should take? If not, why not?
2 Which of the three roads do you think is the safest and which is the most dangerous to take?
3 Which of the things on the list in Exercise 2 would help Jake to make his decision?

5 **Read the final part of Jake's story. Which road does he choose?**

Jake arrives at the crossroads. As he's already planned his journey, he knows which road he'll take. He isn't in a hurry to reach his cousin's village so he can forget one option. And although he loves the idea of an adventure, he knows he might get lost and not meet anyone on one of the other options. So he chooses the road which he knows will be an interesting journey and lead him to his destination.

REFLECT

6 **Discuss the questions with your class. Do you agree with the REFLECTION POINT?**

1 Why do you think people sometimes call life a journey?
2 In what ways could Jake's story be about life?
3 Do you think there's a correct or incorrect answer to the question in Exercise 3? Why?/Why not?

REFLECTION POINT

It's good to think ahead and make plans. A map can show you where you are and where you want to go, but there are different ways to reach your destination. Think about your options and plan accordingly.

EXTEND

7 **Make a 'map' showing your life journey so far. Include your schools, things you've done and places you've been. Where would you like your journey to take you in the next few years? Add more information to the map. How can you prepare now for the next stage of your journey?**

»» Workbook, page 49

SPEAKING Have you got the idea?

Check and correct understanding

SPEAK

1 Work in pairs. Describe the photos. What are Ellie, Luis and Tom doing?

WATCH OR LISTEN

2 2.11 Watch or listen to the scene to check your answers to Exercise 1.

Luis: Stop me if you don't understand. OK? So Ellie, you're standing here and Tom, you walk past her like this. Are you with me?
Tom: (1) .... I don't see her?
Luis: No. What I'm saying is that you walk past her. Of course you see her.
Tom: So, I see her, but I ignore her and keep walking.
Luis: That's not what I meant. She's the girl of your dreams. You want to go out with her, but you're embarrassed when you see her. (2) .... ?
Tom: In other words, I see her, I panic, I don't know what to do, so I continue walking.
Luis: That's correct.
Ellie: (3) .... ?
Luis: Yes, of course.
Ellie: What's my motivation? How should I feel?
Luis: (4) .... You're a zombie.
Tom: You're saying that I want to go out with a zombie.
Luis: No. You don't know she's a zombie yet. (5) .... ?
Ellie: Do you mean I look normal? In the script it says I look blank. It's not very believable.
Luis: It's a film and I'm the director. Do you understand what I'm saying?
Tom: You're saying that we aren't allowed to ask questions.
Luis: (6) .... And ... action! ... Cut!

3 2.11 Watch or listen again and complete the phrases (1–6).

4 Write the phrases from Exercise 3 in the correct section of the PHRASEBOOK.

5 2.12 Listen and repeat the phrases, paying attention to intonation.

6 In groups of three, act out the scene from the video.

PHRASEBOOK 2.13

Checking you have understood

In other words, ...
You're saying that ...
Do you mean ... ?
So, ...
....
....

Checking you have been understood

Do you understand what I'm saying?
Stop me if you don't understand.
Are you with me?
....
....

Confirming or correcting understanding

That's not what I meant.
What I'm saying is ...
That's correct.
....
....

ACT

7 In groups of three, complete the tasks.

- Decide what happens in the next sequence of the zombie film and write the script using two actors.
- Choose one student to be the director. The other students are the actors.
- The director works with another pair of actors and directs the new scene. Use phrases from the lesson to check and correct understanding.

Workbook, page 47

WRITING My job application

Write a formal letter

SPEAK AND READ

1 Work in pairs. Read the job advertisements. Which job would you prefer to apply for? Why?

A

• Part-time assistant needed to start immediately at an electrical shop. Must live in the area and have an interest in electrics.

B

• Student needed to give extra revision classes to 12-year-old twins. If you are interested in languages and other school subjects, please get in touch.

C

• Film producer is looking for someone to walk four pet dogs twice a day. Must love animals and be prepared to get up early.

2 Read Ben's letter. Which of the points in the first advertisement does he mention?

2 Well Walk
London NW6 8QT
4th November

East Heath Electrical Shop
14 East Heath Road
London NW6 4AJ

Dear Sir or Madam,

I am writing about the part-time job working in the East Heath Electrical Shop which I saw advertised on the Young People & Work website.

I am currently still in full-time education, but I would like to learn more about electrics. I am hoping to become an apprentice electrician when I leave school next year.

I live locally and can start work immediately. During term time I am available to work 12 hours per week, but I can work for more hours during holidays.

I hope you will consider me for this position. I look forward to hearing from you.

Yours faithfully,

Benjamin Brooks

STUDY

3 Order the things that Ben mentions in his letter.

___ Why he's the right person for the job
___ What his current school situation is
___ Where he saw the job advertisement
___ When he can start working
___ Which job he's applying for
___ His reasons for wanting the job

4 a Read the tips in the HOW TO box.

HOW TO
write a formal letter

- Follow the letter-writing rules in Exercise 4b.
- Write full forms not contractions.
- Use formal words and phrases whenever possible.

b Complete the rules for writing formal letters using Ben's letter to help you.

address date letter name phrase signature

1 Write your ______ at the top right of the page.
2 Write the ______ underneath.
3 Write the ______ and address of the person you are writing to underneath on the left.
4 Start your ______ with *Dear Mr/Mrs/Ms*, if you know the person's name, or *Dear Sir or Madam*, if you don't.
5 End your letter with the ______ *'I look forward to hearing from you.'*
6 Above your ______, write *'Yours sincerely,'* if you know the name of the person or *'Yours faithfully,'* if you don't.

PRACTISE

5 Make this letter more formal. Use the tips in the HOW TO box and Exercise 4b to help you.

Hi Brian Davis,
My name's Dave and I'd like more information about the job I saw in the ad in yesterday's newspaper. Please get in touch and tell me more. Hope to hear from you soon.
All the best,
Dave

PLAN, WRITE AND CHECK

6 You're going to write a letter applying for one of the other jobs in Exercise 1. Use Exercise 3 to help you plan your letter.

7 Write your letter. Then check it using the checklist in the HOW TO box.

SHARE AND REVIEW

8 Swap your letter with a partner. Read your partner's letter and review it.

Workbook, pages 48–49

VOCABULARY Jobs

1 Write the missing words.

Maribel didn't know what apprenticeship to do. She didn't like plants so she didn't want to be a (1) g________ . She was terrible with numbers so she'd never make a good (2) a________ . If she'd worked harder in her IT class, she could've been a software (3) d________ . 'I'll never be a (4) c________ ,' she thought, 'because I can't make anything, especially out of wood. And I can't change a light bulb so I'll never be an (5) e________ .' She really wanted to be a (6) v________ ________ , but she was scared of dogs. What *could* she do? She made a list to help her decide.

I'd like to...
save people from burning buildings. (7) ________
help people look their best. (8) ________ ________
look after people on flights. (9) ________ ________
help doctors to make people better. (10) ________ ________
help people with their sinks and baths. (11) ________
create the soundtrack for a film. (12) ________ ________

___ /12

Film jobs

2 Maribel chose the final job on her list. On her first day at work she met the people she'd be working with. Name the jobs.

1 The ________ controls the camera.
2 The ________ tells everyone what to do on the set.
3 The ________ helps the actors speak their lines.
4 The ________ prepares the food.
5 The ________ changes the way the actors' faces look.
6 The ________ puts all the pieces of the film together.
7 The ________ controls all the different areas of making a film.
8 The ________ creates the outfits the actors wear.
9 The ________ appear in crowd scenes.
10 The ________ performs dangerous sequences in place of the actor.

___ /10

GRAMMAR *Make, let* and *allow*

3 Complete Maribel's story with the words in the box.

allow allowed let (x2) made (x2)

Maribel thought that working in films would be glamorous, but it wasn't. Her boss didn't (1) ________ her do the important jobs, and she wasn't (2) ________ to speak to the actors. The studio (3) ________ her get up very early in the morning and didn't (4) ________ her to have Saturdays off. But Maribel (5) ________ herself work harder every day. She knew she could be the best sound technician ever if her boss would (6) ________ her show it.

___ /12

Defining and non-defining relative clauses

4 Choose the correct options to complete Maribel's acceptance speech.

First of all, I'd like to thank all the people (1) *which* / *who* have helped me over the years. My first boss, (2) *that* / *who* is in the audience tonight, didn't believe in me when I first started. I think her criticisms, (3) *which* / *where* were unjustified, helped to make me a stronger person. It was when I made my third film, (4) *which* / *whose* title you all know, that my career took off. There are some films (5) *who* / *–* you never forget. *Zombies of London* is a film (6) *that* / *–* will stay with me forever. I'd like to end by thanking the people (7) *that* / *whose* have always believed in me. Thanks Mum and Dad. Home is truly the place (8) *where* / *which* all our careers start.

___ /16

Your score: ___ /50

SKILLS CHECK

✓✓✓ Yes, I can. No problem!
✓✓ Yes, I can. But I need a bit of help.
✓ Yes, I can. But I need a lot of help.

I can recognise formal and informal writing. ________
I can infer meaning when I listen. ________
I can think ahead and make plans. ________
I can check and correct understanding. ________
I can write a formal letter. ________

Workbook, pages 50–51

READ

1 Read the extract from a biography and the questions below. For each question, choose A, B, C or D.

It all started with a job my uncle got me. He was working as a costume designer on a film called *Disaster* – it was about a hurricane that devastated a town, causing floods and landslides and destroying pretty much everything. There was lots of screaming and yelling and crying, death and disease and some terrible dialogue. Everything was so unrealistic that the film itself was a complete disaster.

Anyway, the director needed a few more extras for a school scene, so my uncle suggested me. My parents didn't mind and as it was the school holidays I was allowed to do it. For two days I sat at a desk in a classroom. On the second day, one of the boys just couldn't get his lines right, even though he was a professional actor. I'd heard the lines so many times, I knew them by heart. The director was a bit of a bully. He stopped the boy, who had been trying to get his scene right yet again and groaned loudly. Then he looked round the class. Unexpectedly, he pointed to me.

'You,' he said. 'Come and try.'

'What me?' I said.

'Yes, you. Come here.'

I looked at the other boy who obviously felt terrible. He looked like a dog that had been beaten by its owner. I hated the director for being so horrible to that boy. He *was* a bad actor but he'd been trying really hard.

So I looked for an excuse. 'Erm, I don't know how to act,' I said.

Unfortunately it had the wrong result. 'Well, this boy can't act either!' said the director cruelly. 'Come here!'

So I did the scene. I knew the lines, of course. But I could also feel myself becoming the boy in the film, thinking like him, feeling like him. It was as if I was growing into his skin. When I'd finished my lines, I suddenly became aware of everybody looking at me in silence. Then I felt the director hit me hard on the back. 'Well done, kid,' he said. 'Good job for somebody who can't act.'

Everybody started clapping. Even the real actor, who the director had embarrassed, gave me a small smile and a thumbs up. I smiled back. A whole new world of future possibilities had opened up.

Two weeks later, a letter dropped through the letter box with my name on it and the logo of a big film studio. I opened it. 'Dear Mr Lee,' the letter began. 'We are writing to inform you that we would like to consider you for the lead part in our new film. Please phone me to make an appointment for an audition. Yours sincerely, Davina Estelle (personal assistant).' At the bottom of the letter was a handwritten note from the director. 'Hi kid. You've got an awesome future. See you soon, Ken.' It was the start of a great career on the big screen – but I never ever worked with that director again.

1 What did the writer think of *Disaster*?
 A It had everything a good disaster film should have.
 B It wasn't successful because it didn't have enough action.
 C It failed because it wasn't believable.
 D The dialogue was the best part of the film.

2 The writer uses the phrase 'like a dog that had been beaten by its owner' to describe …
 A how upset the boy looked.
 B how angry the boy was.
 C how stupid the boy was.
 D how proud the boy felt.

3 The writer didn't want to do the scene because …
 A he didn't like the director.
 B he was worried that he wouldn't remember the lines.
 C he couldn't act and didn't want to embarrass himself.
 D he didn't want to make the other boy feel worse.

4 How did the writer feel about the scene?
 A He was happy that he had remembered the lines.
 B Acting the part came very easily to him.
 C He felt it wasn't a bad performance for his first scene.
 D He felt uncomfortable in his own skin.

5 What did the writer do after he got the letter?
 A He made lots of films with the director.
 B He made films with other directors.
 C He decided not to go into film.
 D He became a film director.

EXAM TIPS

do a multiple-choice reading exercise

- Read the whole text first.
- Read each question or the first part of the sentence carefully.
- Find the correct place in the text and choose the best option.
- Check that the meaning of the answer or the completed sentence matches the text.

recognise and understand similes
See page 30.

recognise formal and informal writing
See page 40.

Reading: _______ /10

LISTEN

2 2.14 **You will hear an interview with a writer called Beth Lastoria. Complete the sentences with no more than three words.**

1 Beth thinks that reading stories ________ her to write her own.
2 She started to write in her free-time because she had so many stories in her ________ .
3 Beth was always interested in ________ worlds.
4 She likes characters who ________ and do the unexpected.
5 She sent her work to lots of different publishers but ________
6 One day she thought, 'I'll publish them ________ .'
7 You can publish ________ as an e-book.
8 The author gets more money and ________ their work.
9 Beth had soon sold ________ copies.
10 It's easier and cheaper for Beth's readers to ________ books that she publishes online.

Listening: ______ /10

WRITE

3 You've seen the advert below on a theatre website. Write a letter (140–190 words) and ask for more information. Explain what your special interest is (acting, producing, etc). You don't need to include an address.

Writing: ______ /10

Progress check score ______ /30

EXAM TIPS

listen and complete notes

- Read the sentences carefully before you listen.
- Think about what type of information is missing.
- Listen for the words <u>before and after</u> the missing information.
- Write the exact words that you hear (1–3 words).

focus on important information
See page 32.

infer meaning when you listen
See page 42.

EXAM TIPS

write a letter

- Read the task carefully and underline the most important parts.
- Decide if you need to use formal or informal language.
- Make a plan. Decide how many paragraphs to use.
- Make sure you cover every part of the task.
- Use appropriate linking words and phrases to make your letter clear and easy to read.
- Check your work. Is it the right length?

write a formal letter
See page 46.

UNIT 5 STREET ART

IN THE PICTURE Art

Talk about different types of art

RECALL AND READ

1 **Work in pairs. Add other words to the network. You have three minutes.**

- **ART**
  - **Works of art**: a sculpture, a video clip
  - **Artists**: painter, musician
  - **Places where you can see art**: museum, exhibition

2 **Work in pairs. Complete the definition below. Then compare your definition with the class and agree on a class definition. Write it on the board.**

Art is …

3 **Read Natasha's essay about art. Is her definition of art the same as the one on the board? If not, what differences are there?**

WHAT IS ART AND WHERE DO WE FIND IT?

Is art a Monet landscape of the countryside or an installation of a functional object such as a toilet? Is it a portrait of a well-known person in a museum or a collage of old magazine pictures? Is it a seventeenth-century still life of fruit or flowers or the black and white sketch I made in my exercise book at school?

What about 3-D pavement art on the street, a mural in an underground tunnel or graffiti on a wall? And performance art created with the artist's own body?

What if I put an unmade bed in an art gallery – is that art? If I can wear it, is it art? If I can live in it, is it art?

My answer is that art can be anything and anywhere. Anything that is made or performed with imagination and shared with others is art.

WORK WITH WORDS

4 a **Underline ten words for different types of art in the essay. Match the pictures (1–10) to the correct words.**

1 *sketch*

b 2.15 **Listen and check. Then listen and repeat.**

5 a **Which works of art do you think have the picture captions below? Write the correct works of art from Exercise 4a.**

a A beautiful picture of a river under a cloudy sky ....
b It's an amazing achievement not to move for hours. ....
c The face in the painting is as realistic as a photo. ....
d This is a great way to beautify the walls inside a building. ....
e A creative use of an everyday item ....
f A perfect image, created with just a few lines ....

b **Write your own captions for the other works of art in the pictures.**

9

8

7

10

5

4

6

EXTEND

6 **Write sentences about the materials the artists have used in some of the pictures. Use the words in the box and a dictionary if necessary. Then add materials to your art network.**

canvas	chalk	ink	paint	paper	plaster	spray paint

In picture 5, the artist has used paint on canvas.

7 **THE MOVING PICTURE** **Watch the video. What sort of art do the students like?**

SPEAK

8 **a** **Work in pairs. Student A: look at picture 9 and picture 5. Compare and contrast them. Say how you think the people in the pictures felt.**

b **Student B: look at picture 4 and picture 8. Compare and contrast them. Say which one you like best and why.**

PHRASE BYTES

In the … , you can see … whereas in …

At the top/bottom …

On the left/right …

In the foreground/background …

The image/performance/style is …

GO BEYOND

Do the Words & Beyond exercise on page 134.

Workbook, page 52

READING On the wall

Transfer information to a different text

SPEAK AND READ

1 **Look at the wall art on this page. Where and when do you think it was created?**

2 a (2.16) **Read the article and check your answers from Exercise 1.**

b **Choose from sentences a–e below the one which fits each gap (1–4). There's one extra sentence.**

a It represented the history of his country.
b There was also computer-generated art.
c Most of them are many thousands of years old.
d It is therefore an art form which divides opinions.
e It also gives them a long-lasting surface.

3 a **Read the tips in the HOW TO box.**

HOW TO
transfer information to a different text

- ☐ Identify the purpose of the new text, who the readers are and which information is important.
- ☐ Decide if the text should be notes or full sentences.
- ☐ Decide if the style is formal or informal. (See page 40.)
- ☐ Use your own words. Give sources if you quote or copy information.

b **You're going to put the art photos on your blog. Use information from the article and write captions.**

4 **Which tips in the HOW TO box did you use for help with Exercise 3b? Tick (✓) them.**

REACT

5 **Work in pairs. Answer the questions.**

1 What examples of wall art have you seen?
2 Is graffiti art or a crime? Give reasons for your opinion.

A short history of wall art

Early self-expression

Making your personal mark on a wall with spray paint is nothing new. Thirty-seven thousand years ago one of our earliest ancestors left his signature on the walls of Chauvet Cave in France. Holding his hand on the rock, he put a type of red paint in his mouth and spat around it to leave a perfect handprint. Early man later painted scenes of animals and hunters on rock using chalk and charcoal. (1) .... Experts believe that some of the one million 'rock art' sites in Africa could date back as far as 50,000 years.

A new technique

In the 16th and 17th centuries in India, many palaces, temples and mosques were decorated with beautiful frescoes. A fresco is a mural which is painted on walls and ceilings onto fresh wet plaster. Painting onto wet plaster means that the paint dries into the material, giving the colours a special brightness. (2) .... 'Fresco' is actually the Italian word for 'fresh' and in Europe some of the most famous frescoes are found in Italy (for example, on the ceiling of the Sistine Chapel in Rome).

Wall art as politics

Mexico is famous for its bright murals, full of people and life. Between 1920 and 1940, after a long civil war, public buildings were decorated with huge murals to celebrate the birth of a new, more equal society. Artists painted giant scenes in which everyday people worked in the fields, fought for their country or celebrated together – such as this 20th century mural by Amado de la Cueva. (3) .... The 'muralists' strongly believed that art could educate people and change society.

An art form with many faces

In the 21st century, wall art is a feature of many cities and much of it has a social or political message. While some is commissioned by companies or public offices as advertising or to improve ugly urban spaces, much is illegal graffiti on other people's property. (4) .... In some cities, graffiti is a way for gangs to mark their territory. But for many graffiti artists, graffiti art is simply about spray painting their own name on an empty wall. Wall art is right back where it started.

GO BEYOND
Add new words to your art network on page 50.

Workbook, page 53

GRAMMAR *-ing* forms

Use gerunds and participle clauses

READ

1 Look at the photo at the bottom of the page and read the description. What is important when looking at this type of art?

Pavement artists create amazing 3-D pictures using chalk or paint. They plan how to do this before starting the picture. But how do they actually do it? Well, firstly, the technique isn't new: artists used it in the 15th century when painting church ceilings. Secondly, 3-D artwork is actually 2-D, but looking at the picture from the correct angle gives the 3-D effect. From the wrong angle the picture looks flat and out of shape. Having a real person in the picture is important too. Artist Julian Beever loves being in his own pictures. In this pavement art photo, he's sitting in the picture fishing.

STUDY

2 Complete the examples from Exercise 1.

-*ing* forms (1): gerunds

Use: As a noun.

Form:
Gerunds can be:

– the object of a sentence:
Julian Beever loves .... in his own pictures.

– the subject of a sentence:
.... at the picture from the correct angle gives the 3-D effect.

See GRAMMAR DATABASE, page 124.

3 Complete the explanations with more examples from Exercise 1. Then underline the main clause and circle the -*ing* form.

-*ing* forms (2): present participles

Use: As a verb to connect two clauses in a sentence.

Form:
Use a present participle if:
– two things happen at the same time *and*
– the main clause and participle have the same subject.

main clause with main verb	participle clause with present participle
Artists create pictures	***using** chalk and paint.*

(= Artists create pictures and they use chalk and paint.)

....

Present participles are common after *when*, *while*, *before* and *after*:

....

See GRAMMAR DATABASE, page 124.

PRACTISE

4 a Complete the sentences with the correct gerund from the box.

doing going listening making playing watching

1 .... to museums is fun.
2 .... 3-D films in the cinema makes me dizzy.
3 .... a piece of art is very satisfying.
4 .... video games is a waste of time.
5 .... to live music is very different to listening to recorded music.
6 .... graphic art on the computer is more interesting than painting or drawing.

b Make the sentences in Exercise 4a true for you. Tell your partner. Does he/she agree?

I think going to museums is boring.

Really? I think going to museums is fascinating.

5 a Write about this famous picture in the National Gallery in London. Use a main verb and a participle clause.

1 Two men / stand / look / at the artist.
Two men are standing looking at the artist.
2 Between the two men / be / a shelf / contain / different objects.
3 The man on the left / lean / on a shelf / hold / something in his right hand.
4 A long flat object / lie / on the floor / fill / the bottom part of the picture.
5 Every year, thousands of visitors / stand / in front of the picture / try / to work out what the object is.

b Can you see the object? Look at the picture from the right, from the side. If you can't see it, look at page 142.

WRITE

6 Look at page 141. Describe what's happening in the picture.

Workbook, pages 54–55

LISTENING AND VOCABULARY Sand sculptures

Recognise general statements and exceptions

SPEAK AND LISTEN

1 Look at the photos. How do you think sand sculptures are made?

2 2.17 Listen to an interview with sand sculptor Tim Handford. Put the drawings in order and check your answer from Exercise 1.

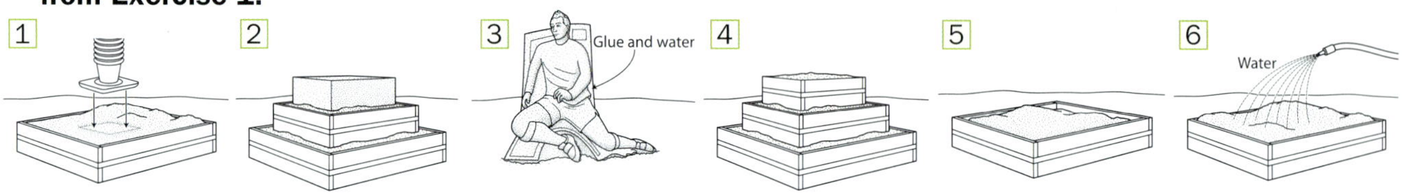

3 a Read the tips in the HOW TO box.

b 2.18 Listen to part of the interview again. For each sentence, write which part is a general statement (*G*) and which part is an exception (*E*).

1 By and large, it lasts a month or two unless there's heavy rain.
2 On the whole, it's really hard work except when a technical team compacts the sand before we arrive – then it's easier.
3 With the exception of a few really talented artists, most people need to apply their art to some sort of practical use.

4 Underline the words in the HOW TO box which helped you to do Exercise 3b.

HOW TO

recognise general statements and exceptions

General statements say something is true in most situations, but there may be exceptions.

- General statements: listen for the phrases *As a rule, By and large, Generally, In general, On the whole … , Most people … .*
- Exceptions: listen for *except for, except when, unless, apart from (when), with the exception of.*

REACT

5 What do you think of Tim's advice to young artists? Should art be both beautiful and functional? Why?/Why not?

WORK WITH WORDS

6 Choose the correct definitions for the adjectives.

1 I started doing quite elaborate sculptures on the beaches in Spain.
A expensive B complicated C soft
2 My main job at the moment is a bit quirky, a bit different.
A unusual B useless C silly
3 Wow, that's very impressive.
A stupid B boring C skilful

7 Read the adjectives and their definitions (1–9). Work in pairs. Which adjectives could describe the things (a–e) in the box?

1 unique (very special, unusual or good)
2 dramatic (with an exciting appearance or effect)
3 average (of usual or ordinary standard)
4 controversial (makes people disagree)
5 powerful (strong and very effective)
6 dull (boring)
7 subtle (not obvious or direct)
8 moving (makes you feel strong emotions)
9 stunning (surprising and beautiful)

a a sad film about a young boy
b a work of art made from a plastic bag
c a fighting scene in a play
d a beautiful watercolour in soft colours
e a still life of a dead bird and some grapes

GO BEYOND

Do the Words & Beyond exercise on page 134.

SPEAK

8 Give your opinion about the works of art on pages 50–51.

Workbook, pages 56–57

GRAMMAR Question tags

Ask questions and confirm ideas using question tags

READ AND LISTEN

1 2.19 **Read and listen to the comic. What's the joke?**

STUDY

2 Choose the correct options to complete the explanations. Use Exercise 1 to help you.

Question tags

Use: At the end of sentences to make questions.

Form:

auxiliary verb + subject

*It could be about energy waste, **couldn't it**?*

Use a positive question tag (*could you?*) with a ***positive*** / ***negative*** sentence.

Use a negative question tag (*isn't it?*) with a ***positive*** / ***negative*** sentence.

If the sentence doesn't have an auxiliary verb:

- Use *do*/*does* for the present simple.
- Use *did* for the past simple.

See GRAMMAR DATABASE, page 124.

Workbook, page 58

3 2.19 PRONOUNCE **Listen again to the conversation in Exercise 1. Mark the question tags where the voice goes up (↗) and the question tags where the voice goes down (↘). Then complete the explanations with the correct symbols.**

1 If the voice goes ________ , the person wants information or help and is asking a real question.
2 If the voice goes ________ , the person is asking the other person to agree or confirm an opinion.

PRACTISE

4 Match the sentences to the correct question tags.

1	That's a very dull picture,	a	is it?
2	You couldn't lend me that book,	b	do you?
3	He painted that himself,	c	won't you?
4	It isn't a very good day for the sand sculpture competition,	d	could you?
5	You'll send me the link for these photos,	e	didn't he?
6	You don't know how much that painting costs,	f	isn't it?

5 a 2.20 **Complete the conversations with the correct question tags. Then listen and check.**

Pippa: You're going to the photo exhibition, (1) ________ ?
Hong: Yes, I am. My mum got tickets. It looks really interesting, (2) ________ ?
Pippa: Yes, it does. You don't know how much the tickets cost, (3) ________ ?

Akim: You know we're painting that mural on Saturday, (4) ________ ? Well, you couldn't help us, (5) ________ ?
Jade: No, sorry. I told you it's my dad's birthday on Saturday, (6) ________ ?

b Work in pairs. Read the conversations with the correct pronunciation of the question tags.

SPEAK

6 a Work in pairs. Write five things that you think you know about your partner.

- something your partner can do
- something your partner is like (*cheerful, generous*, etc)
- something your partner often does
- something your partner did yesterday
- something your partner didn't do yesterday

b Tell your partner your ideas using question tags. Make sure your voice goes down. Your partner confirms or rejects your ideas.

You can't sing very well, can you?

No, I can't. / Well, actually I can.

LANGUAGE & BEYOND

HOW OPEN ARE YOU TO OTHER CULTURES?

1. Have you ever listened to music in a foreign language (not English)?
2. Have you eaten food from different countries?
3. Have you watched a film or a TV show in another language?
4. Have you ever 'travelled' on the internet and found out about another country?
5. Do you watch programmes on TV about other cultures or countries?

>>> Value the art and culture of different societies

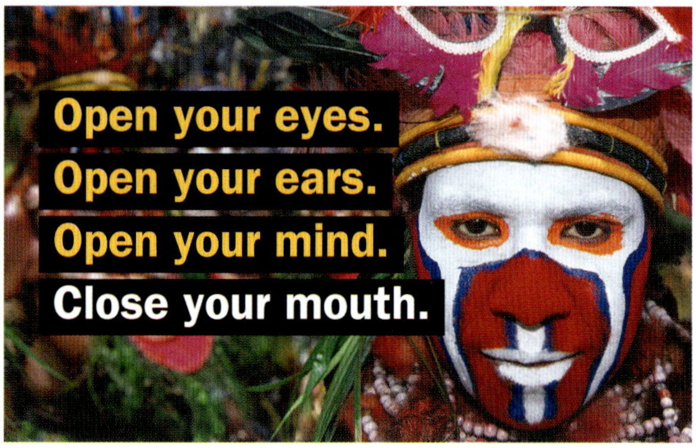

SPEAK AND READ

1 Explain what the postcard on the right means in your own words.

2 2.21 Read and listen to the conversation and answer the questions.

1 What's Lulu so excited about?
2 Why didn't she do this before?
3 What changed her mind?

Ella: Hi Lulu. What are you watching?
Lulu: It's a Bollywood film.
Ella: A 'bolly' what?
Lulu: Bollywood. The place where they make Indian films used to be called 'Bombay' in English, so people called the place 'Bollywood'.
Ella: Oh, like Hollywood, OK, I get it. But why are you watching it? It's not even in English, is it?
Lulu: Well, it has English subtitles. … You know my aunt came over yesterday evening? Well, she had this Bollywood film and she wanted me to watch it with her. As a rule I don't like foreign films with subtitles and I knew there was singing and dancing – and I generally hate musicals … but I didn't want to be rude so I watched it and …
Ella: … you liked it, didn't you?
Lulu: Yes, it was so good I have to watch it again. Come on, it's only just started.
Ella: Ah, no, I hate films with subtitles … and musicals …

DO

3 Work in pairs. Ask and answer the questionnaire above, giving reasons or more details for your answers.

REFLECT

4 Discuss the questions with your class. Do you agree with the REFLECTION POINT?

1 How often do you have contact with other cultures? When?
2 What positive experiences have you had when meeting people from other cultures or visiting other countries?
3 Why do we sometimes hesitate to try something new or 'foreign'?

REFLECTION POINT

We all belong to a certain culture and it's a big part of our identity. It's normal to want to stay in the 'comfort zone' of your own culture and be a little afraid of unfamiliar things. But if you don't open your mind to other cultures, you'll miss some fantastic experiences.

EXTEND

5 Work in pairs. Role-play a situation in which a visitor comes to your home and is not keen to try your food, listen to your music or watch your TV programmes. How can you convince him/her?

Workbook, page 61

SPEAKING So do I

Agree or disagree with an opinion

SPEAK

1 Work in pairs. Look at the things in the box and answer the questions.

art books clothes film music

1 What tastes do you have in common with members of your family or friends?
2 What differences are there in the things you like?

WATCH OR LISTEN

2 2.22 Watch or listen to the scene. What things do Ava and Sasha agree on? What do they disagree on?

Ava: Listen to this! I think it's one of the best songs I've heard for a long time. The lyrics are really moving.
Sasha: OK, let me listen … um … um … um … wow, I totally (1) .... I just love her voice.
Ava: So (2) .... I. It makes me cry every time I hear it. … I don't like that new song by The Roberts, though, do you? As far as I'm concerned, it's totally overrated.
Sasha: I think (3) .... too. I don't understand why it's so popular.
Ava: (4) .... do I. It's not very original, is it? … Talking about original … that book that you lent me …
Sasha: Yeah, I know. Isn't it great? The characters are so realistic, aren't they?
Ava: Well, (5) .... , I thought they were pretty average. To be (6) .... , I didn't like the book that much. I'm not into science fiction.
Sasha: Neither (7) .... I, but I liked this book.
Ava: Look, I'm sorry. Let's just agree to disagree this once. OK?

3 Look at the conversation again and underline all the opinions.

4 a 2.22 Watch or listen again and complete the phrases (1–7) in Exercise 2.

b 2.23 Listen and repeat the phrases, paying attention to stress and intonation.

ACT

5 a Work in pairs. Think of a song and a film which are popular at the moment. Act out a conversation in which you give your opinion and your partner agrees or disagrees.

b Choose one of the following topics (or your own topic) and practise another conversation where you give opinions, agree and disagree.

bungee jumping CCTV cameras heavy metal music sushi voting at 16

PHRASEBOOK 2.24

Giving an opinion
I think/believe (that) …
As far as I'm concerned …
Isn't it great/awful … ?

Agreeing
I think so too.
So do I. / So am I.
Neither do I. / Neither am I.
I totally agree.

Disagreeing
Well, actually …
To be honest …
I'm afraid I don't agree.

Workbook, page 59

WRITING I recommend it

Use linking words

SPEAK AND READ

1 **Have you ever been to a music festival or concert?**

YES: What singers or bands did you see? What was the best thing about it?
NO: Would you like to go to a music festival or concert? Why?/Why not?

2 **Read Mark's review of a cultural event. Where did he go and what were the highlights for him?**

Last summer, my dad and I went to Roskilde Festival in Denmark. Roskilde Festival isn't only one of the biggest music festivals in Europe, attracting nearly 100,000 fans, but it also donates all its profits to charity.

Bruce Springsteen was the main act (my dad was there because of him). There were also 200 other music acts from around the world. However, the festival wasn't just about music. There were food events, video competitions and art installations too – including a huge sculpture made from (used!) chewing gum.

Although Springsteen gave a powerful performance, for me rap band The Roots and Brazilian singer Criolo were the most impressive acts. The organisation was amazing and as a result, the festival was a peaceful event on the whole. Despite the mud (that's part of music festivals, isn't it?) life on the campsite was great.

I can thoroughly recommend going to Roskilde Festival. It'll open your mind to all kinds of new music and you'll meet new people.

STUDY

3 **Look at Mark's review again. Write the descriptions next to the correct paragraphs.**

- What you liked or couldn't stand
- A good experience or a big mistake?
- What happened, who took part
- Basic facts: what, when, where

1 Introduction: ....
2 More detailed description: ....
3 Your impressions and opinions: ....
4 Your recommendation: ....

4 a **Read the tips in the HOW TO box.**

HOW TO
use linking words

Use these linking words to join sentences and ideas together.

- To add ideas, use *and, also, too* or *not only … but also*.
- To contrast ideas, use *despite, but, however, although* or *even though*.
- To express a cause, use *because, because of* or *as*.
- To express a result, use *so, as a result* or *therefore*.

b **Find eight linking words from the HOW TO box in the review. Where do they come in a sentence (beginning, middle or end)?**

c **Work in pairs. Write example sentences for the other words in the HOW TO box. Make sure you put the linking words in the correct place. Use a dictionary if necessary.**

Get it right

although + subject + verb: *Although Springsteen gave a powerful performance, …*

despite + noun: *Despite the mud, …*

PRACTISE

5 **Join the ideas with a correct linking word from the HOW TO box.**

1 I love rap music, ... the lyrics are sometimes really rude about women.
2 .... the rain, we really enjoyed the festival.
3 The tickets are cheap and the venue is .... popular with students.
4 .... my friend was going, I decided to go to the concert.
5 The band was excellent, ... they only played for half an hour.
6 We really enjoyed the performance, ... we're going to download their songs.

PLAN, WRITE AND CHECK

6 a **You're going to write a review of a cultural event you've been to. It can be a festival, an exhibition, a theatre play, a circus or a carnival – or something else. Use the plan in Exercise 3 and make notes.**

b **Write your review. Remember to include linking words.**

SHARE AND REVIEW

7 **Swap your review with a partner. Read your partner's writing and review it.**

Workbook, pages 60–61

VOCABULARY Art

1 Complete the sentences with the correct art from the box.

collage	graffiti
installation	landscape
mural	pavement art
performance art	portrait
sketch	still life

1 A(n) ______ of old trainers with video.
2 A classic countryside ______ of the local area.
3 Original ______ with music by the artists.
4 An interesting ______ of pictures of dead spiders.
5 A large piece of 3-D ______ in chalk.
6 A head and shoulders ______ of the Head.
7 A black and white ______ in ink of the artist's girlfriend.
8 A small ______ of a fruit bowl.
9 A large ______ on the school wall by 8b.
10 A piece of ______ art with the artist's name.

___ /10

Words to describe art

2 Complete the judge's comments about the works of art in Exercise 1 with the correct adjectives.

- Clever use of original, (1) qu______ objects.
- (2) Su______ colours and beautiful brushwork.
- (3) Im______ costumes and (4) dr______ movements.
- (5) Co______ use of wildlife but interesting effect.
- An (6) el______ and detailed piece of art.
- A realistic image of a (7) un______ subject.
- A (8) mo______ picture painted with love.
- A good solid painting that makes a (9) du______ subject look interesting.
- (10) St______ wall art. Well done!
- (11) Av______ use of imagination but (12) po______ colours.

___ /12

GRAMMAR *-ing* forms

3 Complete the interview with Kyle, the winner of the competition. Use the correct form of the words in the box.

ask collect get lie make put think

home | competition | winners | forum

Us: How did you get the idea?
Kyle: Well, I was sitting in the changing room (1) ______ changed after sports class. All the trainers (2) ______ round on the floor looked really artistic. (3) ______ about it, I realised this could be a really cool installation.
Us: Did it take a long time?
Kyle: (4) ______ enough old trainers was the hard part. I put up a notice in school (5) ______ people to donate their old ones. (6) ______ them together and (7) ______ the installation didn't actually take very long.

___ /14

Question tags

4 Complete the comments overheard at the exhibition with question tags.

1 *Those white trainers are yours,* ______ *?*
2 *Nobody wears those trainers now,* ______ *?*
3 *You can't explain that to me,* ______ *?*
4 *It's a comment on consumerism,* ______ *?*
5 *Kyle has got a great imagination,* ______ *?*
6 *You gave Kyle that idea,* ______ *?*
7 *My shoelace is broken. You don't think I could take one,* ______ *?*

___ /14

Your score: ___ /50

SKILLS CHECK

✓✓✓ Yes, I can. No problem!
✓✓ Yes, I can. But I need a bit of help.
✓ Yes, I can. But I need a lot of help.

I can transfer information to a different text. ______
I can recognise general statements and exceptions when I listen. ______
I can value the art and culture of different societies. ______
I can agree or disagree with an opinion. ______
I can use linking words. ______

Workbook, pages 62–63

UNIT 6 CRIME SCENE

IN THE PICTURE Crime

Talk about crimes and criminals

RECALL AND READ

1 2.25 **Listen and take notes on what you hear. What do you think happened? Compare with a partner.**

2 Work in pairs. Read the magazine feature and do the tasks.

- Find words that you used in your notes in Exercise 1.
- Underline the names of eight crimes and criminals.
- Decide which statistics surprise you the most and why.

CRIME DOESN'T USUALLY PAY

There's been a crime. At the scene, police car lights flash, an ambulance stops, police officers talk on radios. Two detectives arrive. They examine the victim, take photos, collect evidence. They use the latest technology to identify and arrest the criminal. The message? Crime doesn't pay.

That's how it works in TV series, but how many crimes are solved in real life? Statistics depend on the crime and where you live, but recent figures for the USA show that not all criminals are caught.

- Sixty-five per cent of murders are solved, but one in three murderers doesn't pay for their crime.
- The average bank robbery makes less than $10,000 and over half of bank robbers are caught.
- Just fifteen per cent of burglars are caught, which means preventing burglary is the only solution.
- Twenty-five per cent of cybercrimes go unsolved, so protecting yourself against identity theft is essential.

WORK WITH WORDS

3 Complete the table with words from the article in Exercise 2.

Crime	Criminal	Verb
theft	thief	steal
		rob
		burgle
	murderer	murder
	cybercriminal	

4 Match the crimes in the box to the photos (1–6).

burglary murder pickpocketing piracy shoplifting ~~vandalism~~

vandalism – photo 1

5 Match the crimes in the box to the definitions.

blackmail cybercrime kidnapping mugging robbery theft

1 .... : stealing something
2 .... : illegally taking someone and making them a prisoner
3 .... : using private information to make a person do something
4 .... : stealing from a person or place, often using violence
5 .... : attacking people in a public place to steal something
6 .... : a crime that's committed on the internet

6 Make a table for the crimes in Exercise 5. Try to add the criminals and verbs. Check your answers on page 142.

7 (2.26) **Listen and repeat the crimes.**

8 (2.27) **Listen to eight situations. Write the name of the crime and a short description of the situation.**

9 **THE MOVING PICTURE** **Watch the news story. What problem does it describe? What solutions are mentioned?**

EXTEND

10 **Work in pairs. Decide which punishment below is best for each of the crimes in Exercise 3.**

- a fine *(How much money?)*
- community service *(What job for the community? For how long?)*
- a prison sentence *(How long in prison?)*

SPEAK

11 **Work in pairs. Do one or both of the tasks.**

A Think of a crime that's been on the local, national or international news recently. Have the police solved the crime?

B How common are the crimes in Exercises 3–5 in your country? What could the government and police do to prevent these crimes?

PHRASE BYTES

There's been a lot in the news recently about …

I think … is a real problem, especially in …

To tackle the problem of … I think the police/government should / have to …

GO BEYOND

Do the Words & Beyond exercises on page 135.

Workbook, page 64

READING Chicago

>>> Infer meaning when you read

SPEAK AND READ

1 **Make a class list of things you know about Chicago. Think about its location, and who and what it's famous for.**

2 (2.28) **Quickly read the website article and do the tasks below.**

- Decide who it was written for.
- Add information to your list from Exercise 1.
- Match the photos to three underlined places.

1

2

3

Where to stay | Things to do | Getting around | Eating out | Crime & safety

1 Like most big cities, crime forms part of Chicago's past and present. Mention Chicago and people will immediately think of the famous mafia boss Al Capone. Capone made his fortune by illegally selling alcohol during the prohibition years of the 1920s and early 30s; the era of organised crime and police corruption that was recreated in the movie *The Untouchables*.

2 Today, Chicago still makes headlines for its gang-related violence, but it's generally a safe place to visit. As in any modern metropolis, there are areas where you mustn't go if you want to avoid problems, but you shouldn't let any bad press stop you from visiting this amazing city.

3 If this is your first visit, you'll probably spend much of your time in and around The Loop, the city's central business district, and neighbourhoods immediately to the north like Old Town and Lincoln Park, with its zoo and museums. These are busy, popular areas. There's safety in numbers, as they say, so you don't have to take any special precautions, though you ought to keep your valuables out of sight.

4 Further north, you'll move into areas where you have to be more careful, especially after dark. Parts of Uptown fall into this category. Some locals say you ought not to use the elevated 'L' railway on the north side at night.

5 Most of the real trouble spots are in South Side or West Side, where there are some areas you'd better not go, and others that you must avoid at all costs. If you do wander into these areas, you should keep an eye on the cars. A street full of old cars with the occasional expensive one means you ought to turn back. The owners of those cars probably don't make their money doing a nine-to-five job.

3 **a** **Read the tips in the HOW TO box.**

b **Match the definitions to expressions and sentences in the article in the paragraph indicated.**

1 is famous because it's in the news (2)
2 criticism in the media (2)
3 it's less dangerous if you're with other people (3)
4 places where there's a lot of crime (5)
5 they're probably criminals (5)

4 **Which tips in the HOW TO box did you use for help with Exercise 3b? Tick (✓) them.**

REACT

5 **Work in pairs. Answer the questions.**

1 What did you learn about Chicago that you didn't know before?
2 Would you like to visit Chicago? Why?/Why not?

HOW TO

infer meaning when you read

If you infer meaning in written texts, you understand what the writer doesn't express directly.

- ☐ Identify the writer's general opinion. This helps to understand individual sentences.
- ☐ If you don't recognise names, use the context to work out why they're mentioned.
- ☐ Look for idioms (see page 8) and other expressions that say things indirectly.

GO BEYOND

Make a list of words and phrases in the article that are related to criminal activities.

Workbook, page 65

GRAMMAR *Should, must, have to, ought to, had better*

Use modal verbs to give advice and make recommendations

READ

1 **Read the advice. Where's it about? How difficult is it to avoid street crime?**

"You'd better get street-wise"

In any city around the world there are places you ought not to visit at night and others you must avoid at any time of the day. You should find out about these places before you travel, but you mustn't let what you read spoil your trip because you don't have to change your behaviour much to stay safe. You just have to use your common sense. It will usually tell you what you ought to do in any given situation.

STUDY

2 **Complete the explanations with the words and phrases in the box. Use Exercise 1 to help you.**

necessary prohibited not necessary a good (or bad) idea

Should, must, have to, ought to, had better

Use: For advice and recommendations.

should(n't) *ought (not) to* *Should you ... ?*	It's ....
had better (not)	It's a good (or bad) idea in a particular situation.
have/has to *must* *Do you have to ... ?*	It's .... , important or strongly recommended.
don't/doesn't have to	It's ....
mustn't	It's .... or dangerous.

Form:
modal verb + infinitive without *to*

***have to* or *must*?**
You can often use both with the same meaning.
Use *have to* when you can't choose to do something:
You have to get a visa.
Use *must* for strong recommendations:
You must visit the old town.

See GRAMMAR DATABASE, page 125.

PRACTISE

3 **Write complete sentences using the words in brackets. Decide if the verb needs to be positive or negative.**

Eight tips for staying street-wise in the city

1 You / keep away / from streets with poor lighting (must)
You must keep away from streets with poor lighting.
2 You / stay / on busier streets (ought)
3 You / behave / too much like a tourist (should)
4 You / hide / phones and cameras in public (better)
5 You / walk around / with headphones on (ought)
6 You / leave / valuables at your hotel (better)
7 You / visit / every part of the city (have)
8 If someone tries to rob you, you / resist (must)

4 **Choose the best options to complete the forum answers.**

Q: I'm going to London with my class soon. What (1) *should I* / *had I better* do when I'm there?

A: You really (2) *ought* / *must* to go to the British Museum. It's amazing and it's free. In general, I think central London's safe, but you (3) *mustn't* / *don't have to* forget the basic safety advice for any big city. Also, cars (4) *must* / *have to* drive on the left, so be careful when you cross roads. Finally, (5) *you'd better* / *you must* practise your English before you go because not many people speak other languages!

Add a comment

Q: I'm going to Kenya with my family this summer. (6) *Must we* / *Do we have to* get a visa? And what about vaccinations?

A: Visitors (7) *ought to* / *have to* have a visa, but you (8) *don't have to* / *shouldn't* get one before you go because you can get one at the airport when you arrive. As for vaccinations, I don't think (9) *you have to* / *you'd better* have any, but I think some are recommended, so you (10) *must* / *ought to* consult your doctor.

Add a comment

WRITE AND SPEAK

5 a **You see a question on the forum in Exercise 4 asking for advice about visiting your town or city. Write an answer. Include practical advice and advice for staying safe.**

b **Work in pairs. Talk about the advice in your answers. Do you agree with all your partner's advice? Why?/Why not?**

Workbook, pages 66–67

LISTENING AND VOCABULARY No place to hide

Recognise turn-taking

SPEAK AND LISTEN

1 **Work in pairs. Describe what you can see in the pictures. Talk about who might live there.**

2 **a** 2.29 **Listen to the first part of a radio crime series. Take notes on the owner of the house.**

b **Compare your notes with your partner from Exercise 1. Decide which of your ideas were right or wrong.**

3 **a** **Read the tips in the HOW TO box.**

b 2.29 **Listen again and answer the questions.**

1 Who says these words and expressions from the HOW TO box, Mitch (*M*) or Shirley (*S*)?

- a Actually, M/S
- b That reminds me, M/S
- c Well, M/S
- d Just a minute! M/S
- e Sorry to interrupt you, but M/S
- f By the way, M/S

2 Who asks more questions, Mitch or Shirley?

3 Who takes more turns?

HOW TO

recognise turn-taking

- ☐ *That reminds me*, *By the way*, and *Well*, can be used to change the subject.
- ☐ *Actually,* adds surprising information.
- ☐ *Sorry to interrupt you, but …* and *Just a minute!* are used to interrupt somebody.
- ☐ Questions and pauses invite somebody to speak.

4 **Which tips in the HOW TO box did you use to help with Exercise 3b? Tick (✓) them.**

5 2.30 **Work in pairs. Decide what Mr Smith has done. Then listen to the second part of the series. Check your answer and answer the questions below.**

1 Whose house did Mr Smith burgle?

2 What deal does Shirley offer Mr Smith?

REACT

6 **Work in pairs. Talk about TV crime series in your country. Which ones are there? How popular are they? Why do people like watching them?**

WORK WITH WORDS

7 **Match the definitions (1–10) to the words in bold in the extracts on the right from the radio programme.**

1 .... : a dirty area that you can see on the surface of something
2 .... : somebody who sees a crime
3 .... : evidence that shows something is definitely true
4 .... : a chemical substance that contains genetic information
5 .... : an object or fact that helps solve a crime
6 .... : marks made by shoes or feet
7 .... : the part that's left when the rest has been finished
8 .... : evidence that a crime suspect was somewhere else
9 .... : marks made by fingers
10 .... : a line of marks left by somebody or something moving

'the **remains** of his evening meal'
'that **trail** of **footprints** on the floor'
'there's another **clue** in the sink'
'this **mark** on the wall'
'You need **proof** to arrest me.'
'It wasn't me. I've got an **alibi**!'
'A **DNA** test will show that it's your blood.'
'I'm sure we'll find **fingerprints** too.'
'And we have a **witness**.'

8 2.31 **Listen and check your answers. Then listen and repeat the types of evidence.**

9 **Work in pairs. Do the following tasks.**

- Look at the extracts in the box in Exercise 7. Which evidence is proof of where Mr Smith was, and which evidence gives a clue, but not proof?
- If detectives went to your house, what evidence would they find to show that you lived there?

GO BEYOND

Do the Words & Beyond exercise on page 135.

Workbook, pages 68–69

GRAMMAR *Can't have, could/may/might have, must have*

Talk about possible explanations for things in the past

READ AND LISTEN

1 2.32 **Read and listen to the conversation. What's happened to Kim's phone?**

Kim: I can't find my phone.
Mary: You **must** have left it at home. You always forget something.
Kim: I **can't** have left it at home. I showed you that photo this morning.
Mary: Well, it **could** have fallen out of your bag.
Kim: No. I always keep it closed.
Mary: Do you think someone **may** have stolen it?
Kim: It's possible. But when?
Mary: Hang on, you sent a message just after class. You **might** have left it on your desk.
Kim: You're right. I'd better go back and see.

STUDY

2 Complete the explanations with modal verbs from Exercise 1.

Can't have, could/may/might have, must have

Use: To talk about possible explanations for things in the past that are based on evidence.

could/ .... */* .... *have*	You think an explanation is possible.
.... *have*	You're sure an explanation is true.
.... *have*	You're sure an explanation is impossible.

Form:
can't/could/must, etc + *have* + past participle

See GRAMMAR DATABASE, page 125.

PRACTISE

3 2.33 **Rewrite the underlined sentences with *can't have*, *could*, *may*, *might* and *must have*. Use all the verbs. Then listen and check.**

Mary: Have you asked at lost property? (1) Maybe someone has found it.
Someone may have found it.
Kim: (2) I'm sure Tom picked up my phone by accident. He's got the same one.
Mary: (3) It's not possible that Tom took it. He's not at school today.
Kim: I need to find it fast. (4) It's possible someone's used all my credit by now!
Mary: Have you checked your coat? (5) Maybe it fell through a hole in the pocket.
Kim: (6) I'm sure it didn't do that. We didn't hear it when you rang me.
Mary: It's here! (7) The battery obviously ran out. That would explain why you didn't hear it.

4 2.34 **Complete the conversation with *can't have*, *could have*, *may have*, *might have* or *must have* and the verbs in the box. Then listen and check.**

~~be~~ get hear imagine leave make

Pete: Mum, I heard someone downstairs. It (1) *must have been* a burglar.
Mum: You (2) .... a burglar. There are never any burglaries in this part of town. You (3) .... it.
Pete: I didn't! There it is again.
Mum: Anything (4) .... that noise. The wind, for example.
Pete: But it's not windy at all.
Mum: OK, let's go and have a look … Oh, it's an owl! But how did it get in?
Pete: I'm not sure, but I (5) .... a window open.
Mum: If you did, it (6) .... in through it. There's no other way into the house.
Pete: The question is, how do we get it out again?

5 a 2.35 PRONOUNCE **Listen to the sentence from Exercise 4.**

It must have been a burglar.

- Which two words are stressed the most? Underline them.
- Which two words aren't stressed? Circle them.

b 2.36 **Listen and repeat other sentences from Exercise 4. Pay attention to the rhythm created by stressed and unstressed words.**

WRITE AND SPEAK

6 a Write two possible explanations for each situation using *could*, *may* and *might have*.

Situation 1: You went to a local shop at 9am and it was closed. It's normally open at this time.
The owner might have overslept.
Situation 2: During the night you heard two people shouting next door. Then you heard a loud bang, and everything went quiet.
Situation 3: You live in a house with a garden. Last night, your cat didn't come home.

b Work in pairs. Tell each other your explanations.

- Decide if any explanations are impossible and explain why using *can't have*.
- Choose the best explanation for each one, then tell the class using *must have*.

LANGUAGE & BEYOND

3: DAVID

'I used to paint graffiti around our neighbourhood. Occasionally, I had to run away from the police and angry neighbours.'

Three case studies

We look at how three teenagers learned to take responsibility for their actions.

BEFORE

1: GORKA

'I was a difficult student. I arrived late, took ages to get my books out and spent the class messing about and talking.'

2: NAOMI

'I love R&B music. I used to look for albums on the Net, then download them illegally from file-sharing sites.'

»» Take responsibility for your actions

KNOW YOURSELF

SPEAK AND READ

1 a Work in pairs. Look at the magazine article above. What are the people doing?

b Read the three 'before' case studies. Do you know anyone like Gorka, Naomi and David?

DO

2 a Gorka, Naomi and David met some of the people who were affected by their actions. Work in pairs. Discuss how you think they answered the questions below.

1 Why do you do what you do?
2 How do you think your actions affect other people?
3 Who do you blame for your actions?
4 Who's really responsible for your actions?

b Read what the teenagers said after their meetings. Check to see if your predictions were correct.

REFLECT

3 Discuss the questions with your class. Do you agree with the REFLECTION POINT?

1 Do you think Gorka, Naomi and David are completely responsible for their actions? If not, who else is?
2 Who has benefitted most from their change of behaviour? Why?
3 Why can it be hard to take responsibility for your actions?

EXTEND

4 Work in pairs. What do some people say about not paying tax and dangerous driving? What might they say after a meeting like the one in Exercise 2?

AFTER

1: GORKA

'I was bored in class and wanted attention, and I always complained about how teachers picked on me. After talking to teachers and other students, I realised I was wasting their time and mine.'

2: NAOMI

'I downloaded music because everyone does it. But I spoke to a group that broke up because people didn't buy their music. I realised that illegal downloads are bad for other people, and I buy music now.'

3: DAVID

'Painting graffiti's really exciting. But when I spoke to neighbours and local shopkeepers, I realised how much they have to pay to clean their walls. I've found a place where it's OK to paint, so now we're all happy.'

REFLECTION POINT

Our behaviour sometimes has negative consequences for other people. If we can understand those consequences and stop blaming other people for our actions, we can make life better for them and for us.

»» Workbook, page 73

SPEAKING You shouldn't have done that

»» Give and react to criticism

SPEAK

1 If you criticise something, you say what you think is wrong or bad about it. Work in pairs. Answer the questions.

1 When was the last time you criticised somebody? What for? How did they react?
2 When was the last time somebody criticised you? What for? How did you feel?
3 Why is it difficult to accept criticism?

WATCH OR LISTEN

2 2.37 Watch or listen to three conversations and answer the questions.

1 Why does one person criticise the other?
2 Who is more careful with their criticism?

3 2.37 Work in pairs. Complete the conversations. Write one word in each gap. Then watch or listen again to check or complete your answers.

1 **Ruth:** You're late! We've missed the film.
Tom: I'm sorry, but it wasn't my fault. The bus was stuck in traffic.
Ruth: You (1) ______ have got an earlier bus. You (2) ______ the film started at six.
Tom: Yes, but there must've been an accident.
Ruth: I'm (3) ______ of your excuses. You (4) ______ have sent a message.
Tom: You're right. It won't happen again.

2 **Nora:** Ruth, I know you're stressed out with exams, but you (5) ______ have shouted at Tom.
Ruth: I know, but he made us miss the film.
Nora: That's true, but you were (6) ______ aggressive. We've all got angry before, but imagine how he must have felt.
Ruth: You're right. I shouldn't have shouted.

3 **Tom:** Er, Ruth, I've got a bit of bad news. Somebody stole my bag on the bus and it had your book in it.
Ruth: Tom! I (7) ______ you to look after it! How (8) ______ you be so careless?
Tom: I'm sorry. It was right next to me, but I obviously wasn't careful (9) ______ .
Ruth: Oh, well, these things happen.

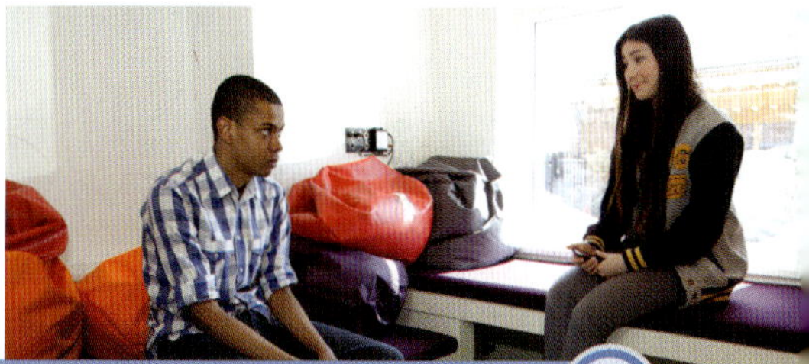

4 In different colours, underline:

- three expressions Nora uses to make her criticisms easier to accept.
- three excuses Tom and Ruth make, including the word that comes before them.
- two different expressions Tom and Ruth use to accept criticism, and what they say next.

5 2.38 Listen and repeat, paying attention to intonation.

ACT

6 Work in pairs. Prepare two conversations and present them to other students.

- Think of a situation in which one person criticises another person for something.
- Conversation 1: Criticism is given angrily. The other person reacts badly and makes excuses.
- Conversation 2: Criticism is given carefully, and the other person accepts it well.

PHRASEBOOK 2.39

Criticise

You should/shouldn't have got/left ...
You could have sent a message / told me ...
You know/knew ...
I told you to be ...
You were too aggressive / weren't careful enough.
I'm tired of ...
How could you be/leave ... ?
I know ... but ... / We've all ... but ...

React to criticism

I'm sorry, ... / I know, ... / Yes, ...
... but it wasn't my fault.
You're right.
It won't happen again.
I shouldn't have got so angry / shouted.

»» Workbook, page 71

WRITING In my opinion

»» Use paragraphs and topic sentences

SPEAK AND READ

1 **Work in pairs. Look at the question and discuss your opinions.**

Are prisons the best way to stop crime?

2 **Read an essay that answers the question. Does the writer agree with your opinions?**

Most people would agree that if you commit a crime, you should be punished. The idea is that punishment stops you committing another crime. However, I don't think prison is the best way to stop crime.

The first reason is that every year, thousands of people go to prison, but statistics show that over 50% of criminals commit another crime later. It's clear, therefore, that sending criminals to prison doesn't stop crime.

Also, shouldn't we think about how to make criminals take responsibility for their actions? I think we need to educate them about the consequences of their crimes. That way, they might change their behaviour.

And finally, keeping people in prison is expensive, and our prison population is growing. I don't think we can afford to send so many people to prison if it doesn't stop crime.

To sum up, sending criminals to prison doesn't work. It would be better to spend money on educating them so they learn why crime doesn't pay.

STUDY

3 **Read the essay again and answer the questions.**

1 What's the role of the first and last paragraphs?
2 How many main arguments do each of the other paragraphs include?
3 What facts does the writer use to support his or her arguments?

4 a **Read the tips in the HOW TO box and check your answers to questions 1 and 2 in Exercise 3.**

b **Find the topic sentence in the second, third and fourth paragraphs of the essay.**

HOW TO

use paragraphs and topic sentences

- Start with an introduction. Mention your opinion and what other people think.
- Write one of your arguments in each of the following paragraphs.
- Include a **topic sentence** in each paragraph that summarises its argument.
- Include other sentences to support or explain the topic sentence.
- End with a conclusion. State your opinion again and summarise your main argument.

PRACTISE

5 **Choose one of the essay titles below. Think of three arguments to defend your opinion and write a topic sentence for each argument.**

- *People should lose their internet connection if they download music and films illegally.*
- *All bullies should be expelled from school.*
- *Phones should be banned from schools.*

PLAN, WRITE AND CHECK

6 **You're going to write an essay. Write about the title you chose in Exercise 5, or choose another one. If you choose another one, think of three new arguments to defend your opinion.**

7 **Write your essay. Use tips from the HOW TO box to help you organise it. Then check it.**

SHARE AND REVIEW

8 **Swap your essay with a partner. Read your partner's essay and review it.**

Workbook, pages 72–73

VOCABULARY Crime

1 Complete the crimes and criminals.

Joey: We're the Teenage Crime Busters, or TCB for short. Our mission is to stop and solve crime in the city. We stop bank (1) r________ before they happen, keep (2) b________ out of your home and (3) s________ out of your store. We stop (4) m________ from killing, make sure (5) k________ don't take people prisoner and that (6) b________ don't try to make money from your secrets. On the street, we stop (7) m________ before they attack people, (8) p________ before they steal your purse or wallet and make sure (9) v________ don't go round breaking things. We also stop (10) p________ from selling illegal copies of films and games. And on the Net we stop (11) c________ from committing identity (12) t________ .

___ /12

Types of evidence

2 Choose the correct options.

Susie: OK, this is the crime scene. We need to find as many (1) *clues* / *proof* as we can. We need (2) *alibi* / *proof* before the police can arrest the criminal. Sally, check for (3) *fingerprints* / *footprints* on that car door, and then see where that (4) *mark* / *trail* of (5) *footprints* / *witnesses* in the snow goes. Tommy, check out the (6) *fingerprints* / *remains* of the pizza on the back seat. You might be able to get a (7) *clues* / *DNA* sample from where it's been bitten. Joey, there's a (8) *mark* / *remains* on the side of the car. Find out what made it. Then talk to the man over there. He's our only (9) *trail* / *witness*. Ask him what he saw. The suspect says he was at the cinema when the crime took place, so I'll check out his (10) *alibi* / *DNA* to see if he was really there.

___ /10

GRAMMAR *Should, must, have to, ought to, had better*

3 Complete with the words in the box.

better don't have to have to must mustn't ought should shouldn't

Susie: I think you'd (1) ________ tell us where you really were at 6pm this evening.

Mr Gold: Why (2) ________ I tell you anything? You're just a kid. You (3) ________ to be at home watching TV.

Susie: You (4) ________ say anything. But you (5) ________ think I won't solve this crime because I'm a kid. Do I (6) ________ remind you how many crimes the TCB has solved?

Mr Gold: Listen. If you value your own life, you really (7) ________ stop investigating this crime. The man behind it is the most dangerous criminal in the city. You (8) ________ become his enemy.

___ /16

Can't have, could/may/might have, must have

4 Complete with *can't*, *could*, *may*, *might*, *must have* and the correct form of the verbs. Use each modal verb at least once.

Susie: Gold told me the most dangerous criminal in the city is behind this crime, so Al Perone (1) ________ (organise) it. I think Gold (2) ________ (steal) the money, but I'm not sure. But Gold can't eat gluten, so he (3) ________ (eat) that pizza. So if Gold was in the car, there (4) ________ (be) a second person too. What did you find out?

Joey: The man who saw what happened says he (5) ________ (see) two people in the car, but he can't be sure. One person ran down to the river. We think he (6) ________ (cross) the river, but the water's very fast, so that's unlikely.

___ /12

Your score: ___ /50

SKILLS CHECK

✓✓✓ Yes, I can. No problem!
✓✓ Yes, I can. But I need a bit of help.
✓ Yes, I can. But I need a lot of help.

I can infer meaning when I read. ___
I can recognise turn-taking. ___
I can take responsibility for my actions. ___
I can give and react to criticism. ___
I can use paragraphs and topic sentences. ___

Workbook, pages 74–75

READ AND COMPLETE

1 **Read the article below and think of the word which best fits each gap. Use only one word.**

TOP THREE ART CRIMES

THEFT

In the art world, truth is often stranger (**1**) ______ fiction. In 1990, two thieves walked into the Gardner Museum in Boston wearing police uniforms and false moustaches and stole 13 unique paintings. The works (**2**) ______ art, (**3**) ______ were worth more than $500 million, have never been found. Twelve years later, a group of criminals stole five valuable paintings from the National Fine Arts Museum in Asunción, Paraguay, (**4**) ______ digging a huge tunnel into the building.

LOOTING

In 2003, at the time of the Iraq war, 15,000 pieces of Iraq's cultural history (**5**) ______ stolen from the National Museum in Baghdad. The museum's (**6**) ______ important piece, the Warka Vase dating from 3200 BC, was also stolen, although it was later taken (**7**) ______ to the museum – broken into several pieces. Only a third of the lost treasures have (**8**) ______ returned.

VANDALISM

In 2006, a 12-year-old boy visiting a gallery in Detroit on a school trip stuck a piece of chewing gum onto a $1.5 million painting. The canvas (**9**) ______ have been very badly damaged, but luckily the gum only left a small mark.

A copy of the Thinker statue by August Rodin was also the victim of vandalism in Buenos Aires. In 2011, vandals used spray paint (**10**) ______ give the sculpture green hair and a pink body, and add a black shoulder tattoo. Unfortunately, the statue was damaged even more by water when it was cleaned.

Reading and completing: ______ /10

EXAM TIPS

complete a gapped text

- Quickly read the text. What's it about? Where would you expect to see it?
- Read the text again and look at the words before and after each gap.
- Use only one word in the gap. Typical words include articles, prepositions, pronouns, verbs and linking words.
- Make sure you use the correct form for verbs and always check your spelling.

infer meaning when you read
See page 62.

LISTEN

2 2.40 **You will hear people talking in five different situations. For questions 1–5, choose the best answer (A, B or C).**

1 You hear a police officer talking.
What crime is she dealing with?
A mugging
B pickpocketing
C vandalism

2 You hear two friends talking.
What's their opinion of the photo exhibition?
A They prefer looking at colour photos.
B The boy doesn't think the portraits are very good.
C The girl thinks the quality isn't good enough.

3 You hear a father talking to his son.
What does he think about what his son's doing?
A He's annoyed that his son's using his computer.
B He tells his son it's dangerous and against the law.
C He says it's unfair to the film industry.

4 You hear a teacher talking.
Why does a student interrupt her?
A The teacher forgot to tell them about the art competition.
B The teacher told them some wrong information.
C The teacher put some wrong information on the school website.

5 You hear part of a TV programme.
What has happened?
A One of the girls has taken something without paying.
B One of the girls has bought a new bag.
C A store detective has stopped one of the girls.

Listening: ______ /10

WRITE

3 You've seen this announcement on a website for English language learners. Follow the instructions.

Short story
competition

Take part in our competition. All you have to do is write a short story (140–190 words). Your story must begin with this sentence.
Although I didn't know for sure who had stolen my new bike, I had a strong idea who it could be.

Your story must include:
- a conversation.
- a description of a place.

Writing: ______ /10

Progress check score ______ /30

EXAM TIPS

do a multiple-choice listening exercise (several audio texts)

- Read and listen to the question: it identifies the speaker(s) and the situation or topic.
- Listen for the main message and the speaker's attitude or feelings.
- Think about your answer. Then look at the options. Is your answer there?
- Choose an option because of its meaning, not just because it has similar words to the audio. When you listen again, check your choices.

recognise general statements and exceptions
See page 54.

recognise turn-taking
See page 64.

EXAM TIPS

write a story

- Read the task carefully. What do you need to include in your story?
- Make a plan with a clear storyline. Use your imagination!
- Make sure your story links to the opening or closing sentence.
- Use different past tenses, linking words and time expressions to connect events.
- Use adjectives, adverbs and descriptive expressions to add interest.
- Make sure your story is the right length and includes everything in the task.

use linking words
See page 58.

UNIT 7

TURNING POINTS

IN THE PICTURE Money verbs and nouns

Talk about money

a

READ AND RECALL

1 **Work in pairs. Look at the photos and describe what you can see. What's the connection between the photos?**

2 **Read the magazine tips. Which of the tips do you already follow? Which would you like to follow?**

3 **THE MOVING PICTURE Watch the video. What questions are the people answering? Ask your partner the questions.**

Seven Money Tips for Teens

1 It's never too soon to start saving money. If you put money into a savings account now, you'll quickly start making money.

2 If your parents give you an allowance or if you have some part-time work, save a fixed amount and then spend the rest on what you want.

3 You can save money when you shop. Don't waste money by spending it on something in an expensive shop when another shop is selling it cheaper.

4 Think twice before you buy something. Do you really need it or are you throwing your money away?

5 Keep a record of the money you spend.

6 Don't carry a lot of cash when you go out. If you only take what you need, you'll spend less.

7 Don't borrow money from your friends if you can't pay it back.

WORK WITH WORDS

4 **2.41 Match the verbs in the box to the definitions. Then listen and repeat.**

donate inherit owe pay back raise withdraw

1 collect money for a particular purpose
2 take money from a bank
3 give money or goods to a charity or other organisation
4 return money that you borrowed from someone
5 receive money or property from someone who has died
6 have to give money to a person that you borrowed from

5 **a** **2.42 Complete the sentences with the verbs from Exercise 4. Then listen and check.**

1 'We encourage people to ________ clothes. We sell them and the **profit** goes to the cause.'
2 'One day, I'll ________ the house, but I'll probably have to sell it to pay all the legal **fees**.'
3 'Mum? I know it's wrong to get into **debt**, but can you lend me ten pounds? I'll ________ you ________.'
4 'I don't believe it. It says I can't ________ anything because my **bank account** is in the red.'
5 'We sold our computer games and old phones to ________ money for charity but we made a **loss**.'
6 'I had a job and an **income** but now I'm homeless and I ________ money to the bank.'

b **Match the sentences in Exercise 5a to the photos (a–f).**

6 **2.43 Match each verb to one of the nouns in bold from Exercise 5a. Listen and check. Then listen and repeat.**

1 open	4 make
2 get into	5 have
3 pay	6 make

c

b

d

e

f

7 a 2.44 PRONOUNCE **Listen and repeat the words, focusing on the different vowel sounds.**

not /nɒt/ — note /nəʊt/

b 2.45 **Listen and circle the vowel sound you hear. Then listen and repeat the words.**

1	profit	/ɒ/	/əʊ/	3	donate	/ɒ/	/əʊ/
2	loss	/ɒ/	/əʊ/	4	owe	/ɒ/	/əʊ/

EXTEND

8 Write the noun forms of the verbs. Use *-ings*, *-al*, *-ion* or *-ance* and make any necessary spelling changes.

donate earn inherit save withdraw

SPEAK

9 Work in pairs. Invent a story using three of the photos. Use some of the money verbs and nouns in Exercises 4 and 5 to tell your story.

PHRASE BYTES

The story could be about …

We could use this photo to show …

Then what happens?

GO BEYOND

Do the Words & Beyond exercise on page 136.

Workbook, page 76

READING The power of half

Make notes for a summary

SPEAK AND READ

1 Work in pairs. Complete the tasks.

- Describe what you can see in the photo.
- Discuss what type of family you think the Salwens are.

2 a Read the tips in the HOW TO box.

b 2.46 **Read the magazine article and make notes for a summary. Then compare your notes with a partner.**

HOW TO

make notes for a summary

- [ ] Read the whole text and note important information.
- [ ] Read again and add any interesting details to your notes.
- [ ] Copy a quote if it's important.

THE POWER OF HALF

Sometimes if you want to make a difference in this world, you have to do something radical. Hannah Salwen was just 14 years old when she realized that she wanted to change things.

It all started when her dad, a reporter and editor at the *Wall Street Journal*, was driving her home from a sleepover at a friend's house.

They were almost home when they stopped at a street junction. Hannah looked left out of her dad's side window and saw a homeless man sitting on the ground holding a cardboard sign. Then she looked right at a man sitting in an expensive black Mercedes convertible. After looking left and right again, she said: 'If that man had a less nice car, that man there could have a meal.' Her dad replied that the homeless man could also have a meal if they changed their own car.

Later that evening, as she was eating with the rest of her family, Hannah described what had happened. 'It's not fair,' she said. 'We should fix this.' When she brought up the subject again a few days later, her mom asked: 'What do you want to do? Sell our house? Move into a smaller one and give what's left over to charity?' Hannah didn't think twice. 'I'll give up my bedroom. We should sell the house and give away the money. Definitely.'

Hannah's mom, dad and brother, Joseph, discussed the idea together and agreed to sell their house and give half the money to charity. They eventually found a new house a few blocks away that was almost exactly half the size of the family's current home and half the price. After moving in, they had regular meetings to decide what to do with the $800,000 they'd made on the sale.

3 a Decide if the sentences are true (*T*) or false (*F*). Correct the false sentences.

1 Hannah's father worked for a newspaper. T/F
2 The story started when she was on her way to stay with a friend. T/F
3 The homeless man was sitting on a wall. T/F
4 Hannah's brother said he'd give up his bedroom. T/F
5 The new smaller house was on the other side of the city. T/F
6 The whole family decided what to do with the money. T/F

b Which details from Exercise 3a would you include in a summary?

4 Which tips in the HOW TO box did you use for help with Exercises 2b and 3? Tick (✓) them.

REACT

5 a Work in pairs. Answer the questions.

1 What do you think the Salwens decided to do with the money they made from selling the house?
2 What do you think 'The power of half' in the title refers to?

b Student A: read the text on page 141. Student B: read the text on page 142. Summarise and exchange the information you read. Then decide what you would have done with the money.

GO BEYOND

Find these words and phrases in the article. What do they mean? Use a dictionary to help you.

radical, sleepover, convertible, It's not fair

Workbook, page 77

GRAMMAR Conditionals review

>>> Talk about possible or imaginary situations in the present and future

READ AND LISTEN

1 2.47 **Read and listen to the conversation. What's 'a saying'?**

Ben: Can you lend me £10?
Matt: If I lend it to you, will I ever see you again?
Ben: Of course you will. What are you talking about?
Matt: There's a saying that if you lend someone money and never see that person again, then it's worth the money.
Ben: What does that mean?
Matt: Well, for example, if I lent you £10 and you never gave it back, then I'd know you weren't a real friend. It cost me £10, but I discovered something important. It's a saying. Like – 'money doesn't grow on trees'.

STUDY

2 Read the explanations. Then underline an example of a zero, first and second conditional sentence in Exercise 1.

Conditionals review

In conditional sentences an *if*-clause describes a situation, and a second clause describes its results.

Zero conditional

Use: To talk about situations that are always true.

Form:
If + present simple, … present simple

First conditional

Use: To talk about possible situations in the future and their results.

Form:
If + present simple, … *will/may/might* + infinitive without *to*

Second conditional

Use: To talk about unlikely or imaginary situations in the present or future and their results.

Form:
If + past simple, … *would/wouldn't* + infinitive without *to*

See GRAMMAR DATABASE, page 126.

PRACTISE

3 Choose the correct options.

1 If you pay for things in advance, (*you*) / *you'd* often get a discount.
2 If money grew on trees, it *won't* / *wouldn't* be worth much.
3 If Dad gives me some money for my birthday, *I'd* / *I'll* buy a new phone.
4 I'd lend you the money if I *had* / *have* it.
5 We'll go to the concert if we *can* / *could* afford it.
6 I always carry some cash if *I'll* / *I* go out with friends.

Workbook, pages 78–79

4 a 2.48 **Complete the conversation with the correct form of the verbs. Then listen and check your answers.**

Carla: What would you do if (1) *you found* (you / find) £50 on the street?
Matt: In general, I think if (2) ________ (you / find) something that belongs to someone else, you should return it.
Carla: I agree. But imagine you're on an empty street and you know that if you don't take it, someone else (3) ________ (see) it and keep it.
Matt: If the street was definitely empty, then (4) ________ (I / take) the money. But (5) ________ (I / not spend) it if (6) ________ (it / belong) to someone else. Why do you ask?
Carla: Because I just found £50 on the street. What (7) ________ (you / do) if (8) ________ (you / be) in my shoes?

b Work in pairs. Answer Carla's question at the end of Exercise 4a.

5 a Match the question halves.

What would you do?

1 What would you do ___
2 If you go out with friends, ___
3 If a friend asked to borrow some money, ___
4 If you visit the UK or US, ___
5 If you spend all your money by Saturday, ___
6 What should you do ___

a what would you say?
b if someone lends you money?
c how will you survive the weekend?
d what do you all usually spend money on?
e if you inherited $5,000?
f what currencies do you need?

b Write answers to the questions.

SPEAK

6 Work in pairs. Ask the questions in Exercise 5a. Compare and discuss your answers.

7 Work in pairs. Read the sayings and explain what you think they mean, giving examples.

- Early to bed and early to rise makes a man healthy, wealthy and wise.
- A rich man doesn't know his friends.
- The best things in life are free.

LISTENING AND VOCABULARY *If ...*

»» Predict what a story will be about

SPEAK AND LISTEN

1 Work in pairs. Answer the questions.

Do you know of any famous people who have had a turning point in their lives? What happened to them?

2 a Read the tips in the HOW TO box.

b Work in pairs. Describe what you can see in the pictures. What do you think happened to the people?

Kath

Mark

Corey

HOW TO

predict what a story will be about

- Look at any pictures or visual clues.
- Think about typical information in a story:
  - Setting the scene (Where and when did the story happen? Who was involved?).
  - Describing events (What happened? How did the speaker feel?).
  - Talking about consequences (What was the result?).

3 ▶2.49 Listen to three people talking about turning points in their lives. Make notes, using the tips in the HOW TO box to help you. Were your predictions in Exercise 2b correct?

4 ▶2.49 Listen again and complete the sentences with the correct name – *Kath*, *Mark* or *Corey*.

1 ________ learned a valuable lesson from the turning point.
2 ________ used to have a more relaxing life.
3 ________ doesn't remember exactly what happened.
4 ________ would probably have a different career now.
5 ________ had problems making new friends.
6 ________ improved because of the support of another person.

REACT

5 Work in pairs. Do the tasks.

- Which of the stories did you find most interesting?
- Describe a turning point in your life or in the life of someone you know. Include the ideas from the HOW TO box.

WORK WITH WORDS

6 ▶2.50 Complete the extracts from the interviews with the adjectives ending with *-ful* and *-less*. Listen and check.

careful forgetful grateful peaceful stressful

endless helpless hopeless motionless pointless

1 The place we lived before was really quiet and ________ .
2 At first, city life was really ________ .
3 My life here had felt ________ until then.
4 We were staying at a resort – ________ beaches and lots of sun.
5 I was really ________ at playing at first.
6 I'm really ________ for what my uncle did.
7 All I remember is lying ________ on the road.
8 I couldn't see anything and … I felt so ________ .
9 Mom says I'm more ________ than I used to be.
10 I'm definitely more ________ than I used to be.

7 ▶2.51 Listen and repeat the adjectives from Exercise 6.

8 Work in pairs. Ask and answer questions. Student A: ask the questions on page 141. Student B: ask the questions on page 142.

GO BEYOND

Do the Words & Beyond exercise on page 136.

»» Workbook, pages 80–81

GRAMMAR Third conditional

Talk about imaginary situations in the past

READ

1 Read the article. Why are the students in the picture studying Spanish?

Writers and historians have always been fascinated by alternative histories. What would have happened if the *Titanic* hadn't hit an iceberg? Would Marilyn Monroe have become such an icon if she hadn't died at the age of 36? What would have happened if Pizarro hadn't found potatoes in Peru? The history of the world could have been very different if certain events had or hadn't taken place. If the Spanish Armada had landed in England in 1588, life would have been very different for the English (and your English class).

It's the same with our own lives. A decision you take today might have a dramatic effect on your future. One day, you might look back in time and wonder – 'What would have happened if … ?'

STUDY

2 Choose the correct options to complete the explanations. Then underline three more third conditional sentences in Exercise 1.

Third conditional

Use: To talk about imaginary situations in the past and their results.

Form:
Positive and negative
If + past **participle/perfect** … , …
If the Spanish Armada had landed in England,
… *would(n't) have* + past **participle/perfect**
life would have been very different.

Questions and short answers
would + subject + *have* + past participle
Would Marilyn Monroe have become such an icon if …
Yes, she would. / No, she wouldn't.

Note
would have > *would've*
You can also use *should*, *could* and *might* in the result clause.

See GRAMMAR DATABASE, page 126.

PRACTISE

3 Match the sentence halves.

1 If the *Titanic* hadn't hit an iceberg, ____
2 If Pizarro hadn't found potatoes in Peru, ____
3 The Beatles would never have existed ____
4 If Mount Vesuvius hadn't erupted, ____
5 If the Spanish Armada had landed in England in 1588, ____
6 Marilyn Monroe might have become a singer ____

a if she hadn't died at the age of 36.
b we wouldn't have started eating crisps.
c the city of Pompeii would have survived.
d James Cameron wouldn't have made the film.
e if Paul McCartney hadn't met John Lennon.
f this book wouldn't have existed.

4 2.52 Complete Marta's 'consequences' story with the third conditional. Then listen and check.

1 If I *hadn't gone away* (not go away) at the weekend, I *would've stayed* (stay) at home.
2 If I ____ (stay) at home, I ____ (can do) more revision.
3 If I ____ (do) more revision, I ____ (not fail) my history exam.
4 If I ____ (not fail) my exam, Dad ____ (not be) angry.
5 If Dad ____ (not be) angry, we ____ (might go) to the match.
6 I ____ (be) very happy if we ____ (go) to the match.

5 Write your own consequences story using the third conditional. Use Exercise 4 to help you. Then read your story to your partner.

6 Write the questions using the third conditional.

1 What / happen / if / the internet / not be invented?
What would have happened if the internet hadn't been invented?
2 What / you / do / if / you / not come / to school today?
3 If / you / be given / one superpower when you were ten, / which superpower / you / choose?
4 If / you / be born / in another country, / where / you / like / be born?

SPEAK

7 Work in pairs. Ask and answer the questions in Exercise 6, giving as much information as you can.

LANGUAGE & BEYOND

COMMUNICATE & COOPERATE

»» Adapt to changing situations

SPEAK AND READ

1 **Work in pairs. Read the statements. Choose the statement that best describes you.**

1 'I like my routine and don't enjoy change.'
2 'I like looking for new ways to solve problems.'
3 'I can adapt to almost any situation.'

2 **Read the questionnaire individually and decide what you would do in each situation.**

3 **Work in pairs. Compare your answers to the questionnaire. How many are the same?**

WHAT WOULD YOU DO?

Read the situations. Choose the option that is most accurate for you or write your own answer.

1 **One evening you arrange to meet three classmates at your home to work on a school project. Just before the agreed time, one of them phones to say the others have decided to meet at a new coffee shop instead. How do you feel?**

a Angry. The others changed the plan without consulting you.
b Excited. Meeting in a new coffee bar will be more fun than meeting at home.
c Other (write your response): ______

2 **You've arranged to spend the weekend camping with some friends. When you wake up on Saturday, it's raining heavily. You're supposed to meet the others in an hour. What do you do?**

a Call your friends to cancel the trip and arrange to do it another time.
b Get ready to go, but pack some waterproof clothes to take with you.
c Other (write your answer): ______

3 **You have to write an essay for tomorrow's history class, but you don't know what to write. It's late and you've been staring at a blank piece of paper for 40 minutes. What do you do?**

a Decide to tell your history teacher that you couldn't do the homework.
b Set the alarm to get up at five in the morning and try to write it then.
c Other (write your answer): ______

DO

4 **In small groups, answer the question.**

Which of the changes in the questionnaire was caused by …
1 yourself? 2 other people? 3 other circumstances?

5 **Being flexible means being able to make changes or deal with a situation that is changing. Look at the answer options in the questionnaire, including any that you've added. Order them from the most to the least flexible.**

6 **Match the answer options in the questionnaire to these pieces of advice.**

1 Change your approach and try a different method.
2 Don't always think about yourself.
3 Be prepared for things that might force a change.

REFLECT

7 **Discuss the questions with your class. Do you agree with the REFLECTION POINT?**

1 Why do you think people don't like change?
2 How can being flexible help you overcome problems?
3 What can you do to make yourself a more flexible person?

REFLECTION POINT

In general, people don't like change. However, changes happen constantly, and the more we learn to adapt to those changes, the more creative and flexible we become.

EXTEND

8 **Work in groups. Think of two more situations to continue the *What would you do?* questionnaire. Give your situations and answer options to another group to answer.**

Workbook, page 85

SPEAKING At the post office

»» Send letters and parcels at the post office

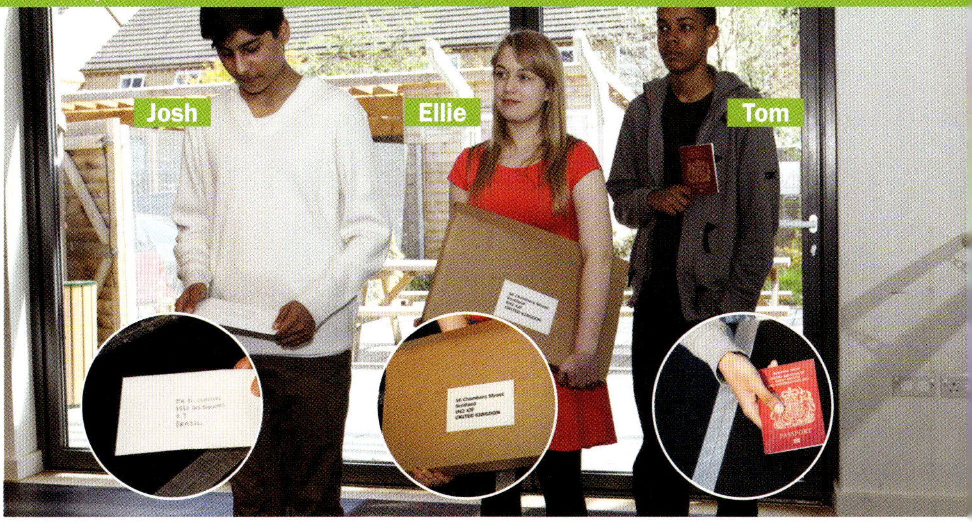

SPEAK

1 a Work in pairs. Look at the photo. What do you think each person wants to do at the post office?

b What information will they need to ask for and give?

WATCH OR LISTEN

2 2.53 Watch or listen to the scenes and check your answers to Exercise 1.

Assistant: Hello. How can I help you today?
Josh: I'd like a stamp to send a letter to Brazil, please. Can you tell me how much it would cost?
Assistant: That would be (1) ______ p by airmail.
Josh: Is there a cheaper way to send it?
Assistant: You can send it by normal post, but it could take up to (2) ______ weeks to get there.
Josh: OK, I'll send it by airmail. Can I have one (3) ______ p stamp, please?

Ellie: Hi. I need to send this parcel to Scotland. How much will it cost?
Assistant: It's just under (4) ______ kilos so that would cost (5) £ ______ with our Standard parcel service.
Ellie: How long will it take to get there?
Assistant: (6) ______ days.
Ellie: That's too long. It's a birthday present. Are there any other options?
Assistant: With our Express (7) ______ service it would get there the next day. That would cost (8) £ ______ plus VAT.

Tom: Hello. I'd like to send some money to someone in Spain.
Assistant: Do you have some form of ID?
Tom: I've got my passport.
Assistant: That's fine. How much do you want to send?
Tom: (9) £ ______ . Do I have to pay anything extra?
Assistant: There's a (10) £ ______ fee. If you still want to go ahead, then you'll need to fill out one of these forms.

3 2.53 Watch or listen again and write numbers in gaps 1–10.

4 Answer the questions.

1 What's the difference between airmail and normal post?
2 Why does Josh decide to send the letter by airmail?
3 Why does Ellie want the parcel to reach its destination quickly?
4 How long does the Express service take?
5 Why do you think the assistant asks Tom for ID?
6 Does Tom have to pay anything extra?

5 2.54 Listen and repeat some sentences from the conversations. Pay attention to intonation.

ACT

6 Work in groups. Complete the tasks.

- Make a list of different things you can do at a post office. Each student chooses one of the things.
- Think of the language you need to explain what you want to do.
- Some students are the post office assistants. The others form a queue and take it in turn to explain what they want.

PHRASEBOOK 2.55

Explaining what you want

I'd like a stamp to send a letter to Brazil, please.

I need to send this parcel to Scotland.

I'd like to send some money to someone in Spain.

Can I have one 87p stamp, please?

Asking for information

Can you tell me how much it would cost? / How much will it cost?

Is there a cheaper way to send it?

How long will it take to get there?

Are there any other options?

Do I have to pay anything extra?

»» Workbook, page 83

WRITING Join our appeal

Use persuasive language

SPEAK AND READ

1 Work in pairs. Look at the top of the poster and answer the questions.

1 What do you think is the message of the title?
2 What kind of charity or good cause do you think the poster is promoting?
3 What kind of information would you expect to find on the poster?

Put yourself in their shoes

How would you feel if you had to sleep on the street? Could you find enough to eat if you had no money in your pockets? Where would you wash? Who would you trust? This year's appeal is in aid of homeless teenagers on the streets of our city.
The Street Trust is a charity that helps young homeless people by providing them with food and support. If any teenagers in our city have nowhere to sleep, The Street Trust will help them.
Our aim is to raise more money than we did last year for the Africa School appeal. If you hadn't given generously then, the aid workers in Kibaale, Uganda, wouldn't have finished building the school. Help us again. Take action now by giving money, clothes, anything you don't need anymore. Or donate your time. We need volunteers to help at the jumble sale on Saturday. Contact Suzie or Neil in Class 4B and become involved.

2 Look at the rest of the poster and check your answers to Exercise 1. Where would you expect to see the poster?

STUDY

3 a Read the tips in the HOW TO box.

HOW TO
use persuasive language

- Use imperatives with action words like *help*, *donate* and *give*.
- Use second conditionals to make people identify with the situation.
- Use 'you' to address the reader directly.
- Use first and third conditionals to describe how an action will help or helped in the past.

b Work in pairs. Find examples of persuasive language in the poster.

PRACTISE

4 Rewrite the sentences using more persuasive language.

1 People can help us with our appeal by contacting Mrs Harris.
Help us now! Call Mrs Harris.
2 Homeless people don't usually have any contact with their families.
3 With the money we raise, the charity will be able to give clothes to the homeless.
4 We'd be very grateful if you could give as much money as you can.
5 Because of your support last year, we were able to help the earthquake victims.

PLAN, WRITE AND CHECK

5 a It's one year later. You're going to create a poster for the school's new appeal.

- Think of a charity or cause you'd like to raise money for.
- Think of an attention-grabbing title for your poster and a picture you can include.
- Write the text for the poster. Use the model text in Exercise 2 and the tips in the HOW TO box to help you plan your poster.

b Create your poster. Remember to include conditionals.

SHARE AND REVIEW

6 a Swap your poster with a partner. Read your partner's poster and review it. Then display the posters on the classroom wall.

b Look at the other posters. Which one do you find the most persuasive? Why?

Workbook, pages 84–85

VOCABULARY Money verbs and nouns

1 Complete the story with the correct form of the words.

bank account debt donate fee income inherit
loss owe pay back profit raise withdraw

This is the story of Herbert Drew who thought he had (1) ________ a fortune when his millionaire father died. Herbert's father had owned a newspaper business that made huge (2) ________ in the 1990s, providing the family with a very good (3) ________. Unfortunately, his father never told the family when the business started making a(n) (4) ________ after the arrival of the internet. After his father's death, when Herbert tried to (5) ________ money from the family's (6) ________, he realised the family had no money. Instead, he had inherited all his father's (7) ________. It took him five years to (8) ________ enough money to (9) ________ everything he (10) ________ (including the family lawyer's (11) ________). He (12) ________ the family car to charity.

___ /12

Adjectives ending with *-ful* and *-less*

2 Read Herbert's comments and complete the adjectives with *-ful* or *-less*.

'My father was (1) hope________ at running a business. I, on the other hand, have always been (2) care________ with money. He was also very (3) forget________ and often called me Harry.
When I heard about the debts I stood (4) motion________ for a few minutes, feeling totally (5) help________.
Those five years of debt were very (6) stress________ and every day felt (7) end________. Now life is much more (8) peace________.
It's (9) point________ trying to blame my father. I'm (10) grate________ for everything he did for me.'

___ /10

GRAMMAR Conditionals review

3 After paying back the debts, Herbert wondered what to do with the newspaper business. Complete the conditional phrases.

1 If people continue to get their news from the internet, print newspapers ________ (not exist) in the future.
2 If there ________ (not be) any newspapers, the world would be a worse place.
3 What would happen to all the workers if we ________ (decide) to close down the papers?
4 Mother always says: 'If you ________ (be) flexible in life, you can adapt to change.'
5 If we change the way we think, I know we ________ (find) a solution.
6 What ________ (my father / do) if he was here today?
7 If we ________ (do) the opposite, then maybe we'll survive.
8 There's still time to do something if we ________ (act) quickly.

___ /16

Third conditional

4 Herbert's father had written a letter before he died. Write the verbs in the correct form.

Dear Herbert,

I'm sorry to have left you with the family debts. If I (1) ________ (be) more careful with the business, then things (2) ________ (may be) different. I also believe that the newspapers (3) ________ (can continue) to be successful if they (4) ________ (not invent) the internet. If I (5) ________ (know) how it would change everything, I (6) ________ (do) something. I'm sure you (7) ________ (can help) me if I (8) ________ (ask) you, but I was too proud to tell you what had happened. Anyway, there's no point in thinking about what (9) ________ (may happen) if things (10) ________ (be) different. What would you (11) ________ (do) if you (12) ________ (be) in my place?

Your father

___ /12

Your score: ___ /50

SKILLS CHECK

✓✓✓ Yes, I can. No problem!
✓✓ Yes, I can. But I need a bit of help.
✓ Yes, I can. But I need a lot of help.

I can make notes for a summary. ____
I can predict what a story will be about when I listen. ____
I can adapt to changing situations. ____
I can use persuasive language. ____

Workbook, pages 86–87

UNIT 8

FRENEMIES

IN THE PICTURE Relationships

Talk about relationships

The story so far

RECALL AND READ

1 Make a network or diagram to show the relationships between the people in the box. Compare with a partner.

acquaintance   boyfriend/girlfriend   classmate   close friend
enemy   friend of a friend   guest   neighbour   old friend
online friend   relative   teammate

2 Read the photo story and answer the questions.

1 What was the relationship between Dan and Lily at the beginning of the story?
2 How did their relationship change?
3 What happened then?

3 How do you think the story continues? Work in pairs. Draw another two frames with speech bubbles and captions. Compare your ideas with another pair.

4 THE MOVING PICTURE Watch the video. Is the story the same as or different from your ideas in Exercise 3?

WORK WITH WORDS

5 Write the sentences as captions in the correct place in the story (1–7).

a Dan and Lily had been **going out** for three months. But something was wrong …
b Dan and Lily **fell out**. They had a huge argument.
c Lily had **let Dan down**.
d Dan and Lily had always **got on**. But this was different … *1*
e Dan and Lily **got together** at the concert.
f Dan **asked Lily out**.
g Dan found it hard to **put up with** the sudden changes in Lily's moods.

6 Look at the words in bold in the captions in Exercise 5 and the questions in part 8 of the story. Match them to the correct definitions.

1 .... disappointed Dan
2 .... end their relationship
3 .... accept
4 .... had a friendly relationship
5 .... forget Lily and feel happy again after the end of their relationship
6 .... having a romantic relationship
7 .... become friendly again after their argument
8 .... invited Lily to go on a date with him
9 .... stopped being friendly with each other
10 .... started a romantic relationship

What will happen next?

- Will Dan and Lily **make up** and continue their relationship?
- Or will they say goodbye and **break up**?
- If they say goodbye, will Dan ever **get over** Lily?

To be continued …

8

7 a Write the phrasal verbs in the correct category.

~~ask sb out~~ break up with sb fall out with sb get on with sb get over sb get together with sb go out with sb let sb down make up with sb put up with sb

Start a relationship	Have a relationship and deal with problems	Finish a relationship
ask sb out		

b 3.01 **Listen and check. Then listen and repeat.**

EXTEND

8 Choose the correct words.

- When phrasal verbs are transitive (have an object), the object can go in different positions.
  - With *ask somebody out* and *let somebody down*, the object goes *before* / *between* / *after* the verb and the adverb.
  - With *put up with somebody* and *get over somebody*, the object comes *before* / *between* / *after* the preposition(s).

SPEAK

9 Work in pairs. Do one or both of the tasks.

A Talk about the relationships in your favourite TV series or novel series.

In the first 'Twilight' book, Bella got together with Edward. In the second book, he let her down and they broke up. …

B Talk about relationships in your family.

My brother has been going out with his girlfriend for a year. But they fall out and make up a lot.

GO BEYOND

Do the Words & Beyond exercise on page 137.

Workbook, page 88

READING I wish

Recognise facts and opinions

SPEAK AND READ

1 a **What advice do older people often give you? Work in pairs. Make a list of topics.**

clothes and appearance, …

b **Do you find their advice useful? Tell your partner, explaining why or why not.**

2 3.02 **Read the article. Explain in your own words what the people have regrets about.**

Taylor regrets that …

3 **Choose the correct word.**

1. Taylor *sometimes* / *never* bullied other students.
2. Taylor says it's *important* / *pointless* to pretend to be something you're not.
3. Jasper *wants* / *doesn't want* to persuade teens to talk about problems.
4. Jasper thinks you should live a *full* / *careful* life.
5. Xavier regrets that he didn't have a *high enough* / *low enough* opinion of his teachers.
6. Anna was spoiled as a child and now she finds dealing with money *easy* / *difficult*.

4 a **Read the tips in the HOW TO box.**

b **Read the article again and find examples of facts and opinions. Underline them in different colours.**

5 **Which tips in the HOW TO box did you use for help with Exercise 4b? Tick (✓) them.**

REACT

6 **Work in pairs. Which issue or piece of advice do you think is the most important or the most useful?**

GO BEYOND

Write a heading for a piece of advice like the ones in the article.

Things I wish I'd known as a teenager

Taylor, 25, computer programmer

It's important to be yourself

When I was 15 I desperately wanted to be like everybody else – same clothes, same hairstyle, same interests. The kids who were different often got bullied – and I'm ashamed to say I sometimes joined in. I wish I'd known then that the most important thing is to be true to yourself. In my experience, if your friends are real friends, they won't care if you're different.

Jasper, 21, counsellor

You're not alone

Sometimes when you're a teen, you feel as if you're all alone and there's nobody you can talk to – even your friends. Did you know between 20 and 30% of teens in the USA have a period of depression before they become adults? I think life is so much easier if you share your problems. I really wish I'd been given this piece of advice. If only I'd just talked to somebody. You only get one life – so live it.

Xavier, 27, teacher

Your teachers only want what's best for you

When I was at school I never thought I'd become a teacher. I behaved badly in class and I regret that now. Today, I wish kids understood that teachers push them to do their best – and not just to give them a hard time. I love my job, but in my opinion, it's a very challenging one. If I'd known as a teenager how difficult it is, I'd have shown my teachers more respect.

Anna, 22, dental nurse

Money doesn't grow on trees

When I was a teenager, I never learned how to save money or make a budget – just to spend it! My parents gave me everything I wanted, but I realise now they must have gone without a lot of things themselves. Now I wish I knew more about planning my finances – and I'm not the only one. According to a survey by a big American banking company, teens today know less about money management than teens five years ago.

HOW TO

recognise facts and opinions

- ☐ Look at the text type: decide if it usually has facts or opinions or both.
- ☐ **Facts** can be checked. Look for statistics, sources or phrases like *According to, Research shows*.
- ☐ **Opinions** are based on feelings and experiences. Look for phrases like *I think, In my opinion/experience*.

Workbook, page 89

GRAMMAR Wishes and regrets: *I wish* and *If only*

Talk about wishes and regrets

READ

1 **Read the question and answer from a question-answering site. Can you think of any more differences between real friends and frenemies?**

I know a frenemy is somebody who pretends to be a friend but is really an enemy. But how can you tell a frenemy from a real friend?
Pauline

Best answer
A friend wants what's best for you; a frenemy wants what's best for herself. A friend would say, 'I wish you hadn't hurt your ankle. It must be painful.' A frenemy would say, 'If only you didn't have a bad ankle. Now I have to go jogging on my own.' And a frenemy will let you down if she gets a better offer, so she might say, 'I wish I could come shopping with you as I promised. If only Ravi hadn't asked me out on the same afternoon.'

STUDY

2 **Underline examples of *I wish* and *If only* in Exercise 1. Then complete the explanations.**

Wishes and regrets: *I wish* and *If only*

Use: To express unhappiness with a situation in the present or past.

Form: present
I wish / If only + **past** ....

Form: past
I wish / If only + **past** ....

See GRAMMAR DATABASE, page 127.

PRACTISE

3 **Pauline is writing on her blog. Complete the sentences.**

1 Friendships are so difficult. I wish *friendships weren't so difficult* .
2 I expect friendships to be perfect. I wish I ....
3 I get so angry at little things. I wish I ....
4 I'm annoying at times. If only I .... !
5 My friends get impatient with me. I wish my friends ....
6 My friends don't know how important they are to me. If only my friends ....

Workbook, pages 90–91

4 a **Vadim is telling Pauline about a problem. Complete his regrets with the correct form of the verbs.**

Vadim: I had a really bad argument with Alex yesterday. I wish I (1) .... (not shout) at him.
Pauline: What did you say?
Vadim: I said I wish he (2) .... (not move) to our school and that I wish I (3) .... (not waste) so much time on our friendship.
Pauline: Do you really wish he (4) .... (not become) your friend?
Vadim: No, of course not. I just wish he (5) .... (tell) me he wanted to ask Jina out. If only he (6) .... (speak) to me first, I could have explained that I like her too.
Pauline: Why don't you tell him that you wish …

b **Complete Pauline's last sentence with your own ideas.**

5 **Complete the sentences about you. Then compare with a partner.**

1 I wish I could (sing …)
2 I wish I had (straight hair …)
3 I wish I was …
4 Last week, I wish I had …
5 If only I hadn't …

SPEAK

6 **Student A: look at page 141. Student B: look at page 142.**

Read out a situation to your partner. Your partner has to think of a wish or a regret.

Your brother isn't very well.

I wish he was better. / I wish he hadn't caught the flu.

LISTENING AND VOCABULARY Need to talk?

Understand hesitation

SPEAK AND LISTEN

1 Look at the poster and answer the questions.

1 What is *Teenline*?
2 Who can you speak to?
3 What does *Teenline* do with your information?
4 What sort of issues do you think you can talk about?

2 3.03 Listen to the first part of Jack's call to *Teenline*. How does he sound?

3 a Read the tips in the HOW TO box.

b 3.04 Listen to the rest of the phone call and complete the sentences.

1 Jack says he has made *a big mistake*.
2 Jack upset a ______.
3 Julie didn't want to ______.
4 Jack took a photo of Julie. Then Jack and Al ______.
5 Jack posted the photo ______.
6 Julie's parents were ______.

4 Which tips in the HOW TO box did you use for help with Exercise 3b? Tick (✓) them.

HOW TO
understand hesitation

- ☐ Listen for sounds like *um*, *er*, *ah* and words and phrases like *well*, *you know*, *like*, *kind of*, *I mean* and *actually*. The speaker is thinking what to say.
- ☐ Listen for phrases like *What do you call it? What's the word? How do you say it?* The speaker is trying to find the right words.
- ☐ Listen carefully to what the speaker says next.

REACT

5 Work in pairs. Discuss the questions.

1 What do you think about what Jack has done?
2 What do you think Jack should do about Julie and Al?

WORK WITH WORDS

6 3.05 Work in pairs. Complete the sentences with the correct names. Listen and check.

1 *Julie's parents* **accuse**d Julie of lying to them.
2 ______ **blame**d Julie for posting the photo.
3 ______ didn't **forgive** Julie for seeing her ex-boyfriend.

4 ______ **offer**ed to go to Julie's house with Al.
5 ______ **refuse**d to go.
6 ______ **threaten**ed to say the photo was Jack's idea.

7 ______ **warn**ed Jack not to go to Julie's house.
8 ______ **persuade**d Jack to tell her what happened.
9 ______ **advise**d Jack to tell the truth.
10 ______ **remind**ed Jack to think everything over.

7 3.06 PRONOUNCE Listen to the reporting verbs in bold in Exercise 6 and repeat. Listen again and underline the main stress in the two-syllable verbs.

1 *accuse*

8 Match the groups of verbs in Exercise 6 (1–3, 4–6 and 7–10) to the correct structure.

Infinitive with *to*	Object + infinitive with *to*	Object + preposition + verb + *-ing*

9 a Write five sentences in direct speech and five sentences with gaps for different verbs from Exercise 6.

'Please help me.' – 'OK.'   *He ______ me to help him.*

b Work in pairs. Swap your sentences and complete them.

GO BEYOND
Do the Words & Beyond exercise on page 137.

Workbook, pages 92–93

GRAMMAR Reported speech review

Report what other people say

READ AND LISTEN

1 3.07 **Read and listen to the conversation. What was the misunderstanding?**

Matt: Did I tell you what happened yesterday?
Bolek: No, what?
Matt: Katie's boyfriend Ahmed asked me if it was true that I really liked Katie. I asked him what he was talking about and then asked him to explain. He said that Luke had told him. Luke said he'd overheard me the day before when I'd been talking to Ben. I laughed and he told me to tell him what was so funny. I'd told Ben that I really liked skating!
Bolek: But I thought you really liked Katie.
Matt: I do, but I'm not going to tell Ahmed, am I?

STUDY

2 Complete the examples from Exercise 1.

Reported speech review

Use: To report what people said in direct speech.

Form: statements
told me / said (that) + subject + past form of the verb
'Luke told me.'
→ He said that Luke ______.
For changes to pronouns etc, see page 127.

Form: *wh-* questions
asked me + what/who, etc + subject + past verb
'What are you talking about?'
→ I asked him ______.

Form: *yes/no* questions
asked me + if/whether + subject + past verb
'Is it true?'
→ He asked me ______.

Form: requests
asked me + (*not*) + infinitive with *to*
'Please explain.'
→ I asked ______.

Form: commands
told me + (*not*) + infinitive with *to*
'Tell me what's so funny.'
→ He told me ______.

See GRAMMAR DATABASE, page 127.

PRACTISE

3 Rewrite the sentences in reported speech.

1 'I want to talk to you about gossiping,' our Head said.
Our Head said that she *wanted to talk to us about gossiping*.
2 'The school has introduced a strict anti-gossiping policy,' she said.
She said that ______.
3 'The school will punish all gossips from now on,' said the Head.
The Head said ______.
4 'What will happen to gossips?' asked a student.
A student asked ______.
5 'Will gossips have to leave the school?' another student asked.
Another student asked ______.
6 'I'm going to send out a letter to your parents tomorrow,' the Head answered.
The Head answered that she ______.

4 Complete what Charlie says with the positive or negative form of the verbs in the box. Do you agree with the last question?

do	give	go	gossip	keep	pass	~~tell~~

I didn't want to gossip, but Kasia persuaded me (1) *to tell* her about Lisa. I told her (2) ______ it a secret and warned her (3) ______ the story on to anybody else. I threatened (4) ______ her any more gossip if she did that. Unfortunately, Kasia didn't keep her promise. The Head found out and ordered me (5) ______ to her office. She reminded me (6) ______ at school. I agreed (7) ______ it – but surely gossiping isn't a crime if you tell the truth?

SPEAK

5 a Choose a sentence type from the ones below. Then think of a sentence and write it on a piece of paper. Write your name under it.

- A statement about you or something you did recently
- A *wh-* question
- A *yes/no* question
- A request
- A command

b Make a ball with your paper. In class, throw your paper balls to the other students for one minute. Then open your paper and report what it says.

Joe wrote that he'd got a new bike.

Alice asked if she could have some chocolate.

Ricardo told me to be quiet.

LANGUAGE & BEYOND

FEEDBACK

1 Your friend is wearing a terrible outfit and asks your opinion. What do you do?

A Say he looks great.
B Say you really like his shirt, but you're not sure about his trousers.
C Say you don't like his outfit.

2 Your friend has upset another friend of yours. She asks you why your other friend isn't speaking to her. What do you do?

A Get angry with her and tell her she made a big mistake.
B Explain the problem and suggest how she can put it right.
C Say you don't know.

3 Your friend asks what you think of his essay. You read it and you don't think it's very good. What do you do?

A Smile and say it's fine.
B Say the essay isn't very good.
C Say it's a good essay, but there are some places where it could be improved. When he has changed those parts, it will be really good.

>>> Give and accept feedback

COMMUNICATE & COOPERATE

SPEAK AND READ

1 Work in pairs. Ask and answer the questions in the questionnaire above.

DO

2 Work in a small group. Compare your answers to the questionnaire in Exercise 1. Make a list of tips (DOs and DON'Ts) when giving somebody feedback on their work or behaviour.

3 Are your tips similar to the ones on the right?

4 Work in pairs. Complete the sentences.

1 When you ask for feedback, you have to be prepared for …
2 If you don't like the feedback you get, it's important to …
3 If you don't agree with someone's advice, you should …

REFLECT

5 Discuss the questions with your class. Do you agree with the REFLECTION POINT?

1 Why is it important for us to get feedback and act on it?
2 Is it easier to accept feedback from certain people? Explain why.
3 How does *the way* feedback is given make you feel?

EXTEND

6 Work in pairs. Role-play giving and accepting feedback in the two situations below. Use the feedback sandwich.

- Your friend hasn't done enough work on your joint presentation.
- Your friend has paid too much for a phone on the internet.

Feedback tips

- Never give feedback unless the other person asks you.
- Always give feedback face to face.
- Put yourself in the other person's shoes before you speak.
- Speak in a calm and non-emotional way (don't sound angry).
- Focus on the person's behaviour and not on his/her personality.
- 'Sandwich' negative feedback between positive statements:
  - First say something positive/ praise the other person.
  - Then give negative feedback.
  - Finally, point out ways to improve specific things.

REFLECTION POINT

We all need feedback in order to develop and learn to do things better. But it's easier to accept feedback if it's given in a positive and helpful way. When you get negative feedback, stay calm and listen.

Workbook, page 97

SPEAKING Don't worry about it

Express regret and forgiveness

SPEAK AND WRITE

1 a Work in pairs. Look at the photos. What do you think Nora, Luis, Sasha and Ava are expressing regret about?

I think Nora told … / Nora might have told …

b Make a list of other situations when people often feel regret.

You said something horrible to a friend.
You didn't remember a friend or relative's birthday.

c Have you ever been in any situations like these? Tell your partner and explain what happened.

WATCH OR LISTEN

2 3.08 Watch or listen to the scenes. Check your answers to Exercise 1a.

1

Nora:	I (1) ______ I hadn't told Emma about your parents breaking up. I'm (2) ______ if I upset you.
Ellie:	Don't worry about it. Everybody will know soon.
Nora:	Sorry, I feel (3) ______ .

2

Luis:	I'm sorry, I (4) ______ have shouted at you like that. I know you didn't mean to drop my tablet. I'm really sorry for (5) ______ you.
Ruth:	It doesn't matter. I understand why you were angry. I'm just so clumsy!

3

Sasha:	I (6) ______ for calling Ben a stupid name.
Teacher:	That's all right. I realise Ben was annoying you. But please don't let me hear anything like that again or I'll have to contact your parents.
Sasha:	It won't happen again, I (7) ______ .

4

Ava:	I really (8) ______ letting you down. I wanted to see that film.
Tom:	You couldn't help it. Your parents needed you to babysit.
Ava:	I feel really (9) ______ about it.
Tom:	Ava, it wasn't your fault.

3 a 3.08 Watch or listen again and complete conversations 1–4 with the missing words.

b Check your answers with the phrases in the PHRASEBOOK.

4 Which situation is more formal than the others? Which phrase is used in this situation? Mark it *formal* in the PHRASEBOOK.

5 a 3.09 Underline the phrases which Ellie, Ruth, the teacher and Tom use to express forgiveness. Listen and check your answers.

b 3.10 Listen again and repeat the phrases, paying attention to sentence stress.

ACT

6 Work in pairs. Choose two or more of the situations from your list in Exercise 1b. Act out short conversations in which one student expresses regret and the other student expresses forgiveness.

PHRASEBOOK 3.11

Express regret

I wish I'd/hadn't told …
I'm sorry if I upset you.
I feel awful / really bad about it …
I should/shouldn't have shouted …
I'm really sorry for upsetting you.
I apologise for calling …
It won't happen again, I promise.
I really regret letting you down …

Express forgiveness

Don't worry about it.
It doesn't matter. / That's all right.
You couldn't help it.
It wasn't your fault.

Workbook, page 95

WRITING My role model

»» Add detail to a description

SPEAK AND READ

1 a A role model is somebody whose behaviour you admire and respect. Work in pairs. Make a list of people you think are role models. They can be famous people or people you know.

b Brainstorm a list of qualities you think many role models have. Make a class list on the board.

2 Read Alara's description of her role model. Which of the qualities on the board does she have?

12 AUG *My Blog*

1 **My role model** is my swimming coach, Kristin. She's about 30 and used to be a national champion.

2 Kristin is small and looks as light as a feather, but she has lots of energy and always bounces around. She finds it easy to control the classes. She's quite strict, she makes us train really hard and she checks we do everything properly. She doesn't put up with lazy people but praises hard workers.

3 Everyone gets on well with Kristin. She's very cheerful and never gets down in the dumps. She's always there with the right advice when you need it and you know she'll never let you down if you need help.

4 I once made a bad mistake in a competition and our team lost the championship. Kristin just told me not to worry. She said she knew that I would never do it again – and she was right. I train twice as hard now because I wish I'd never made that mistake.

STUDY

3 Read the description again and match the paragraph descriptions below to the correct paragraphs (1–4).

a an example of the person's behaviour
b Introduction and personal information
c further good qualities that the person has
d main characteristics of the person

4 a Read the tips in the HOW TO box.

HOW TO
add detail to a description

- Use adjectives (*cheerful, generous*).
- Use descriptive verbs (*whisper* instead of *say*, *giggle* instead of *laugh*).
- Use idioms (see page 8).
- Use similes (eg *as busy as a bee*) (see page 30).

b Find one example of each tip from the HOW TO box in Alara's description.

Get it right

Check means to look at something and make sure it's correct.

Control means to make somebody do something.

PRACTISE

5 Work in pairs. Add more details to the paragraph below to make it more descriptive. Then compare your details with another pair.

My dad is very strong and powerful. He walks quickly. His voice is loud. He's never mean and everybody loves him.

PLAN, WRITE AND CHECK

6 a You're going to write a description of your role model. Use the paragraph descriptions in Exercise 3 and the tips from the HOW TO box and make notes.

b Write your description and add detail.

SHARE AND REVIEW

7 Swap your description with a partner. Read your partner's description and review it.

Workbook, pages 96–97

VOCABULARY Relationships

1 **Complete the conversation about the TV series with the correct form of the verbs in the box.**

ask break fall get (x3) go let make put

Harry: So tell me what happened last week in *High School Club*.
Leah: Well, Katie (1) ________ Luke out, but he said no because he was (2) ________ out with Jasmine. They (3) ________ on really well together at that time. But then Jasmine (4) ________ up with Luke, so Luke (5) ________ together with Katie.
Harry: Er, right …
Leah: But Luke couldn't (6) ________ over Jasmine even though she (7) ________ him down. He found it hard to (8) ________ up with Katie's jealous behaviour too. So they (9) ________ out. Then Luke (10) ________ up with Jasmine and they were happy again.
Harry: Oh. Not much happened then.

___ /10

Reporting verbs

2 **Choose the correct reporting verbs for the programme summary.**

MONDAY TUESDAY WEDNESDAY THURSDAY

In *High School Club* today, Katie (1) *offers* / *threatens* to make trouble for Luke and Jasmine. Katie (2) *warns* / *blames* Jasmine for the break-up and (3) *accuses* / *refuses* Jasmine of stealing her boyfriend. She says she'll never (4) *forgive* / *advise* her for doing this. Jasmine (5) *reminds* / *persuades* her that Luke was her boyfriend and (6) *accuses* / *warns* her to stay away from them. Meanwhile, Luke (7) *persuades* / *offers* to take Katie's things to her house although best friend Malik (8) *advises* / *threatens* him to (9) *blame* / *refuse* to do it. When Luke gets to Katie's house, she (10) *persuades* / *forgives* him to go out for a burger …

___ /10

GRAMMAR Wishes and regrets: *I wish* and *If only*

3 **Complete with the correct form of the verbs.**

If only you (1) ________ (stay) with me forever.

I wish I (2) ________ (not come) here.

I wish we (3) ________ (can) be friends again.

I wish I (4) ________ (not had) this horrible burger.

If only you (5) ________ (know) how often I think of you.

If only I (6) ________ (listen) to Malik.
If only I (7) ________ (be) at home.

___ /14

Reported speech review

4 **Leah is telling Harry about today's programme. Complete each gap with one word.**

Leah: Jasmine asked Luke (1) ________ he had seen Katie again. So Luke explained that he (2) ________ visited Katie at her home the day (3) ________, although he hadn't stayed (4) ________ for long. Jasmine said that she (5) ________ trust Katie at all and that she (6) ________ never speak to her again. She told Luke not (7) ________ phone Katie again. Luke said he wasn't interested in Katie but that he wasn't (8) ________ to take orders from Jasmine.
Harry: So they broke up again. What a pity I fell asleep.

___ /16

Your score: ___ /50

SKILLS CHECK

✓✓✓ Yes, I can. No problem!
✓✓ Yes, I can. But I need a bit of help.
✓ Yes, I can. But I need a lot of help.

I can recognise facts and opinions when I read. ____
I can understand hesitation. ____
I can give and accept feedback. ____
I can express regret and forgiveness. ____
I can add detail to a description. ____

Workbook, pages 98–99

READ

1 Read the magazine article and choose the correct people (A–D). You can choose the people more than once.

Which person:

doesn't think their friends are grateful?	1 ......
gets a similar allowance to their friends?	2 ......
doesn't get any money from their parents?	3 ......
does housework for their allowance?	4 ......
feels uncomfortable asking for money?	5 ......
has some money that they won't spend now?	6 ......
would donate their money if they had some?	7 ......
knows their situation is typical?	8 ......
disagrees with their parents about allowances?	9 ......
thinks money makes people unhappy?	10 ......

Reading: ______ /10

EXAM TIPS

do a multiple-matching exercise

- Quickly read the texts. What's the general message of each one?
- Read each question. Use key words in the question to help you find the answer.
- Don't just look for similar vocabulary. Make sure the answer matches the question exactly.
- Check that other texts don't contain a better answer.

recognise facts and opinions

See page 84.

HOT TOPICS

This week, we look at allowances. Do you get one? And if so, what do you have to do for it?

A

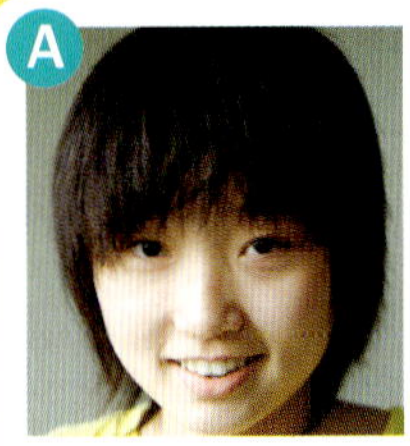

'I get an allowance in exchange for doing jobs around the house – tidying my room, taking out the rubbish, things like that. According to a survey I read recently, that's what most teens have to do where I live. If I don't do a particular job one week, I have to pay back some money, which means I get less the following week. I hate it when that happens, but I think it's a fair system. We all sat down and talked about how much I'd get and what I'd have to do in exchange. My parents even asked me how much my friends got. Maybe if I'd told them my friends got more, they'd have given me more. But the truth is, we all get about the same amount, and I'm sure they'd have talked to my friends' parents if they thought I'd lied to them.'

B

'I don't get an allowance, and I don't want one. In fact, if I had one, I'd give the money to charity. If I really need money, I ask my parents, but that doesn't happen very often. Most of my friends get an allowance. They say it teaches them about money and how to look after it. But they just seem to have endless arguments with their parents about how much they get and what they can't afford. It's all about what they *haven't* got when really they should be thankful for what they do have. I keep reminding them how lucky we are compared to some people in the world, but it's a hopeless case. I really believe they'd be happier if they learned to live on less.'

C

'My case is a little unusual in that my parents don't believe in giving an allowance in exchange for household jobs. They say that we should see jobs as part of our responsibility for keeping the space we share clean and tidy. They say that if I got money for jobs, that would suggest we should only ever do things in life if someone pays us to do them. I don't actually think that's true, but it's pointless trying to argue about it. So I have to ask every time I need money. Sometimes it's stressful trying to persuade my parents that I really need it, and they refuse to give me any if they don't think I'll spend it on something worthwhile. So I wish I had an allowance. It would make life so much easier.'

D

'I come from a big family and my parents can't afford to give us all an allowance, so I've learned to be careful with money. If there are bigger things I want, I save up to buy them with the money I make from doing jobs for the neighbours. At the weekend I often wash neighbours' cars, walk their dogs, cut their grass; things like that. I bought a bike recently, but I'm not saving for anything right now. However, I do actually have some savings. We all inherited some money from our grandparents, but they wanted us to spend it on our education, so we can go to college. Sometimes I think "If only I could spend it now", but I respect their wishes.'

LISTEN

2 3.12 **You will hear a video message recorded by Mason for his ex-girlfriend. For each question, choose A, B or C.**

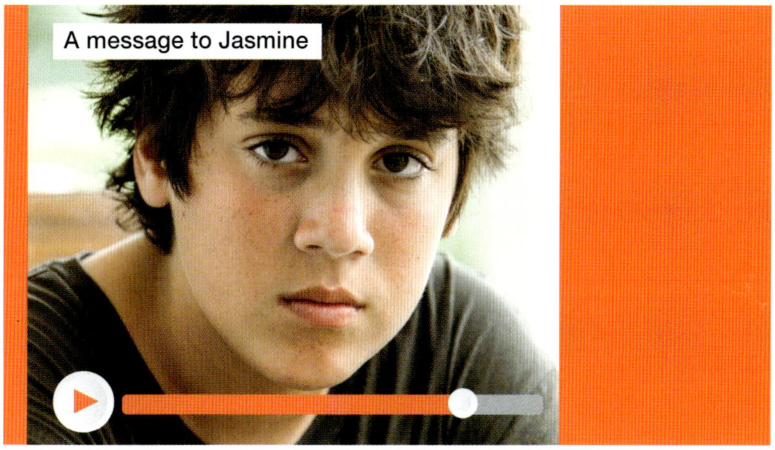

1 What does Mason say about his grandparents?
  A They've had a long and happy relationship.
  B They're unhappy because they have a lot of problems.
  C They used to respect each other but now they argue a lot.

2 How did Mason's relationship with Jasmine start?
  A He asked her out and she immediately said yes.
  B Jasmine told him she'd do anything to go out with him.
  C He asked her out a few times and finally she said yes.

3 What does Mason say about their relationship?
  A He always thought it was pointless.
  B They got on very well at the start.
  C She didn't tell him the truth.

4 Why did they break up?
  A Mason was selfish and never did what Jasmine wanted to do.
  B Jasmine's friends didn't get on with Mason.
  C Mason changed and Jasmine didn't like his new behaviour.

5 What does Mason think now?
  A His friends should have given him better advice.
  B He'd like Jasmine to forgive him, but he knows that's impossible.
  C If you want a relationship to last, you have to be flexible.

Listening: ______ /10

WRITE

3 In your class you have been talking about money. Now your teacher has asked you to write the essay below for homework. Write your essay (140–190 words) using all the notes and giving reasons for your opinion.

Some people think that money can buy happiness. Do you think that's true? Explain why.

Notes

Write about:

1 things that make people happy
2 people who don't have much money
3 ______________ (your own idea)

Writing: ______ /10

Progress check score ______ /30

EXAM TIPS

do a multiple-choice listening exercise (one audio text)

- Find out what the audio's about. Read the instruction, questions and options carefully.
- Listen for the main message and the speaker's attitude or feelings
- Think about your answers to each question. Then look at the options. Is your answer there?
- Choose an option because of its meaning, not just because it has similar words to the audio.
- When you listen again, check your choices.

predict what a story will be about
See page 76.

understand hesitation
See page 86.

EXAM TIPS

write an essay

- Read the task carefully. What's the essay about? Are there any ideas that you have to include?
- Start with an introduction. Say what your opinion is.
- Use a new paragraph for each new idea.
- Give reasons for your opinions: facts, examples or personal experiences.
- Use appropriate expressions to organise your ideas and make them easy to follow.
- Finish with a summary of your opinion.

use persuasive language
See page 80.

add detail to a description
See page 90.

UNIT 9

LOOK AFTER YOURSELF

IN THE PICTURE Food

Talk about street food and how it's made

RECALL AND READ

1 a Make a network for food words (see page 16). Put 'food' at the centre and include these categories: dishes, equipment, cooking verbs, fruit, vegetables, fish, meat and drinks.

b Work in pairs. Add things you can see in the photos to your networks. Then add other words you know.

2 a Match the dishes in photos b–e to the countries in the box.

Mexico Vietnam Japan Bosnia-Herzegovina

b Read the article. Match the descriptions to photos b–e and check your answers to Exercise 2a.

WORK WITH WORDS

3 Match the words in purple in the article to the definitions.

1 cooked in an oven ....
2 cooked over (not in) boiling water ....
3 cooked over a fire ....
4 with something put inside it ....
5 with something around the outside of it ....
6 with a thin layer of soft food on it ....

4 Match the taste adjectives to the foods.

1 hot	a cheese, meat
2 sweet	b curry
3 spicy	c lemon
4 savoury	d sugar, fruit
5 bitter	e chilli
6 sour	f coffee, dark chocolate

5 3.13 Listen and repeat the words in Exercises 3 and 4.

6 a 3.14 PRONOUNCE Listen and repeat the words, focusing on the different vowel sounds.

cook /kʊk/ food /fuːd/

b 3.15 Listen and circle the sound you hear. Then listen and repeat the words.

1 sugar /ʊ/ /uː/
2 fruit /ʊ/ /uː/
3 soup /ʊ/ /uː/
4 good /ʊ/ /uː/
5 should /ʊ/ /uː/
6 too /ʊ/ /uː/

7 Add other food words in the article to the network you drew for Exercise 1a.

TASTY STREET TREATS FROM ROUND THE WORLD

Japanese sushi has become internationally famous. But there's plenty of less well-known street food to discover.

'Bánh Mì is a sandwich made with a French baguette, but the filling is definitely Vietnamese. Mayonnaise is **spread** on the bread, then they add paté, **grilled** meat, crunchy vegetables, fresh herbs and soy sauce. You should ask for a hot chilli sauce on it too.'

'Burek is popular in Bosnia-Herzegovina, and it's sold all over the Balkans, though I think it originally came from Turkey. It's a type of pie made of pastry **filled** with minced beef and spinach or cheese and herbs which is rolled and then **baked**.'

'Tamales are really good for breakfast. They're made of cornflour dough filled with different combinations of meat, chicken, vegetables, beans and cheese. Then they're **wrapped** in banana leaves and **steamed**. There are sweet tamales too, but I like them savoury and very hot and spicy.'

8 THE MOVING PICTURE Watch the video of Mike talking about other Mexican street food. Take notes on when it's eaten, its ingredients and how it's made.

EXTEND

9 Use the word at the end of each sentence to form a word that fits in the gap.

1 This food's really *tasty*. Can I have some more? TASTE
2 I'm going to try one of those chicken and vegetable ________. WRAP
3 I'd like an extra ________ on my pizza. TOP
4 Has that ________ got any meat or fish in it? I'm vegetarian. SPREAD
5 I can't decide what ________ to have in my sandwich. FILL
6 This apple's delicious. It's really ________ too. CRUNCH

SPEAK

10 Work in pairs. Do one or both of the tasks.

A Describe some street food, or food that's quick to prepare, from your country. What ingredients are used to make it? How's it prepared?
B How often do you eat street food or other types of fast-food? What do you eat? Where do you buy it?

GO BEYOND

Do the Words & Beyond exercises on page 138.

Workbook, page 100

READING The right snack

»» Recognise reasons and results

SPEAK AND READ

1 Work in pairs. Answer the questions.

1. Can you buy snacks at your school? If so, what snacks? What do you eat? If not, what snacks do you bring?
2. Think of two healthy snacks and two unhealthy ones. What makes the unhealthy ones bad for your health? Make a list.

2 ▶3.16 **Read the leaflet about a healthy snack campaign. How many of the things on your list from Exercise 1 does it mention? Add other things in the leaflet to your list.**

3 a Read the tips in the HOW TO box.

b Decide if the words in pink in the leaflet are a reason, a result or both. Circle your answer. Then write what they are the reasons for, or the result of.

1. obesity *reason / result* (circled)
   It causes serious health problems.
   It's the result of eating too much junk food.
2. bad fat *reason / result* ....
3. heart disease *reason / result* ....
4. high blood pressure *reason / result* ....
5. change our behaviour *reason / result* ....
6. a ban on junk food in schools *reason / result* ....

4 Which tips in the HOW TO box did you use for help with Exercise 3b? Tick (✓) them.

REACT

5 Work in pairs. Answer the questions.

1. After reading the leaflet, would you sign the petition? Why?/Why not?
2. Do you think students should decide what they can or can't eat during breaks? Why?/Why not?
3. What can schools do to help solve the problem of obesity? Make a list, and then a class list.

HOW TO

recognise reasons and results

- ☐ Look for linking expressions:
  - *because (of), as, since* and *due to* for reasons
  - *so, therefore, as a result* and *as a consequence* for results
- ☐ Look for verbs that introduce results like *cause, change, produce, make* and *result in.*

The Healthy SNACK CAMPAIGN

Read the facts! Sign the petition!

We think something must be done to stop our school selling junk food as snacks – things like chocolate bars, crisps and fizzy drinks. We think healthy options such as fruit, packets of baby carrots and mineral water should be made available instead. We also think shops and stalls around our school should be stopped from selling junk food to schoolchildren.

Here are seven reasons why junk food should be banned.

1. It's high in calories. All over the world, people are eating more junk food and fewer traditional meals. As a result, **obesity** is now a global problem. That's bad because serious health problems like diabetes can be caused by obesity.
2. It's full of empty calories as it fills you up but doesn't give you any of the vitamins and minerals your body needs every day to grow and stay healthy.
3. It contains lots of the **bad fat** that can block your arteries. Doctors have seen the first signs of **heart disease** in primary school children who eat too much junk food.
4. It's often full of sugar. A can of cola contains around 35g of sugar, or nine teaspoons. That's the maximum amount of sugar that should be added to a teenager's diet in a day.
5. Some snacks contain lots of salt, which can give you **high blood pressure**. And **high blood pressure** can harm your heart. One small bag of crisps contains 0.5g, and you're not meant to eat more than 1.5g a day.
6. It contains a lot of artificial additives. Some experts think these additives can **change our behaviour**, making it harder for us to concentrate. It's often impossible to know what additives might have been added, so why take the risk?
7. Bans work. Students in California consume about 160 fewer calories a day due to **a ban on junk food in schools**. That's enough to help maintain a healthy weight as you grow older.

If you feel action must be taken too, sign our petition!

GO BEYOND

Underline all the nouns in the leaflet that are made of two nouns, eg *junk food*.

»» Workbook, page 101

GRAMMAR Modal passives

Use the passive form of modal verbs

READ AND LISTEN

1 3.17 **Read and listen to the conversation. Why is Mo frustrated?**

Mo: Look! I've decided to get a healthy snack. This bread must have been made with about ten different whole grains!

Sue: It looks healthy, but a lot of salt could have been added. Some bread contains more salt per slice than a small bag of crisps. That's why all food should be labelled properly.

Mo: But even if they'd put a label on it, I'm sure I would've been confused by the information. Healthy eating's a lot harder than I'd imagined!

STUDY

2 Complete the explanations with examples from Exercise 1.

Modal passives

Use: With a modal verb (*can, could, may, might, must, should, shall, will, would*) when the action is more important than the person/thing that does the action.

Form: present and future
modal verb + *be* + past participle

They should label all food properly. (active)
________ (passive)

Form: past
modal verb + *have been* + past participle

They could have added a lot of salt. (active)
A lot of salt ________. (passive)
The information would've confused me. (active)
I ________. (passive)

See GRAMMAR DATABASE, page 128.

PRACTISE

3 a Sue's talking to her class about why she's a vegetarian. Complete the first part of her talk with the correct present form of the verbs.

'I don't think animals (1) *should be killed* (should / kill) for their meat. Also, some serious illnesses (2) ________ (can / cause) by eating meat, so it's unhealthy. Eating meat's a waste of food too. The animals we eat (3) ________ (must / give) food. That food (4) ________ (could / grow) for us to eat instead. If we did that, enough food (5) ________ (would / produce) to feed everyone in the world.'

b Complete the second part of Sue's talk with the correct past form of the verbs.

'Also, you never know what chemicals an animal (1) *might have been given* (might / give) to make it grow faster, and its meat (2) ________ (may / change) by those chemicals. Antibiotics (3) ________ (could / add) to its diet too. And millions of trees have been cut down for fields. If hamburgers hadn't become so popular, some of those trees (4) ________ (would / save). I think everyone (5) ________ (should / tell) about this.'

c 3.18 **Listen and check your answers to a and b.**

4 Complete the second sentence so that it means the same as the first.

1 They must label all food properly so we can make healthy decisions.
All food *must be labelled properly so we can make healthy decisions*.

2 We won't solve the world's food problems unless we all become vegetarians.
The world's food problems ________.

3 If governments were less selfish, they could have made hunger a thing of the past.
If governments were less selfish, hunger ________.

4 They should have banned fast-food years ago.
Fast-food ________.

5 Giving free healthy meals at school would reduce obesity.
Obesity ________.

6 They must make unhealthy snacks more expensive so people don't buy them.
Unhealthy snacks ________.

WRITE AND SPEAK

5 a Decide if you agree with the statements in Exercise 4. Make a note of your reasons.

b Work in pairs. Discuss your opinions. If you disagree with your partner, try to persuade them to agree with your opinion.

LISTENING AND VOCABULARY Teen habits

Understand the speaker's attitude

SPEAK AND LISTEN

1 Look at the dictionary entry. Then answer the questions in pairs.

1 How often do you get cold calls at home?
2 What are most cold callers trying to sell?
3 What do you normally do if you answer a cold call? Why?

cold call
NOUN [COUNTABLE]
an unexpected telephone call by someone trying to sell something

2 (3.19) Listen to a phone conversation. Why is the man calling? What's the free voucher for?

3 a Read the tips in the HOW TO box.

b (3.19) Listen again and decide if Elsa's attitude is positive (*P*) or negative (*N*) at these points in the conversation.

1 When she first hears the caller. P/N
2 When she's offered a free voucher. P/N
3 When she's asked about exercise. P/N
4 When she's asked about her blood pressure. P/N
5 At the end of the call. P/N

HOW TO
understand the speaker's attitude

- ☐ Speakers with a positive attitude towards the listener are polite, don't express negative emotions and respect turn-taking.
- ☐ Speakers with a positive attitude towards the topic show interest and ask and answer questions.
- ☐ Speakers with a negative attitude do the opposite.

4 Which tips in the HOW TO box did you use for help with Exercise 3b? Tick (✓) them.

5 (3.20) Match the two parts of the sentences. Listen and check.

1 She phones for a pizza
2 She exercises
3 She had a medical check-up
4 She had an eye test
5 She has a haircut
6 She goes to the dentist's

a a couple of years ago.
b once a year.
c every four months.
d once a week at most.
e about six months ago.
f three times a week.

REACT

6 Work in pairs. Compare yourselves to Elsa. Do you do more or less than her to look after your health and image? Give examples.

WORK WITH WORDS

7 (3.21) Complete the services offered by the shops with the verbs in the box. Listen and check. Then listen and repeat.

alter decorate deliver ~~do~~ dye frame install pierce repair straighten test whiten

1 *do* your **nails** so they look healthy and attractive
2 .... your **eyesight** to see if you need glasses
3 .... your **hair** a different colour
4 .... your **ears** so you can wear earrings
5 .... your **teeth** so they look nice and are easy to clean
6 .... your **teeth** so they look really clean
7 .... a **pizza** to your home
8 .... a **picture** so you can hang it on the wall
9 .... a **computer** so it works again
10 .... your **room** so it looks new or different
11 .... **heating** to keep your house warm in the winter
12 .... **new trousers** because they don't fit properly

8 Work in pairs. Talk about the services that the shops in the picture offer.

The first shop's a hairdresser's, so they cut and dye hair.

GO BEYOND
Do the Words & Beyond exercise on page 138.

Workbook, pages 104–105

GRAMMAR *Have/get* something done

>>> Talk about things you pay someone else to do

READ AND LISTEN

1 (3.22) **Read and listen to the conversation. Why do Maya and her room need to look perfect?**

Dana: You look different. Have you had your hair cut?
Maya: Yes, I have. And do you notice anything about the room?
Dana: Well, I've never seen it so tidy.
Maya: Very funny! But the real difference is that Mum and Dad got it redecorated. Everyone's coming here for my brother's wedding party on Sunday and they want things to look perfect, including me and my room.

STUDY

2 Read the explanations. Then underline two examples of the grammar in Exercise 1.

***Have/get* something done**

Use: For things you pay or ask someone to do for you.

I've just cut my hair. (= I cut it.)

I've just had my hair cut. (= A hairdresser cut it.)

Form:

have/get + object + past participle

Get is more informal.

See GRAMMAR DATABASE, page 128.

PRACTISE

3 Complete the conversation with the correct form of *have* or *get* and the words.

Dana: So (1) *have you had anything else done* (have / anything else / done)?
Maya: Actually, yes. I'm going to be the bridesmaid at the wedding so I (2) ________ (have / a dress / make) specially, and on Saturday I (3) ________ (get / my nails / do).
Dana: What about food?
Maya: We (4) ________ (have / food / deliver), and we (5) ________ (already have / a cake / make).
Dana: Well, I hope you (6) ________ (get / lots of photos / take). I can't wait to see you dressed up like that!

4 Complete the questionnaire with the correct form of *have* and the verbs in the box.

alter	~~cut~~	deliver	pierce	take	test

THE HEALTH & IMAGE QUESTIONNAIRE

How well do you look after your health and image?

Answer the questions to find out!

How often do you ...

1 *have* your hair *cut* ?
2 ________ pizzas ________ to your house?

Have you ...

3 ________ your ears ________ ?
4 ________ your blood pressure ________ ?

When was the last time you ...

5 ________ your eyesight ________ ?
6 ________ new clothes ________ ?

SPEAK AND WRITE

5 a Work in pairs. Answer the questions in Exercise 4. For each answer, ask your partner *Where?*, *When?*, *Why?* or *Why not?* If you don't want to answer, say *I'd rather not say.*

b Write three more questions to ask your partner. Then ask your questions.

>>> Workbook, page 106

LANGUAGE BEYOND

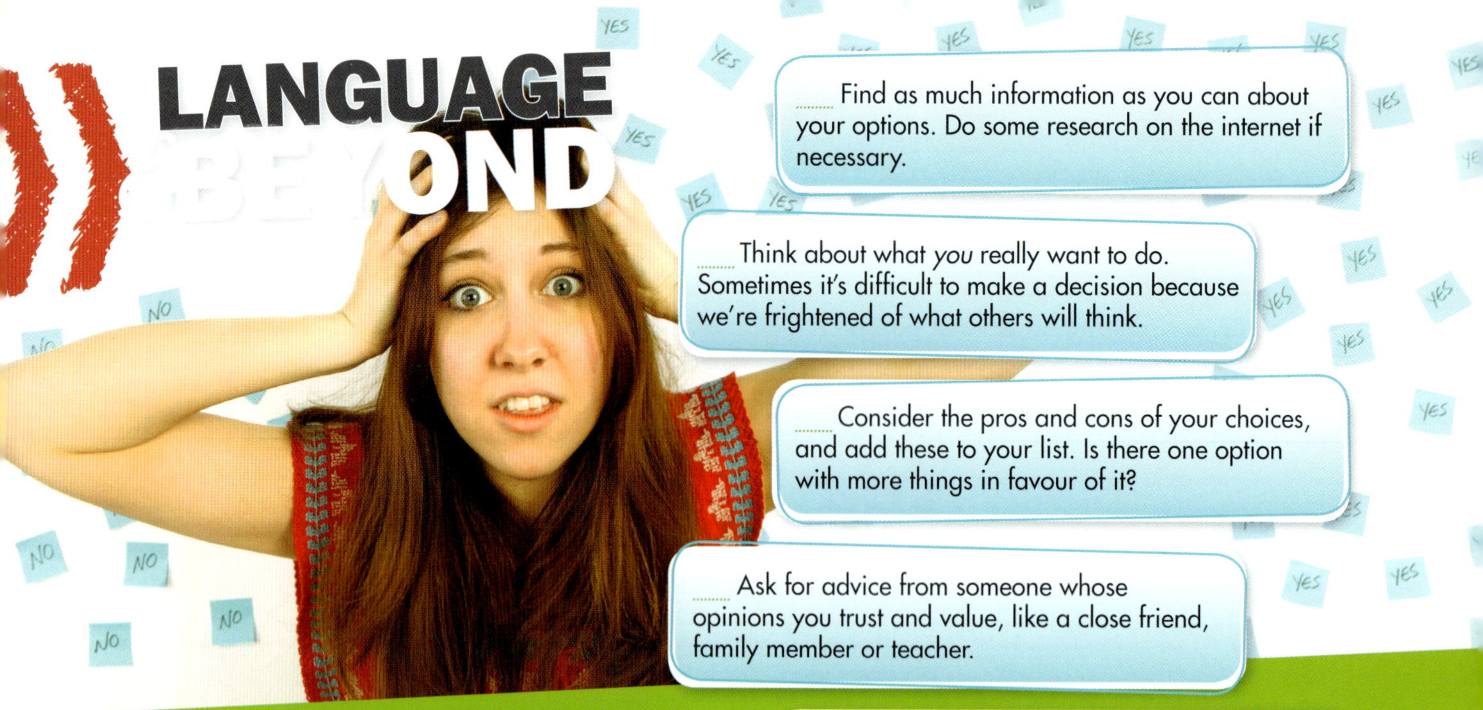

.... Find as much information as you can about your options. Do some research on the internet if necessary.

.... Think about what *you* really want to do. Sometimes it's difficult to make a decision because we're frightened of what others will think.

.... Consider the pros and cons of your choices, and add these to your list. Is there one option with more things in favour of it?

.... Ask for advice from someone whose opinions you trust and value, like a close friend, family member or teacher.

.... It's important to understand what your options are. Make a list, then force yourself to add at least one other option.

>>> Make decisions

SPEAK AND READ

1 Work in pairs. Do the following tasks.

- Tell your partner if you're good or bad at making decisions. To explain why, give examples of decisions you've made recently or need to make now.
- Talk about how you make decisions. Is there anyone you talk to for advice?

2 a Read the five tips above for making the right decision. Then decide which order (1–5) it is best to follow the tips in.

b Work in pairs. Compare your answers to Exercise 2a. If your answers are different, talk about why and try to agree on the best order.

PHRASE BYTES

What tip did you put first?

Really? Wouldn't you ... before you did that?

If it was me, I'd ... next.

3 Which of the tips do you follow?

DO

4 Choose a situation that could apply to you. Then use the tips at the top of the page to help you make the right decision.

- I really want to get fit, but I can't decide what type of exercise to do.
- I'd like to change my image, but I can't decide what look to choose.
- I think I should be a vegetarian, but I can't decide if that's a good idea.
- I can't decide what job I want to do when I leave school.

5 Work in pairs. Talk about the decision you made. Did the tips at the top of the page help you to make the right one?

REFLECT

6 Discuss the questions with your class. Do you agree with the REFLECTION POINT?

1 Why can it be so hard to make decisions?
2 Do the five tips in Exercise 2a work well? If not, how could they be improved?
3 Can you think of any decisions you made that you regretted later? Were you able to learn a positive lesson from them?

REFLECTION POINT

It can be hard to make a decision, but understanding your options better can help you make the right one. No decision is perfect, though, so if you make the wrong one, try to learn from your mistake. This will help you make better decisions in the future.

EXTEND

7 Choose another situation from Exercise 4, or think of a decision you have to make. Use the tips in Exercise 2a to help you make the decision.

Workbook, page 109

SPEAKING Get your hair cut

9

Ask for advice at the hairdresser's

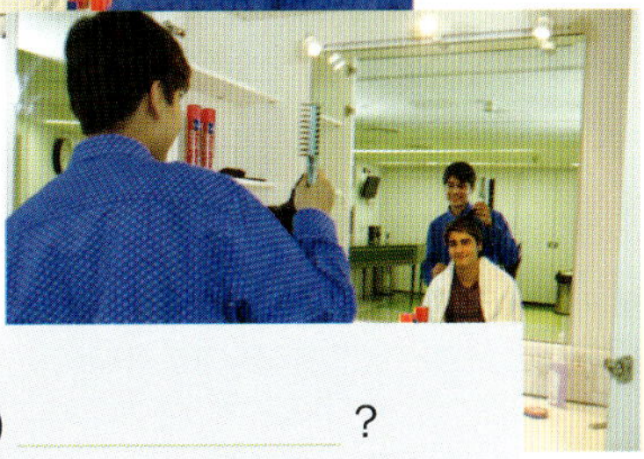

SPEAK

1 Work in pairs. Answer the questions.

1 How often do you have your hair cut?
2 Do you normally have the same haircut, or do you try different styles?
3 Do you like going to the hairdresser's? Why?/Why not?

WATCH OR LISTEN

2 3.23 Watch or listen to the scenes. Who has the clearer idea about the haircut they want, Ruth or Sasha?

1

Hairdresser: How (1) ______________ ?
Ruth: I'm not sure. What would you suggest?
Hairdresser: I think a short cut with a **fringe** would suit you.
Ruth: OK. I'd like some **highlights** too.
Hairdresser: Would you like it **blow-dried** ... you know, smooth or maybe curly?
Ruth: No, thanks.
Hairdresser: And would you like gel or **wax** on it?
Ruth: I'm not sure. What would you recommend?
Hairdresser: I'd choose wax. It leaves your hair more flexible.
Ruth: OK, I'll go for some wax.

2

Hairdresser: What (2) ______________ ?
Sasha: I normally have a **trim**, but this time I'd like it short. Do you think that would suit me?
Hairdresser: Yes, I think that would look good. So how much (3) ______________ ?
Sasha: I don't know. What do you think?
Hairdresser: I'd leave it a bit longer on top so you can put **gel** in it, and have the back and sides really short.
Sasha: OK, that sounds good. Let's see how it looks!

3 3.23 Watch or listen again and complete questions 1–3 in Exercise 2. Then add them to the PHRASEBOOK.

4 Match the words in green to the definitions.

1 ______________ : pieces of hair that are lighter
2 ______________ : a haircut that's only a little shorter but looks tidy again
3 ______________ and ______________ : products that are put on hair to help create a particular style
4 ______________ : hair at the front of your face that's cut in a line
5 ______________ : dried and styled with a hairdryer

5 Underline examples of asking for and giving advice in the conversations.

6 3.24 Listen and repeat some of the expressions in the conversations, paying attention to intonation.

ACT

7 Work in pairs. Role-play a scene at the hairdresser's. Take it in turns to be the hairdresser and the customer.

The customer: You aren't sure what haircut to have. Ask for some advice.
Hairdresser: Give the customer some advice, and ask what else he/she wants done.

PHRASEBOOK 3.25

The hairdresser:
What ______________ ?
How much ______________ ?
How ______________ ?
Would you like it blow-dried/smooth/curly?
Would you like anything/gel/wax on it?

The customer:
I'd like a haircut / a trim / some highlights.
I'd like the fringe shorter.
I don't want much off the back/sides/top.
Could you put some wax/gel on it?

Ask for and give advice
Do you think ... would suit me?
What do you think?
What would you suggest/recommend?
I think ... would look good.
I'd leave it a bit longer / choose wax.

Workbook, page 107

WRITING Our school report

Write a report

SPEAK AND READ

1 Which of these facilities does your school have? Work in pairs. Discuss what's good about them and what could be improved.

- classrooms
- a playground
- playing fields
- a sports hall or gym
- a computer room
- a theatre or auditorium
- a canteen
- a shop or snack bar

2 Read the report. What's it about? Is it generally positive or negative?

To: The head teacher
From: Class 3B

(1) .... : The school canteen

(2) ....

We were asked by our teacher to write a report about the school canteen. We discussed the canteen in class, and we agreed that there are some positive things about it and other things that could be improved.

(3) ....

We all think the canteen is a good facility. It is a big room, and there are enough tables and chairs for everybody. The people serving food are friendly, and it is well organised, so we do not have to queue for too long.

(4) ....

We think the food in the canteen is generally tasty and well cooked. However, we do not think there are enough healthy options on the menu. Also, there is nowhere for us to get our own water.

(5) ....

We think that some healthy options should be added to the menu. These could include a larger variety of vegetables, less fried food and more fruit. We also suggest having a drinking fountain installed so we can get our own water.

STUDY

3 Read the report again and complete it with the headings.

Conclusion Introduction
Negative aspects
Positive aspects Subject

4 Which expressions in the report do these things? Underline them.

1 It says why they're writing the report.
2 They give an opinion.
3 They express suggestions.

5 Read the tips in the HOW TO box and check your answers to Exercises 3 and 4.

HOW TO
write a report

- At the top, write who the report is to, who it's from and the subject.
- Use headings to make the aim of the paragraphs clear.
- Start with an introduction. Say why you're writing the report: *We were asked by ... to write a report about ...*
- Include opinions: We *agreed / (don't) think that ...*
- Finish with a conclusion. Include suggestions with *should* and *could* and with *suggest* + verb + *-ing*.

Get it right

*Talk **about** something.*
Discuss something. (NOT *discuss ~~about~~*)

PRACTISE

6 Write suggestions from the notes (1–4) that class 3B didn't include in their report. Use a different way to express suggestions each time.

1 Add a vegetarian option to the menu.
2 Put on relaxing background music.
3 Install a large TV screen.
4 Have the walls repainted.

PLAN, WRITE AND CHECK

7 You're going to write a report about a facility in your school. Choose one of the facilities in Exercise 1, or another one. Use tips from the HOW TO box to help you plan it.

8 Write your report. Use tips from the HOW TO box to help you organise and express your ideas. Then check it.

SHARE AND REVIEW

9 Swap your report with a partner. Read your partner's report and review it.

Workbook, pages 108–109

VOCABULARY Food

1 Complete the order form with the words in the box.

baked bitter filled grilled hot savoury sour spicy spread steamed sweet wrapped

ECO Home Services

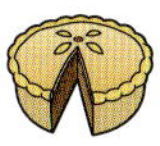

We make a large range of freshly (1) ________ pies with (2) ________ fillings (meat, etc) and (3) ________ fillings (apple, etc). Our (4) ________ curry pie is a favourite and can be ordered with extra chilli if you like (5) ________ food.

Our sandwiches are all (6) ________ with organic ingredients – meat (7) ________ over a fire, (8) ________ or fried vegetables, and bread (9) ________ with butter or margarine. Or have the same ingredients (10) ________ in thin chapatti bread.

To accompany your meal, order a salad with a deliciously (11) ________ lemon, oil and vinegar dressing. Or cake with a (12) ________ but tasty dark chocolate topping.

___ /12

Services

2 Complete the verbs.

ECO Home Services

We (1) d________ food to your house, but that's just one of our services. We can send someone to your home to (2) d________ a room, (3) r________ a computer, (4) i________ heating or (5) f________ a photo. They can even (6) a________ those new jeans you bought that don't fit properly. Our beauty therapists can (7) d________ your hair a new colour, (8) p________ your ears, (9) d________ your nails and (10) w________ or (11) s________ your teeth. And if you have problems reading this, we can even (12) t________ your eyesight!

___ /12

GRAMMAR Modal passives

3 Complete the modal passives with the correct form of the verbs.

OUR COMMITMENT TO QUALITY CUSTOMER CARE

At ECO Home Services no customer should (1) ________ (make) to wait more than an hour for the service they have requested. However, life is unpredictable. The professional we sent you could (2) ________ (delay) by traffic, or may (3) ________ (send) to the wrong address. But if the unexpected happens, and our professional arrives late, you would already (4) ________ (warn) about the delay and would not (5) ________ (ask) to pay for the service. You will (6) ________ (give) a time reference number when you make your request, and this must (7) ________ (show) to our professional in order to avoid payment.

___ /14

Have/get something done

4 Complete the customer comments with the correct form of *have* or *get* and the words.

Testimonials

We (1) ________ (our car / fix) two months ago, and a week later it had stopped working again. This time, we phoned ECO Home Services and (2) ________ (the job / done) properly. It's been running perfectly ever since. ***Brendan Powers***

There have been several burglaries in our area, so we decided to (3) ________ (a safe / install) to keep our valuables in. ECO Home Services did a superb job, so we (4) ________ (locks / fit) on the windows next week. ***Mirna Collet***

We recently (5) ________ (some flowers / send) to my parents for their wedding anniversary. The flowers arrived on time and looked beautiful! If you want to (6) ________ (something / deliver), ECO Home Services is the place to call. ***Molly Stevens***

___ /12

Your score: ___ /50

SKILLS CHECK

✓✓✓ Yes, I can. No problem!
✓✓ Yes, I can. But I need a bit of help.
✓ Yes, I can. But I need a lot of help.

I can recognise reasons and results when I read. ____
I can understand the speaker's attitude. ____
I can make decisions. ____
I can ask for advice. ____
I can write a report. ____

Workbook, pages 110–111

UNIT 10 FUTURE VISIONS!

IN THE PICTURE Life in space

Talk about visions of the future

READ AND RECALL

1 a Do the *Back to the Future* quiz. Compare your answers with a partner and then check on page 142.

1 The Big Bang theory says that the universe began in an explosion when a tiny point began to get bigger. According to this theory, when did our universe begin?

A 13.7 billion years ago B 13.7 million years ago
C 13.7 thousand years ago

2 Six planets can be seen just with the eye. Neptune, however, can only be seen with a telescope and so it was the last planet to be discovered. When?

A ancient times B 1546 C 1846

3 Many of us watch satellite TV channels. The first real communications satellite was called 'Echo', but the first ever satellite, which could not receive signals from Earth but only send them, was called 'Sputnik'. When did the Soviet Union launch it into space?

A 1937 B 1957 C 1977

4 People started using the sun's heat to light fires in the 7th century BC. But when was solar power developed as a source of electricity?

A 1970s B 1990s C 2010s

5 One of the first popular video games was a Japanese game called Space Invaders, which is still produced and played today. When was the first video game ever created?

A 1938 B 1958 C 1978

6 Robot vehicles were designed to explore the moon before the first astronauts landed there in 1969. Robot vehicles have also landed on Mars, including 'Curiosity' which was named by a 12-year-old American student. When did Curiosity land on Mars?

A 1972 B 1992 C 2012

b Underline all the verbs related to making and discovering in the quiz. Circle all the words related to space and start a network about SPACE with these words.

2 Look at the pictures showing illustrations of the future from magazines and books in the 20th century. Match each future vision from that time (1–4) to one or more pictures (a–h).

1 We'll send space tourists to the moon and to other planets in our **galaxy**, using high tech **rockets** and other **spacecraft**.

2 New entertainment devices will allow us to sit in front of a screen and take part in a sport or other activity. Portable TV devices will mean that we can watch our favourite series on the go – on Earth, in **orbit** or on the **surface** of the moon.

3 AS A SOLUTION TO OVERPOPULATION ON EARTH, WE'LL CREATE **COLONIES** ON **SPACE STATIONS**. WE'LL ALSO ESTABLISH A **BASE** ON THE MOON WHERE PEOPLE WILL LIVE IN BIG GLASS **DOMES** FILLED WITH **OXYGEN**.

4 Jet belts with engines will become the new way to travel, allowing people on Earth to fly freely in the air as if there was little **gravity** – like being in space but without leaving the Earth's **atmosphere**.

WORK WITH WORDS

3 a Put the words in colour in Exercise 2 in the correct categories.

- Places to live
- Vehicles
- Describing space and planets

b 3.26 Listen and check. Then listen and repeat.

4 Student A: look at page 141. Student B: look at page 142.

5 Complete the facts with the correct words from Exercise 3a.

6 a 3.27 PRONOUNCE Listen and repeat the words clearly.

big world globe

b 3.28 Listen and repeat. Are the consonants easier to say?

There's a big amazing world outside our globe and beyond.

Moon living: the facts

The international (1) ______ has been in (2) ______ round our globe since 1998.
The moon could be used as a(n) (3) ______ for scientific exploration.
To establish a(n) (4) ______ on the moon, you need power.
You also need access to space by (5) ______ and other (6) ______.
Although the moon is the brightest object in our (7) ______ after the sun, its (8) ______ is very dark.
On the moon there is no (9) ______ for us to breathe.
The moon's (10) ______ means that you'll weigh 8.5kg there if you weigh 50kg on Earth.
As the moon has no (11) ______, temperatures go from 130°C to –170°C. Without protection, like a glass (12) ______, you'll die.

EXTEND

7 3.29 Work in pairs. Put the planets in the correct order from the sun. Listen and check.

Earth Jupiter Mars Mercury Neptune Saturn Uranus Venus

8 THE MOVING PICTURE Watch the video of the International Space Station. What's good and bad about living there?

SPEAK

9 Work in pairs. Discuss the visions of the future in Exercise 2.

1 Which ones have come true? Or come true in a slightly different way?
2 Do you think you will see the other ideas become reality? Why?/Why not?

GO BEYOND

Do the Words & Beyond exercise on page 139.

Workbook, page 112

READING Mission to Mars

»» Understand links between and within sentences

SPEAK AND READ

1 a Work in pairs. Try to answer the questions.

1 What is the planet Mars often called?
2 What does its atmosphere mostly consist of?
3 Approximately how long does it take to get there?

b 3.30 **Read the magazine article to check your answers.**

YOUR FLIGHT LEAVES IN 15 YEARS!

What are you doing in 15 years' time? If you don't have any plans and you enjoy travel and adventure, you might want to consider a trip to Mars. The man who's going to get you there is Elon Musk, the billionaire founder and CEO of SpaceX, the private spaceflight company.

Musk wants to start a colony on 'the Red Planet'. To do this, he's initially going to send a small group of around ten people there. They'll take equipment to create oxygen from the planet's atmosphere, which mostly consists of carbon dioxide. They'll also build transparent domes where they'll be able to grow crops and start farming the planet's surface.
[1] ______

[2] ______ According to Musk, a ticket to Mars will cost $500,000. Musk calculates that there will be eight billion humans on planet Earth by the time the colonisation starts and possibly one person in 100,000 would be prepared to go. Consequently, if all 80,000 colonists pay for their seat, $40 billion will be raised. This will cover the $36 billion the project is likely to cost.

As long as he can develop reusable rockets to make the six-month journey to and from Mars, Musk believes he'll be able to make the project profitable. If he manages to do it, this won't be the first of Musk's achievements. In 2012 he sent the first privately-owned rocket to the International Space Station. [3] ______ However, it looks as if this is going to be his biggest challenge yet.

[4] ______ Since their bodies will go through dramatic changes without gravity, no-one knows for sure what will happen to the pioneers. Neil Armstrong described stepping onto the moon as 'one giant leap for mankind'. How will we describe stepping onto the surface of Mars for the first time?

2 a Read the tips in the HOW TO box.

b Think of one more linking word to add to each group in the HOW TO box.

3 There are four sentences missing from the article. Write the letters (a–e) in the correct place in the article. Use the linking words to help you. There is one sentence you don't need.

a What is more, the entrepreneur developed the Tesla Roadster, the world's first electric sports car.
b Curiously, a Martian year is twice as long as an Earth year.
c Surprisingly, one of the biggest problems facing Musk is how to keep his colonists healthy on the long journey.
d Unfortunately, if you want to be one of these new space pioneers, you'll have to start saving now.
e Once a self-sufficient base has been established, spacecraft will transport up to 80,000 people to live on Mars.

4 Which tips in the HOW TO box did you use for help with Exercise 3? Tick (✓) them.

REACT

5 Work in pairs. What do you think? Tell your partner.

1 Do you think Elon Musk will achieve his dream? Why?/Why not?
2 Would you like to be one of the Mars pioneers? Why?/Why not?

HOW TO

understand links between and within sentences

Look for words and phrases that:

- ☐ link events in time (*once*, *by the time*).
- ☐ add additional or contrasting ideas (*what is more*, *however*).
- ☐ show reasons and results (*since*, *consequently*).
- ☐ express conditions (*if*, *as long as*).
- ☐ express the writer's attitude (*unfortunately*, *surprisingly*, *curiously*).

GO BEYOND

Read the article again and find more linking words.

Workbook, page 113

GRAMMAR Futures review

Talk about arrangements, schedules, plans and predictions

READ AND LISTEN

1 3.31 **Read and listen to the conversation. Why should Mel take a book with her?**

Jon: What are you doing this summer?
Mel: I'm flying to Mars with my sister. The flight leaves next Tuesday. I'm really excited.
Jon: What are you going to do on Mars?
Mel: According to my space travel app, the weather's going to be really good so we'll definitely climb Olympus Mons and we'll probably visit Phobos and Deimos. I'll call you when we get there.
Jon: You won't be able to use your phone on Mars. And you're likely to need a good book. We went to Mars last year. It's really boring.

STUDY

2 Read the explanations. Then underline an example of each form in Exercise 1.

Futures review

Different forms express different ways of talking about the future.

Form:	Use:
present continuous	arrangements
present simple	timetables, schedules
be going to	plans, intentions
will (1)	predictions, often with *probably/definitely*
will (2)	promises, instant decisions
be likely to	things that will probably happen
will be able to	future ability

You can also use *be going to* for predictions when you can see evidence now, or have reliable information:

Look out! The spacecraft's going to hit the planet.

A new report says that space is going to be the next big holiday destination.

See GRAMMAR DATABASE, page 129.

PRACTISE

3 Match the sentences.

1 Oh, no! They're closing the departure gate! *d*
2 Watch out! ____
3 Please fasten your seat belts. ____
4 The Earth looks so small. ____
5 I can see another spacecraft out the window. ____

a We're going to take off in a few minutes.
b Are we going to crash into it?
c You're going to trip on that suitcase.
d We're going to miss the flight.
e It's going to disappear in a minute.

4 Choose the correct options in Mel's e-card.

Greetings from the EasySpacecraft. According to the timetable, (1) *we arrive* / *we're arriving* at 09:07 tomorrow morning. The first thing (2) *we do* / *we're going to do* is find my uncle and aunt. (3) *They're meeting* / *They meet* us at the airport. Then (4) *we probably go* / *we'll probably go* to the hotel. (5) *We're not being able to do* / *We won't be able to do* much on the first day because (6) *we're* / *we're likely to be* tired after the long journey. According to the weather forecast, next week it (7) *is going to be* / *is* very windy with lots of dust storms. (8) *I'm getting* / *I'll get* in touch again soon.

5 Complete Jon's reply with the most suitable future forms of the verbs

Thanks for your e-card. I think you (1) ______ (have) a fantastic time on Mars. Jan (2) ______ (come) round tomorrow. We (3) ______ (watch) the Inter-Galactic spaceball match. It (4) ______ (start) at 20:00. (5) ______ (you / be able / see) it on Mars? Jan says that based on recent results, the Martians (6) ______ (beat) the Earth team. Next week, I (7) ______ (visit) relatives. We (8) ______ (likely / stay) for a few days so I (9) ______ (probably / not be) back until Thursday.

6 Write the complete questions. Then write your answers.

1 What / do / after school today?
What are you doing after school today?
I'm meeting my brother.
2 What time / likely / go / to bed tonight?
3 you / do / any sport this weekend?
4 you / think / you / be / famous one day?
5 When / the English class / end?
6 it / rain / this afternoon?

SPEAK

7 Work in pairs. Ask and answer your questions from Exercise 6. Take notes and then tell the class what your partner said.

Workbook, pages 114–115

LISTENING AND VOCABULARY Futurology

Understand paraphrase

SPEAK AND LISTEN

1

2

3

1 **Work in pairs. Describe the photos. In what ways do you think they might represent the future?**

2 3.32 **Listen to a web TV show. Check your answers to Exercise 1.**

3 a **Read the tips in the HOW TO box.**

b 3.32 **Listen again and complete the sentences.**

1 Futurologists ...
2 In the future, we'll be living ...
3 Self-sustaining communities ...
4 A supersonic passenger plane can ...
5 Building a supersonic passenger plane would ...
6 When 3-D printers print food they ...

4 **Which tips in the HOW TO box did you use for help with Exercise 3b? Tick (✓) them.**

HOW TO
understand paraphrase

Speakers often repeat things in other words to make them clear. Listen for:

- ☐ relative clauses (*who*/*which*/*that*).
- ☐ sentences starting with *In other words*, *So*, ...
- ☐ expressions like *that is*, *which*/*that means* ... .
- ☐ repeated words and synonyms (*problematic*/*difficult*).

REACT

5 **Work in groups. Which thing in the reports do you think will have the biggest impact on your life in the future? Explain why.**

The 2-Minute Science Site
Click on a link to watch a report.

- Providing fresh drinking water in **overcrowded megacities**
- **Mini tablets** with the power of today's **supercomputers**
- Bringing the Net to the world's most **underpopulated** regions
- Three-part **miniseries** on the life of Albert Einstein
- Every **ultra-modern** kitchen needs an **ultra-fast** food printer
- Do not **underestimate** the challenge of **supersonic** airliners!
- How **megastores** encourage you to **overspend**

WORK WITH WORDS

6 a **Complete the table with prefixes from the links on the website.**

Prefix	+ verbs (v), nouns (n), adjectives (adj)	Meaning
super	v, n, adj	better or bigger than
	n	very big or important
	adj	extremely
	v, n, adj	too much
	n	smaller than normal
	v, n, adj	not enough

b **Which word means ...**

1 a very powerful computer?
2 think something is smaller, less important, etc than it really is?
3 containing too many people?
4 a very big shop that sells a lot of different things?

7 3.33 **Listen and repeat the words from Exercise 6a.**

8 **Work in pairs. Add prefixes to these words: *star*, *sleep*, *hero*, *thin*, *paid*. Then check the new words in a dictionary. What do they mean?**

GO BEYOND
Do the Words & Beyond exercise on page 139.

Workbook, pages 116–117

GRAMMAR Future continuous and future perfect

>>> Say if actions will be in progress or completed in the future

READ

1 Read the article and answer the question at the end. Check your answer on page 142.

MAGAZINES

Do you think robots will have taken over the planet by 2112, or will they be working for us? Do you think we'll have found a solution to global warming, or will sea levels still be rising? And will California have become an independent country? In 2012, *BBC News Magazine* asked its readers to make predictions about life 100 years from now. Then a futurologist said how likely he thought they were. What do you think he said about California?

STUDY

2 Complete the explanations. Use Exercise 1 to help you.

Future continuous

Use: For actions in progress at a time in the future.

Form:
will + ... + verb + *-ing*

Future perfect

Use: For actions completed before a time in the future, often with *by*.

Form:
will + ... + past participle

See GRAMMAR DATABASE, page 129.

PRACTISE

3 a Choose the correct options to complete the predictions.

MAGAZINES

Here are some of the predictions sent by BBC readers. Can you guess how likely the futurologist thought they were?

1. We'll ***be learning*** / ***have learned*** to control the weather by 2112. ___ /10
2. In 100 years from now we'll ***be transmitting*** / ***have transmitted*** our thoughts to each other. ___ /10
3. There will only be three languages in the world – English, Spanish and Mandarin. All the others will ***be disappearing*** / ***have disappeared***. ___ /10
4. The world population will ***be increasing*** / ***have increased*** to ten billion, so we'll ***be using*** / ***have used*** the oceans to farm fish. ___ /10
5. We'll ***be living*** / ***have lived*** in one country, under the control of a world government. ___ /10
6. We'll ***be discovering*** / ***have discovered*** how to connect our brains to computers, and we'll all ***be using*** / ***have used*** computers to make our brains work faster. ___ /10

b Write a number between 0 and 10 to show how likely you think the predictions are. Then compare your answers with what the futurologist said on page 142.

4 Complete the phone conversation with the future continuous or future perfect form of the words.

Sean: Hi Kathy. Have you started the project about life in 2112? It's really hard. For example, (1) .... (the North Pole / melt) by then? Some websites say yes, others say no.
Kathy: I'm about to have dinner. Can we talk at seven?
Sean: I (2) .... (have) my dinner then, but I (3) .... (finish) by quarter to eight.
Kathy: I (4) .... (practise) with the choir at that time.
Sean: (5) .... (you / look) at the project at the weekend?
Kathy: We're going away, but maybe on Sunday afternoon. I think we (6) .... (get back) by then.
Sean: But it's for Wednesday! You (7) .... (not do) it on time.
Kathy: I will, but I think I (8) .... (work) late on Tuesday to finish it!

WRITE AND SPEAK

5 a Look at the times. Write a sentence about what you'll be doing and what you'll have done.

- at/by 7pm this evening
- at/by midnight tonight
- on/by Saturday
- in/by 2025
- in/by 2050

b Work in pairs. Ask questions to compare your sentences.

What will you be doing at 7pm?

I'll be studying.

LANGUAGE & BEYOND

AREA	MY RATING	NOTES
Grammar	★★★★	Usually OK
Vocabulary	★★	Know the words but spelling often wrong
Listening and understanding	★★★	Sometimes people speak too fast
Speaking and pronunciation	★★	Find pronunciation hard
Reading	★★★★★	Fine
Writing	★★	Spelling again

»» Rate your progress

SPEAK AND READ

1 a Work in pairs. Decide what sort of feedback on your English is most useful. Put the feedback in order from *most useful* (1) to *least useful* (5).

Comments from your English teacher
Comments from your classmates
Homework marks
Results from class tests and exams
The scores in the review pages in your Student's Book

b Compare with another pair and discuss your reasons.

2 a César has used feedback to rate his progress in English this year. Look at his rating above. In what areas does he need to improve?

b Work in pairs. Write a list of things he can do to improve his English. Then compare with the class.

To improve his spelling, he could practise writing words in a notebook. Or he could ...

DO

3 Complete the *Make Progress* diagram. Write the steps in the correct place.

Follow your plan ~~Get feedback~~
Make an action plan Rate your progress

Are you happy with your results?
- Yes: How can they be even better?
- No: What's the problem?

What can you do to improve how you learn?

4 a Make a rating like César's for your English this year.

b Work in pairs. Show your rating to your partner. How could your partner improve their rating?

REFLECT

5 Discuss the questions with your class. Do you agree with the REFLECTION POINT?

1 How often do you rate the results of your learning at school?
2 In what areas of life outside school could you rate your progress?
3 Who can you ask for help if you need it?

EXTEND

6 Think about another school project, a hobby or a sport. Use the *Make Progress* diagram to think about your progress. Then work in pairs. Tell your partner your ideas.

REFLECTION POINT

Rating our own progress and making action plans helps us to improve and make even more progress. By changing things that don't work, pushing ourselves to do better and asking for help where we need it, we can reach our future goals.

GET ORGANISED

»» Workbook, page 121

SPEAKING We'll miss you

>>> Express hopes, wishes and promises

SPEAK

1 **Work in pairs. Describe the photo. What's the situation?**

WATCH OR LISTEN

2 3.34 **Watch or listen to the video messages. Where's Lily going and why?**

Luis: Hi Lily. Um ... I don't know what to say.
Nora: (1) ______
Luis: Right. I'm definitely going to miss your bad jokes.
Ava: And we hope you won't forget us.
Nora: She's only moving to Wales. We'll be able to call and text each other.
Ava: Ah. I promise I'll call you.
Nora: Marta asked us to pass on her best wishes. (2) ______
Luis: But hopefully they won't be as nice as us.
Nora: That's not a nice thing to say. I'll do my best to keep Dan out of trouble.
Ava: Have a great time.
Nora: Look after yourself.
Luis: Bye!

Dan: Well, Lily. What can I say? (3) ______, but you know how bad I am at writing ... and speaking apparently. So ... I wish you all the best. That sounds so formal. (4) ______, but I know you can't because of your dad's new job, but ... anyway ... hope I'll see you again soon. Bye.

3 3.34 **Watch or listen again and write the phrases 1–4 in Exercise 2. Then add them to the PHRASEBOOK.**

4 3.35 **Listen and repeat the phrases, paying attention to intonation.**

5 3.36 **Complete the message that Lily sent to the other drama group members a few days later. Listen and check.**

I hope I'll do my best I'm going to miss
I promise I wish Pass on my best

Hi everyone! Thanks for your video messages. (1) ______ you all too. Wales is nice, but (2) ______ I could be back with all of you. (3) ______ to keep in touch. (4) ______ I'll send you an update at least once a month. (5) ______ you come and visit me one day. (6) ______ wishes to everyone I know. Keep in touch.

ACT

6 **In groups of three, complete the tasks.**

- Choose another student in the class. Imagine the student is moving to another country.
- Write a video message for the student. Make sure you all say something, but don't say the student's name.
- Read your message to the class. Can the other students guess who the message is for?

PHRASEBOOK 3.37

Hopes

We hope you won't forget us.

I hope I'll see you again soon.

______

Wishes

Marta asked us to pass on her best wishes.

I wish you all the best.

______

Promises

I promise I'll call you.

I'll do my best to keep Dan out of trouble.

______

Saying goodbye

Have a great time.

Look after yourself.

______

>>> Workbook, page 119

WRITING You choose!

Present options

SPEAK AND READ

1 Work in pairs. Answer the questions.

1 Do you have friends in other countries, or other parts of your country? If so, where do they live? Do they ever come to visit you?
2 If someone who doesn't know your town or city came to visit you, what activities would you plan for them?

2 Read the email. How well do you think Francine knows Lola? Give reasons for your opinion.

Hi Lola,

Thanks for sending your flight details. Unfortunately, I won't have finished class by the time you arrive, which gives you two options. I could ask my brother to come and get you in his car. Or would you rather wait for 45 minutes at the airport and I'll come and get you? Either way, you'll be here in time for dinner. I've been thinking about things we could do. I know you're into space travel, so one option would be a Kennedy Space Center Tour on your first day. Another option would be to look around Orlando. Alternatively, we could stay at home. Whatever we do's fine by me.

See you very soon!
Love,
Francine

STUDY

3 Read the email again. How many options does Francine give Lola for these things? What are they?

1 Getting from the airport
2 Things to do on the first day

4 a Read the tips in the HOW TO box.

HOW TO

present options

- To present options, use:
  - *(Either) you could … or*
  - *Alternatively, / Or … / One/Another option would be (to) …*
  - *Would you prefer to / rather go … or …?*
- When options have the same result use:
  - *Either way / Whatever we do* + the result

b Underline expressions for giving options in the email.

Get it right

on time = at the correct time, not late

in time = early enough

PRACTISE

5 Complete the sentences with the words in the box.

alternatively	be	could	or	rather	way

1 We go to the beach in the afternoon.
2 Another option would to go to Walt Disney World™.
3 Either, I'm sure we'll have a great time.
4 Would you have pasta or rice for dinner?
5 , you could sleep on the sofa bed in the living room.
6 On Thursday night you could either come to class stay at home.

PLAN, WRITE AND CHECK

6 A friend is coming to stay in your house for a few days. Think of options for your friend in response to the questions below.

I'll be arriving at 5pm on Wednesday. Can you pick me up? If not, what's the best way to get to your house? So I know what to bring, do you have any activities planned for the week? Finally, where will I be sleeping? Should I bring a sleeping bag?

Oh, no! I can't at 5pm!

7 Write your email. Use expressions from the HOW TO box to give options.

SHARE AND REVIEW

8 Swap your email with a partner. Read your partner's email and review it.

Workbook, pages 120–121

VOCABULARY Life in space

1 Complete the text with the correct words.

MOVE TO VENUS!

Bored of living on Earth or Mars or being in (1) o__________ around Earth on the (2) s__________ s__________? Move to our new (3) b__________ on Venus! Venus is situated next to Earth in our (4) g__________ and is lovely and warm with a (5) s__________ temperature of 460°C. (6) G__________ on Venus is very similar to the Earth so you'll have no problems with weight. Each glass (7) d__________ house has (8) o__________-making equipment as Venus' (9) a__________ is not suitable for breathing. The price of each house includes transport to Venus on the new V22 (10) r__________ or public (11) s__________. Join our (12) c__________ on Venus now!

___ /12

Prefixes of size, quantity and degree

2 Jett and his dad are the first colonists on Venus. Complete the words with the prefixes in the box.

mega mini over super ultra under

Dad: Are you on your (1) __________ tablet again?
Jett: I was just watching *Cyber City*, that new Earth (2) __________ series.
Dad: I'm glad I don't live in one of those (3) __________ crowded (4) __________ cities, aren't you? You shouldn't (5) __________ estimate how lucky we are.
Jett: Mmm. But Venus is a bit (6) __________ populated, Dad. We're the only people here!
Dad: Yes, but we're lucky to have all this (7) __________-modern equipment. I don't know what we'd do without our (8) __________-fast food printer and our powerful home (9) __________ computer. Just imagine if we had to take a(n) (10) __________ sonic plane every day to go shopping. And those (11) __________ stores just make you (12) __________ spend. It's good there are no shops here.
Jett: Is it?

___ /12

GRAMMAR Futures review

3 Complete Jett's chat messages with the correct form of the verbs.

B: What are your plans for next week?
J: I think I (1) __________ (probably / play) virtual reality games most evenings as usual. On Tuesday I (2) __________ (do) sport. Real sport! Computer school (3) __________ (finish) on Friday for the summer. Yes! Then Dad and I (4) __________ (visit) some friends on the moon for a holiday. It's all arranged. We (5) __________ (likely / come back) in two weeks.
B: What's the weather going to be like on the moon?
J: It's the moon! There (6) __________ (not be) any weather! There's never any weather there. Anyway, bye for now. I (7) __________ (get) in touch again soon – promise!

___ /14

Future continuous and future perfect

4 Complete the website update with the correct future continuous or future perfect form of the verbs.

NOTICE

We're sorry to say that we (1) __________ (not build) any more homes on Venus. By the time you read this, we (2) __________ (close) the colony and the two people there (3) __________ (move) to the moon. But the good news is: we (4) __________ (start) a new colony on Mercury next year. We (5) __________ (take) reservations from next week although we (6) __________ (not calculate) the exact price by then. See you soon!

___ /12

Your score: ___ /50

SKILLS CHECK

✓✓✓ Yes, I can. No problem!
✓✓ Yes, I can. But I need a bit of help.
✓ Yes, I can. But I need a lot of help.

I can understand links between and within sentences when I read. ______
I can understand paraphrase when I listen. ______
I can rate my progress. ______
I can express hopes, wishes and promises. ______
I can present options in an email or letter. ______

Workbook, pages 122–123

READ AND COMPLETE

1 Read the article and choose the correct word (A, B, C or D) for each gap.

SPACE FOOD

What happens when you're hungry in space and there's nowhere to order a pizza?

The answer, of course, is space food. But what's it like? (1) ______, it's very similar to food on Earth. However, since all the food for a mission needs to be stored on board, it (2) ______ stay fresh for up to six months even though there's no fridge. It's therefore frozen and dried and put in ultralight packets. But it's also very sticky (3) ______ it sticks to spoons and doesn't fly around the ship in zero gravity.

But what will happen when missions to Mars last for years rather (4) ______ months? Experts predict that astronauts will have to grow fruit and vegetables. But will they be happy eating a salad while orbiting Mars or will they be calling down to the planet's (5) ______ to order a mega-sized Martian pizza?

	A		B		C		D	
1	A	Surprisingly	B	However	C	Unfortunately	D	Therefore
2	A	can	B	has to	C	are to	D	mustn't
3	A	so to	B	so when	C	so that	D	in order
4	A	less	B	for	C	three	D	than
5	A	top	B	surface	C	galaxy	D	space

Reading and completing: ______ /5

2 For questions 1–5, complete the second sentence so that it has a similar meaning to the first sentence. You must use between two and five words, including the word given. Do not change the word given.

1 Visitors from outer space could have built the pyramids.
COULD
The pyramids ______ by visitors from outer space.

2 I've got some homework to do, but I can finish it by six.
FINISHED
I've got some homework to do, but I ______ it by six.

3 We might be late because the traffic will probably be very heavy.
LIKELY
We might be late because the traffic ______ be very heavy.

4 I'm going to the hairdresser's for a haircut tomorrow.
CUT
I'm going to ______ tomorrow.

5 In the future, they'll make everything with 3-D printers.
BE
In the future, everything ______ with 3-D printers.

Reading and completing: ______ /5

EXAM TIPS

complete a gapped text with multiple-choice answers

- Quickly read the text. What's it about? Where would you expect to see it?
- Read the text again and look at the words before and after each gap. Think what the missing word might be.
- Look at the answer options. Is your word there? If not, which option fits best?
- Read the whole sentence with your choice in it. Does it make sense? If not, try another option.

recognise reasons and results
See page 96.

understand links between and within sentences
See page 106.

LISTEN

3 3.38 **You will hear five different people talk about making decisions. Choose the type of decision each person has to make (A–H). There are three extra letters which you do not need to use.**

A what to do after leaving school
B where to have something done
C which colour to choose
D what to do at the weekend
E where to go on holiday
F how to change their appearance
G whose advice to follow
H how to make something

Speaker 1 ____
Speaker 2 ____
Speaker 3 ____
Speaker 4 ____
Speaker 5 ____

Listening: ______ /10

EXAM TIPS

do a multiple-matching exercise
See page 27.

understand the speaker's attitude
See page 98.

understand paraphrase
See page 108.

WRITE

4 **Your school has some money to spend on improvements and has asked students to write a report on how to spend the money. Two options to consider are a new library or a new swimming pool.**
Write a report for the head teacher (140–190 words). Include your opinion of the two options and suggest another option of your own.

EXAM TIPS

write a report

- Read the task carefully. Who's it for? What information do you need to include?
- At the top, write who the report is to and from, and the subject.
- Start with an introduction. Say why you're writing the report.
- Divide your report into clear sections. You can use headings to make sections clearer.
- Include factual information, opinions and suggestions.
- Finish with a conclusion. Summarise your opinions and suggestions.

present options
See page 112.

Writing: ______ /10

Progress check score ______ /30

EXTRA READING King Arthur

BEFORE YOU READ

1 Look at the cover of the book and read the descriptions. Which do you think is the correct description?

a This is the true story of how a young man called Arthur became King of Britain in the 14th century.
b The stories of King Arthur are more than a thousand years old. They are stories; they are not history.
c King Arthur and the Knights of the Round Table is a traditional poem about the adventures of a knight.

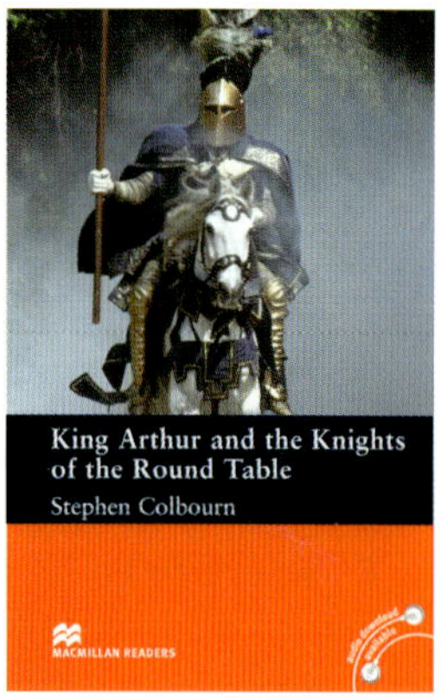

WHILE YOU READ

2 3.39 Read the extract from *King Arthur and the Knights of the Round Table.* Was your answer to Exercise 1 correct?

For fifteen summers and winters, there was no king in the south and the people suffered because there was no order in the land. Then, one night, Merlin the Magician came secretly to Winchester. He went to Winchester Cathedral – the great church in the town – and spoke to the Archbishop.
'Tell all the people to come to the Cathedral on Sunday,' he said.
On Sunday, the knights and the people of Winchester came to the cathedral.
They prayed for peace and a good king. And while they were praying, they heard a sound like music outside the cathedral.
The people went outside. In the field by the church, they saw a large stone. The stone was half as big as a man. A bright, metal sword was standing in the stone.

HOW TO
recognise and understand similes
See page 30.

The people could see only the handle of the sword. The archbishop looked at the stone and the sword. Words were written on the stone in gold letters:

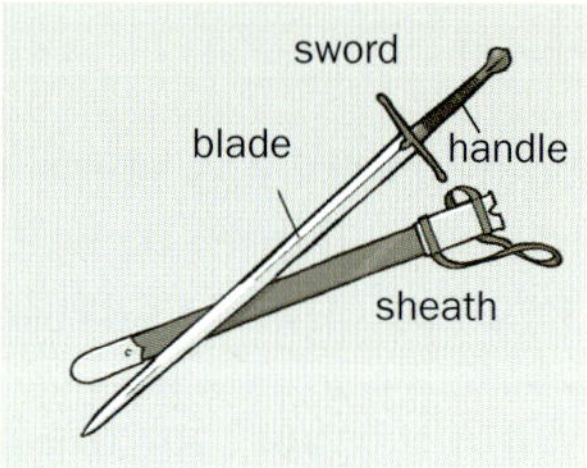

THE MAN WHO PULLS THIS SWORD FROM THE STONE IS THE TRUE KING OF ALL BRITAIN.

Then one by one, the men tried to pull the sword from the stone. All the knights of Winchester tried, but they all failed. The sword did not move.
'The true king is not here today,' said the archbishop. 'I will send messages through all the lands of Britain. Soon, everyone will know about this sword. Anyone who wants to pull the sword out of the stone must come here at Christmas. On New Year's Day, we will have a contest. We will see who can draw the sword from the stone.'

All the knights of Britain came to gather at Winchester. They put their tents in the fields near the cathedral. It was winter and very cold so the men lit fires to keep warm.
Sir Ector was an old, brave and honest knight. He came to Winchester with his two sons – Kay and Arthur. The three men rode their horses towards the cathedral. It was New Year's Day and they were going to the gathering of the knights.
Kay was eighteen years old and ready to become a knight. But only a king can give a man this title. And there was no king in the land.
Arthur was nearly sixteen years old. He did not look like his brother, Kay. Kay was dark-haired. But Arthur had fair hair, which was almost the colour of gold. Arthur was taller and stronger than his older brother.

Kay stopped his horse. Then he put his hand on his sheath and felt for his sword. But the sheath was empty. 'I have forgotten my sword,' he said to Arthur. 'I helped father to put on his armour but I forgot to put my own sword in my sheath.'
'I will ride back to our tent,' said Arthur. 'The knights are gathering near the cathedral. Go there. I will fetch your sword and bring it to you.'
'Ride quickly,' said Kay.
So Arthur rode his horse back across the field. Then, in the middle of the field, he saw the stone and the sword. The bright sunshine shone on the sword.
'No-one is using this sword,' Arthur thought. 'I will borrow it for my brother Kay.' Then the young man pulled the sword from the stone and took it to his brother.

Arthur did not know why the sword was in the stone. But Kay knew about the sword and the other knights knew too. They all gathered around Kay and Arthur.
'Who gave you this sword?' asked a knight. 'What are you doing with it?'
'Arthur, this sword does not belong to you,' said Sir Ector. 'Put the sword back in the stone. The sword belongs to the true king.'
All the knights watched as Arthur put the sword back into the stone.
'Kay,' said Sir Ector. 'Draw the sword from the stone.'
So Kay put his hand around the handle of the sword and pulled. But the sword did not move. Then all the other knights tried to pull the sword out of the stone, but it did not move.
'Arthur,' said Sir Ector. 'Draw the sword from the stone.'
Arthur put his hand on the sword and drew the sword from the stone easily. Then he raised the sword above his head and the metal flashed brightly in the sunlight. Everyone could see that Arthur held the sword.
Sir Ector got off his horse. He drew his own sword from its sheath and knelt down on the ground. He lowered his head and held the handle of a sword towards Arthur.
'Arthur,' said Ector. 'You are the true king of all the land and I am your servant.'
Arthur was astonished. 'Father, put your sword away,' he said.
'Arthur. You must know the truth,' said Sir Ector. 'I am not your father. Merlin the magician brought you to me more than fifteen summers ago when you were only a few days old. 'Take this child into your home,' Merlin told me. 'The boy's name is Arthur. Take care of him. Arthur and Kay will be brothers.'
When they heard these words, everyone knelt down. Arthur was astonished and could not speak.
Three months passed. At the beginning of spring, Arthur was crowned king in Winchester Cathedral. When the Archbishop put the crown on his head, all the people shouted, 'LONG LIVE THE KING!

AFTER YOU READ

3 Copy the organiser. Then make notes about the characters, places and objects that appear in the extract. Use the notes to retell the story in your own words.

Title: ____________________

Characters	**Places**	**Objects**

4 Write the answers to the questions in your own words.

1 In what ways are Arthur and Kay different?
2 Why does Sir Ector tell Arthur to put the sword back in the stone?
3 Which part of the story does the picture show?

HOW TO
take notes
See page 10.

5 3.40 Listen to an audio extract of one of the most famous parts of the legend. Who gives Arthur the sword and what must he do with it one day?

6 Read about *King Arthur* and answer the questions.

Many of the characters and events from the *King Arthur* stories have been used in other books, plays, video games, TV series and films. In *The Lord of the Rings* and *The Hobbit* by J.R.R. Tolkien, Gandalf the Wizard is based on Merlin the Magician. In the *Star Wars* films, the Jedi Knights are based on the Knights of the Round Table.

1 Can you think of other examples in which similar characters and events from *King Arthur* have been used?
2 The people and events in legends often change over time. Why?
3 Which myths and legends are associated with your country? In what ways are they similar or different to King Arthur?

EXTRA READING An Adventure at Brownville

BEFORE YOU READ

1 3.41 **Read about the author of *Owl Creek Bridge and Other Stories*. What do you think his short story *An Adventure at Brownville* might be about?**

Ambrose Gwinnett Bierce was an American journalist and writer. When the American Civil War began in 1861, he became an officer in the Union Army. His stories about the American Civil War made him famous. Bierce admired the American writer, Edgar Allan Poe. He liked Poe's stories about ghosts, horror and mystery. Many of Bierce's own stories are about strange mysteries and ghosts.

WHILE YOU READ

2 3.42 **Read the extract from *An Adventure at Brownville* and check your answer to Exercise 1.**

There was only one school in Brownville and I was the only teacher. Brownville was a small town and had few young people, but many visitors stayed there in the summer.

Brownville has some of the finest views in the state of California. The town lies between hills that are covered in beautiful, colourful trees. In the hills, the air is fresh and clear. Many visitors came to Brownville to improve their health. They walked on the hills and breathed the good, clean air.

I saw many of these visitors because I lived in a boarding house. In summer, the house was full of guests and I talked to most of them. I ate breakfast and supper in the boarding house and spent the rest of the day at the school.

The school was not far away. It was on the other side of a hill. The distance by road was about one and a half miles, but I knew a shorter way. I could walk over the top of the hill in fifteen minutes. There was a path that ran through the forest on the hill.

I came back along this forest path late one evening. It was the last day of term. Tomorrow, the students' vacations would begin. I had stayed late at the school because I had been writing reports.

Suddenly I heard voices. One was a woman's voice, and she sounded angry. The second voice belonged to a man. It was a deep and musical voice — the voice of a singer. I could not see who was speaking, but I could hear the words clearly.

'*Don't* threaten me!' the man said. 'You can do nothing. Don't try to change anything, or you will both suffer.'

'What do you mean?' said the woman's voice angrily. It was a cultivated voice — she spoke clearly and well. 'Do you mean that you'll murder us?'

It was almost dark now, but suddenly I saw the two people among the trees. They were standing on the path. The man was tall and slim. He seemed to be wearing black clothes. But there were too many shadows and I could not see clearly.

The woman wore a pale grey dress. They did not see me.

As I watched, the woman knelt on the ground in front of the man. She held her hands together in front of her face. Was she begging for the man's help? Or was she praying that he would not hurt her? I did not like this scene. There was trouble here. I stepped behind a large tree.

When I looked at the path again, the man and woman had disappeared. I walked on until I saw the light of the lamps shining from the windows of the boarding house. The scene of the man and the woman in the forest stayed in my mind. It had made me feel unhappy and uncomfortable.

I saw some new guests at breakfast the next morning. A young woman sat at a table opposite mine, but she was not the woman who I had seen last night.

Then a younger lady entered the dining room. The two young women looked very similar. And they were both extremely pretty.

When the second young lady spoke, I recognised her voice immediately. I had heard it in the forest. The two ladies were sisters. I guessed that they were about 18 and 20 years old.

I finished my coffee and left the dining room quickly. I did not see the tall, slim man, but I heard him. He was in the garden of the boarding house. As I had guessed, he was a singer. He was practising his singing. He was singing 'La donna é mobile' — a song from Verdi's opera, *Rigoletto*.

The singer had a very good, strong voice. Maybe it was too good. Why was he in a simple boarding house in Brownville and singing in this way? I walked away quickly.

HOW TO

infer meaning when you read

See page 62.

When I returned to the boarding house later, I saw the elder sister. She was standing in the garden with the singer. He was dressed in black clothes. His back was turned towards me, so I could not see his face.

The singer was talking easily to the young woman. I guessed that they knew each other well. When I came into the garden, he stopped talking and turned around. He looked straight at my face. The man was not young. I guessed that he was about 50 years old. His face was extremely handsome. His hair was thick and black – as black as the clothes that he wore. And the clothes were very fine. They were smart, fashionable and well made. They looked expensive. He could not have bought clothes like these in Brownville. I have seen pictures of opera houses in the fashionable cities of Europe. This man reminded me of the men in those pictures.

The man looked at me as if he knew the thoughts in my head. Did he know what I was *thinking*? The expression on his face was not angry or frightening. But I suddenly felt afraid. Why? I could not explain it. I only knew that I was afraid of this dark and handsome man. He was dangerous. I did not like him.

AFTER YOU READ

3 a Copy the organiser. Then make notes for the three different scenes in the extract.

Title: ____________________
Author: ____________________

Scene 1	Scene 2	Scene 3
Time of day:	Time of day:	Time of day:
Location:	Location:	Location:
Events:	Events:	Events:
Key sentence:	Key sentence:	Key sentence:

b Use your notes to help you write a short summary of the extract.

HOW TO

make notes for a summary

See page 74.

4 Write the answers to the questions in your own words.

1 How would you describe Brownville?
2 The narrator says that maybe the singer's voice is 'too good'. What does he mean?
3 Why does the narrator feel unhappy and uncomfortable at the end of the extract?

5 a Look at the illustration from the book. What do you think happens next?

b 3.43 Listen to the next part of the story and check your answer to 5a. Why did the girls come to Brownville?

6 Read the five tips for writing a short story and answer the questions.

1 Describe the setting quickly. ☐
2 Make sure the reader can identify with the narrator or a character. ☐
3 Describe the events of your story quickly. ☐
4 Create conflict and include exciting or frightening situations. ☐
5 Build your story to a climax. ☐

1 Which of the tips are covered in *An Adventure at Brownville*? Tick (✓) them.
2 What are the main differences between writing a short story and a novel?
3 What do you think happens in the rest of the story? Would you like to read more to find out?

Present tenses review

Present simple

- Use the present simple to talk about habits, routines and things that are generally true:
  Wheelchair rugby ***combines*** *elements of rugby, basketball and handball.*
  All extreme sports ***involve*** *an element of risk.*
- Use adverbs and expressions of frequency such as *usually, always, every day* with the present simple:
  She ***usually*** *trains every day.*

Present continuous

- Use the present continuous to talk about things in progress now or around now and also to refer to temporary or changing situations:
  She's ***training*** *hard for next year's Paralympics™.*
  We're ***practising*** *for Saturday's match.*
- Use time expressions such as *now, right now, at the moment* and *these days* with the present continuous:
  And ***now*** *the Kenyan athlete is crossing the finishing line!*
  Are you still playing tennis ***these days****?*

WATCH OUT! State verbs

Don't use the present continuous with **state verbs**. *Use the* present simple. State verbs often express mental states and opinions (eg *believe, feel, know, think, remember, understand*) and preferences (eg *like, love, hate, need, want*):
She ***wants*** *the Brazilian team to win.* (NOT ~~*She is wanting*~~ …)
I ***don't think*** *they are a very strong team.*

Present simple passive

USE

- Use the present simple passive when the person or thing that does the action is unknown, obvious, or less important than the subject of the sentence or not important at all:
  Wheelchair rugby ***is played*** *in more than 30 countries around the world.*

FORM

- Form the present simple passive with *am/are/is (not)* + past participle:
  Wheelchair rugby ***is*** *also* ***known*** *as 'Murderball'.*
- To form questions in the present simple passive, put *am/is/are* before the subject:
  Is *wheelchair rugby* ***played*** *indoors or outdoors?*
- To say who or what does the action, use *by*:
  Wheelchair rugby is played ***by*** *both men and women.*

Past tenses review

Past simple

- Use the past simple for completed actions in the past:
  Abby Sunderland ***left*** *home to sail solo around the world at the age of 16.*

Past continuous

- Use the past continuous for actions in progress at a particular time in the past:
  In 2009, she ***was living*** *a normal life in California.*
- Use the past simple and past continuous together to say something happened [past simple] while another action was in progress [past continuous]:
  – You usually use *while* before the past continuous:
  She lost contact with the outside world ***while*** *she was sailing in high winds.*
  – You usually use *when* before the past simple:
  He was sailing off the coast of New Zealand ***when*** *he spotted a whale.*

WATCH OUT! State verbs

Don't use the past continuous with state verbs such as *like, need, want, know* and *understand*:
I ***felt*** *a real adrenaline rush during the 60 seconds of free fall.* (NOT ~~*I was feeling*~~ …)

Past perfect simple

USE

- Use the past perfect simple to show that an action happened before another action or time in the past. Use the past simple for the other action/time:
  Jordan Romero ***had trained*** *for months before he climbed Everest.*
- You often use the past perfect with the time expressions *by* + time/age, *before, just, yet* and *already*:
  Jordan ***had achieved*** *his dream of climbing the world's seven highest mountains* ***by*** *the age of 15.*
- You often use the past perfect with *because* to give an explanation:
  They were successful ***because*** *they* ***hadn't taken*** *any risks.*

FORM

Positive

- Form the past perfect with *had* + past participle of the verb:
  He ***had reached*** *the summit.*
- The contracted form of *had* is *'d*:
  *He'****d*** *already climbed several of the world's highest mountains.*

Negative

- Form the past perfect negative with *had* + *not* + past participle of the verb:
  He ***hadn't taken*** *any risks.*

Questions and short answers

- Form questions in the past perfect with *had* + subject + past participle of the verb:
  Had *they* ***taken*** *many risks?*
  Yes, they had. / No, they hadn't.

Past simple passive

USE

- Use the past simple passive when the action is unknown, obvious or less important than the subject of the sentence:
  Abby ***was rescued*** *the following day.*
  Jordan ***was*** *always* ***supported*** *by his family.*

FORM

- Form the past simple passive with *was/were* (*not*) + past participle:
  A rescue mission ***was launched****.*
- To form questions in the past simple passive, put *was/were* before the subject:
  Where ***was*** *she* ***found****?*
- To say who or what does the action, use *by*:
  She was found ***by*** *the rescue party.*

Present perfect simple

USE

- Use the present perfect to talk about past actions when we don't know the exact time:
  *Someone**'s hacked** into my email account.*

ever

- Use the present perfect with *ever* to ask about experiences in your life:
  ***Have** you **ever written** a blog?*
- Use *ever* with a superlative adjective to emphasise how good or bad something is:
  *It's **the funniest** thing I**'ve ever read**.*

never

- Use the present perfect with *never* to say you have not done something in your life:
  *I**'ve never laughed** so much in my life!*

just

- Use the present perfect with *just* to talk about very recent events:
  *He**'s just uploaded** some photos from the party.*

already

- Use the present perfect with *already* to talk about actions completed before now:
  *I**'ve already seen** the photos on his phone.*
  *I**'ve copied** the photos to my phone **already**.*

yet

Use the present perfect with *yet* in questions and negative sentences to
- ask if an action is completed or not:
  ***Have** you **updated** your profile **yet**?*
- talk about an action that isn't completed:
  *I **haven't changed** my password **yet**.*

for* and *since

- Use the present perfect with *for* and *since* to answer the question *How long … ?*
  - Use *for* with periods of time:
    *I**'ve had** my new phone **for** two weeks.*
  - Use *since* with dates and points in time:
    *We **haven't had** any internet connection **since** yesterday.*

Present perfect continuous

USE

- Use the present perfect continuous with *for/since* when an action starts in the past and continues to the present:
  *I**'ve been waiting** at the library **for** half an hour. (= I'm still waiting.)*
- Use the present perfect continuous to describe an action in progress recently where there is a result in the present:
  *Meera looks tired. She**'s been doing** her homework all evening.*
- Use time expressions such as *all afternoon/week*, *recently* and *lately* with the present perfect continuous:
  *I've been trying to phone you **all afternoon**.*

FORM

Positive

- Form the present perfect continuous with *have/has* + *been* + *-ing* form of the verb:

I**'ve**/You**'ve**/We**'ve**/They**'ve**	**been**	**revising**	all afternoon.
He**'s**/She**'s**			

Negative

- Form the present perfect continuous negative with *have/has* + *not* + *been* + *-ing* form of the verb:

I/You/We/They	**haven't**	**been**	**doing** enough revision.
He/She	**hasn't**		

Questions and short answers

- Form questions in the present perfect continuous with *have/has* + subject + *been* + *-ing* form of the verb:

Questions				Short answers
Have	you/we/they	**been**	**working** too hard?	**Yes**, I/we/they **have**. **No**, I/we/they **haven't**.
Has	he/she			**Yes**, he/she **has**. **No**, he/she **hasn't**.

WATCH OUT!

Don't use short forms in positive short answers:
Yes, I have. (NOT ~~*Yes, I've.*~~)

Present perfect simple or continuous?

- Use the present perfect continuous to emphasise how long or difficult an action has been. The activity has not finished:
  *I**'ve been uploading** these photos for over an hour.*
- Use the present perfect simple to emphasise the result of an activity, especially when you answer the questions *How much/many?* or *How many times?*:
  *I**'ve uploaded** 20 photos from our holiday.*
- The present perfect simple and continuous with *for/since* often have the same or similar meaning:
  *I**'ve been studying** English for five years.*
  *I**'ve studied** English for five years.*

Past perfect simple and past perfect continuous

USE

- Use the past perfect simple and the past perfect continuous to show that an action happened before another action or time in the past:
  *Harry **had left** the area before the avalanche happened.*
  *Lucy **had been living** a normal life before a series of natural disasters destroyed the city.*
- Use the past perfect continuous for an action in progress up to a time in the past:
  *She **had been surviving** off wild animals and plants.*
- Use the past perfect simple for a finished action before another action or time in the past:
  *The earthquake **had** completely **changed** the landscape.*
- You often use the past perfect simple with *before*, *after*, *just*, *yet* and *already* and verbs like *thought* and *realised*:
  *She **realised** he **had run** away.*
  *We**'d just eaten** breakfast when then tsunami struck.*
- The past perfect simple and continuous with *for/since* often have the same or similar meaning:
  *She **had been hiding** in Central Park for several days.*
  *She **had hidden** in Central Park for several days.*

WATCH OUT! State verbs

Don't use the past perfect continuous with state verbs such as *like, need, want, know, think* and *understand*:
*I **had known** him for a long time.* (NOT ~~*I had been knowing*~~ …)
Be careful: the verb *think* has different meanings. When *think* means *believe*, don't use it in the continuous form. But when *think* means *consider*, you can use it in the continuous form:
*I **had thought** that he was a friend, but I was wrong.*
*She **had been thinking** for a long time that she should run away.*

Past perfect continuous

FORM

Positive

- Form the past perfect continuous with *had been* + *-ing* form of the verb:

I/You/He/She/We/They	**had been**	**waiting.**

Short forms

I'**d**/You'**d**/He'**d**/She'**d**/We'**d**/They'**d**	**been**	**talking.**

Negative

- Form the past perfect continuous negative with *had* + *not* + *been* + *-ing* form of the verb:

I/You/He/She/We/They	**hadn't been**	**listening.**

Questions and short answers

- Form questions in the past perfect continuous with *had* + subject + *been* + *-ing* form of the verb:

Questions				Short answers
Had	I/you/he/she/we/they	**been**	**sleeping?**	**Yes**, I/we/he/she/you/they **had**. **No**, I/we/he/she/you/they **hadn't**.

Sense verbs + *-ing* or infinitive

USE

- We use sense verbs with an object and another verb to talk about things we can see, hear, feel and smell:
  *I can **smell** something **burning**.*
  *I **heard** the door **slam**.*
  *Dasha **felt** something **crawling** up her arm.*

FORM

- Use *see/watch/hear/listen to/feel/smell* + object + verb + *-ing* for an action in progress:
  *I **listened to** my brother **playing** his guitar.*
- Use *see/watch/hear/listen to/feel/smell* + object + infinitive without *to* for a completed action:
  *I **heard** the window **smash**.*

Make, let and *allow*

USE AND FORM

- Use *make* + object + infinitive without *to* to talk about obligation:
  *They didn't **make us do** work experience last year but I chose to do it.*
- Use *(not) let* + object + infinitive without *to* to talk about giving or not giving permission:
  *My uncle **let me work** in his garage.*
- Use *(not)* + *allow* + object + infinitive with *to* to talk about giving or not giving permission in more formal situations:
  *The regulations didn't **allow me to fix** the cars because I was under 16.*
- Use *(not) be allowed* + infinitive with *to* to say you have or don't have permission:
  *But I **was allowed to wash** them!*
- Both *let* and *allow* have the same meaning, but *allow* is usually used in more formal situations.

Defining and non-defining relative clauses

USE

- Use defining relative clauses to identify or describe people, things and places:
  *A clapper is a board **that somebody shows at the start of the shot.***
- Use non-defining relative clauses to give extra information about people, things and places:
  *Skyfall, **which was directed by Sam Mendes**, was the most successful Bond movie ever.*

WATCH OUT! Defining or non-defining?

- A defining relative clause tells us exactly which person, place or thing we are talking about. The clause is not separated from the main part of the sentence by commas. The sentence does not make sense without it:
  *The dialogue coach is the person **who helps the actors with accents and pronunciation**.*
- A non-defining relative clause gives us extra information about a person, place or thing. The sentence still makes sense without it. Use commas to separate the clause from the main part of the sentence:
  *The film, **which stars Daniel Craig**, was released in 2012.*

FORM

- Use *who* for people, *which* for things and *where* for places:
  *The author Ian Fleming, **who** wrote the original James Bond novels, died in 1964.*
  *Titanic, **which** won 11 Oscars, was the first film to make over a billion dollars.*
  *Hollywood is an area in Los Angeles **where** many film studios are based.*
- In defining relative clauses, you can often use *that* instead of *who* or *which*:
  *My brother works for a company **that/which** makes documentary films for the BBC.*
- Non-defining relative clauses don't start with *that*.
  *My sister told me all about Skyfall, **which** (not that) she'd enjoyed very much.*
- Use *whose* for possessions:
  *Lewis Carroll, **whose** real name was Charles Lutwidge Dodgson, wrote Alice's Adventures in Wonderland.*
- In defining relative clauses, when *who*, *which*, *that* and *where* are the object of the verb, they can be left out:
  *The film **(that)** I saw last night was terrible!*
- You can't leave out the relative pronoun in non-defining relative clauses:
  *The casting director, **who** chooses the actors, has a very important job.*

WATCH OUT!

Non-defining relative clauses have a comma at the start and a comma or full stop at the end.
Don't use commas with defining relative clauses.

-*ing* forms

USE

- When we use the *-ing* form as a noun, it's called a gerund. We can use the gerund as the object of the sentence:
  I enjoy ***painting*** *still-life pictures of everyday objects.*
- You can also use the gerund as the subject of the sentence:
  Going *to art galleries is very inspiring.*
- When you use the *-ing* form as a verb to connect two clauses in a sentence, it's called a present participle. The actions in the two clauses need to happen at the same time and the main clause and the participle clause need to have the same subject:
  This artist creates works of art ***using*** *stones, leaves and mud.*
- The subject of the main clause and the participle clause must be the same:
  This artist creates *works of art* ***using*** *stones, leaves and mud.*
- Present participles are common after adverbs like *when*, *while*, *before* and *after*:
  He collects his materials ***while walking*** *in the mountains near his home.*

Question tags

- You can use question tags at the end of sentences to make questions.
  You're very good at art, ***aren't you?***
- Use a positive question tag with a negative sentence:
  The after-school art club isn't on today, ***is it?***
- Use a negative question tag with a positive sentence:
  They'll let us know if it's on next week, ***won't they?***
- If the sentence has an auxiliary verb, use the auxiliary verb (*can*, *have*, *is*, *will*, etc) in the question tag:
  Your dad ***is*** *showing some of his paintings at the exhibition,* ***isn't he?***
- For present simple and past simple question tags, use *do/ does* and *did*:
  He ***sold*** *a few of his paintings at last year's exhibition,* ***didn't he?***
- Put a comma before the question tag and a question mark at the end.
- Use a falling intonation (your voice goes down) when you are sure of the answer and are asking someone to agree with you:
  He's a very talented artist, isn't he?
- Use a rising intonation (your voice goes up) when you are not sure of the answer and are checking if something is true:
  He uses watercolours, doesn't he?

Should, must, have to, ought (to), had better

should / ought to

- Use *should* (*not*) and *ought* (*not*) *to* + infinitive without *to* to say something is a good (or a bad) idea:
  *You **shouldn't** pack too much for your holiday – you're only going away for a week.*
  *You **ought to** weigh your suitcase before you leave for the airport.*
- *Should (not)* and *ought (not) to* have the same meaning, but *should (not)* is more common.
- Only use *should* in questions. You can't use *ought to* in questions:
  *What **should** I pack for my trip to India?*
- The contracted form of *should not* is *shouldn't*.
- The contracted form of *ought not* to is *oughtn't*.

had better

- Use *had better* + infinitive without *to* to say something is a good (or a bad) idea in a particular situation, not in general:
  *You**'d better** find out if you need any vaccinations for your trip.*
- Use *had better* to talk about the present or the future.
- You usually use *had better* in speech or informal writing.
- You can use a contracted form of *had* in *had better ('d)* but you cannot contract *not*.
  *You**'d better not** forget to pack your passport.*

(don't) have to / must

- Use *have/has to* and *must* + infinitive without *to* to say something is necessary, important or strongly recommended:
  *You **have to** carry an ID card.*
  *You **must** avoid that area late at night.*
- Use *have to*, not *must*, in questions:
  ***Do** I **have to** carry an ID card?*
- Use *don't/doesn't have to* to say something is not necessary:
  *You **don't have to** carry an ID card.*
- Use *mustn't* + infinitive without *to* to say something is prohibited or dangerous:
  *You **mustn't** walk alone at night.*

have to or must?

- Use *have to* when a situation makes it necessary to do something:
  *You **have to** get a visa.*
- *Must* is more common for strong recommendations:
  *You **must** visit the old town.*
- *Should* is not as strong as must.

WATCH OUT!

Mustn't has a very different meaning to *don't have to*. *Mustn't* means you are forbidden or not allowed to do something or that it is strongly recommended not to do something:
*You **mustn't** forget to take a guidebook.*
Don't have to means there is no need to do something (but you can do it if you want to):
*You **don't have to** have any vaccinations.*

Can't have, could/may/might have, must have

- Use *can't have*, *could have*, *may have*, *might have* and *must have* + past participle to talk about possible explanations for things in the past that are based on evidence:
  *The TV's still on. He **must have left** in a hurry.*
- Use *could have*, *may have* and *might have* when you think an explanation is possible:
  *He **could have cut** himself shaving.*
  *He **may have been** in the shower when we arrived.*
  *He **might have gone** out through the back door.*
- Use *must have* when you're sure an explanation is true:
  *There's a plate with the remains of a meal on the table. He **must have had** dinner already.*
- Use *can't have* when you're sure an explanation is impossible:
  *He **can't have gone** very far – his car keys are still on the table.*

99% certain it happened	He	**must**	**have**	
		might **could** **may**		**stolen** the money.
99% certain it didn't happen		**can't**		

Conditionals review

Zero conditional

USE

- Use the zero conditional to talk about situations that are always true:
  If I spend all my money on computer games, my parents get cross.

FORM

- A zero conditional sentence uses the present simple in both clauses. The *if*-clause describes the action and the result clause says what happens:
  if-clause (action) result clause
  If + present simple + (subject), ... present simple:
  ***If** you **want** to make a difference in this world, you **have to** do something radical.*
- You can also use the imperative or *should* + verb in the result clause:
  *If your parents give you an allowance, **save** a fixed amount and **spend** the rest on what you want.*
  *If you borrow money from someone, you **should** pay it back as soon as you can.*
- You can also use *when* in zero conditional sentences:
  ***When** my friends and I go out, we usually spend all our money on milkshakes.*

First conditional

USE

- Use the first conditional to talk about possible situations in the future and their results. The *if*-clause describes a possible action. The other clause describes its predicted result:
  If you only take the money you need when you go shopping, you'll spend less.

FORM

- Use the present simple in the *if*-clause and *will* (not) + infinitive in the result clause:
  if-clause (action) result clause
  If + present simple + (subject), ... *will (not)* + infinitive:
  ***If** you **put** money into a savings account now, you**'ll** quickly **start** making money.*
- Use the present simple in the *if*-clause and *may* or *might* (not) + infinitive in the result clause if you are not sure about the result:
  *If I **buy** that new top, I **might not** have enough money left to go to the cinema.*
- Use *unless* with a positive verb in the *if*-clause to mean 'if ... not':
  ***Unless** I finish my homework, my parents won't let me go to the cinema with you.*
  (= If I don't finish my homework, my parents won't let me go to the cinema with you.)
- You can start the sentence with either clause:
  If you talk to them, they might let you go.
  They might let you go if you talk to them.
  Remember: if the *if*-clause comes second, don't use a comma.

Second conditional

USE

- Use the second conditional to talk about an unlikely or imaginary situation in the present or future and its result:
  If I found a wallet on the street, I would hand it in to the police.

FORM

- Use the past simple after *if* in the *if*-clause. Use *would* (*not*) + infinitive without *to* in the result clause. The contracted form of *would* is *'d*.
  if-clause result clause
  If + past simple + (subject), ... *would (not)* + infinitive without *to*:
  ***If** I **won** the lottery, I**'d buy** a house with a swimming pool.*
- To form questions, use *would* + (subject), ... infinitive without *to*:
  *What **would** you **do** if you won the lottery?*
- You can use *If I was* or *If I were* for the first person:
  *If **I was/were** a parent, I'd give my kids pocket money.*
- Use *unless* with a positive verb in the *if*-clause to mean 'if ... not':
  ***Unless** my kids helped with the housework, I wouldn't give them pocket money.*
- You can start the sentence with either clause:
  If I won the lottery, I would give half the money to charity.
  I would give half the money to charity if I won the lottery.
  Remember: if the *if*-clause comes second, don't use a comma.

Third conditional

USE

- Use the third conditional to talk about imaginary situations in the past and their results. Use the *if*-clause to imagine a change to what really happened in the past. Use the other clause to imagine the result of that change.
  If the Titanic hadn't hit an iceberg, 1,500 people wouldn't have died.

FORM

- Use the past perfect after *if* in the *if*-clause. Use *would(n't) have* + past participle in the result clause:
  if-clause result clause
  If + past perfect + (subject), ... + *would(n't) have* + past participle:
  *If the Titanic **hadn't hit** an iceberg, the ship **would have sailed** many more voyages.*
- To form questions, use *would* + subject + *have* + past participle / perfect:
  *What **would have happened** if the Titanic **hadn't hit** an iceberg?*
- In the result clause, you can use other modals like *should*, *could* and *might*:
  *If there had been enough lifeboats on the Titanic, more lives **might have been saved**.*
- You can start the sentence with either clause:
  If it hadn't been such a dark night, they might have seen the iceberg.
  They might have seen the iceberg if it hadn't been such a dark night.
  Remember: if the *if*-clause comes second, don't use a comma.

Wishes and regrets: *I wish* and *If only*

USE

- Use *I wish* or *If only* to express unhappiness with a situation in the present or in the past:
  I wish *I could play a musical instrument.*
  If only *I had studied harder for the maths exam.*

FORM

- Use *I wish* or *If only* + past simple to express unhappiness with a situation in the present:
  I wish I ***was*** *more confident.*
  If only I ***wasn't*** *so shy.*
- Use *I wish* or *If only* + past perfect to express unhappiness with a situation in the past:
  If only I ***hadn't been*** *so impatient with her.*
  I wish I ***hadn't lost*** *my temper.*
- You can use *were* instead of *was* after *If only* and *I wish*:
  If only I ***were*** *taller.* (or *If only I was taller.)*
  I wish it ***were*** *the weekend.* (or *I wish it was the weekend.)*

Reported speech review

Reported statements

USE

- Use reported speech to report what people said in direct speech:
  'I'm sorry.' > He said that he was sorry.

FORM

- Use *said* or *told* in reported speech. You can use reported speech with or without *that*:
  *He said (****that****) he was sorry.*
- Use *told* + object pronoun if you say who the person is talking to:
  He ***told me*** *that he was sorry.*
- Tenses 'move back' one tense in reported speech:
  *Ahmed: 'I'****m*** *sorry.' > Ahmed said that he* ***was*** *sorry.*

Direct speech	Reported speech
present simple	past simple
present continuous	past continuous
present perfect	past perfect
past simple	past perfect
future with *going to*	*was going to*
future with *will*	*would*
can	*could*
may	*might*

- Pronouns (*me*, *you*, etc) and possessive adjectives (*mine, yours*, etc), expressions of time (*now, today*, etc) and adverbs of place (*here, there*, etc) change in reported speech:
  Ahmed: 'Luke told ***me****.' > Ahmed said that Luke had told* ***him****.*
  Matt: 'I'm going to ask Katie to the cinema ***tonight****.' > Matt said* ***he*** *was going to ask Katie to the cinema* ***that night****.*

Direct speech	Reported speech
now	*then*
today	*that day*
here	*there*
tonight	*that night*
yesterday	*the day before / the previous day*
tomorrow	*the next/following day*
last week	*the week before / the previous week*
next week	*the following week*

Reported questions

USE

- Use reported speech to report what people ask in direct speech:
  'What's the matter?' > I asked him what the matter was.

FORM

- The word order in reported questions is different to direct questions. In reported questions, the verb comes *after* the subject:
  Matt > Ahmed: 'What are you talking about?'
  Matt asked Ahmed what he was talking about.
- Form reported *wh-* questions with: *asked* + person + question word + *I/you,* etc + verb:
  Ahmed > Matt: 'What did you say to Ben?' > Ahmed asked him what he had said to Ben.
- Form reported *yes/no* questions with: *asked* + person + *if/whether* + *I/you,* etc + verb:
  Ahmed > Matt: 'Is it true that you like Katie?' > Ahmed asked him if it was true that he liked Katie.

Reported requests and commands

USE

- Use reported requests and commands to report what people ask and tell you to do:
  Matt > Bolek: 'Don't tell her.' > Matt asked Bolek not to tell her.

FORM

- To form reported requests, use *ask/asked* + object + (*not*) + infinitive with *to:*
  'Please phone me tonight.' > I ***asked her to phone*** *me that night.*
- To form reported commands, use *tell/told* + object + (*not*) + infinitive with *to:*
  Ahmed to Matt: 'Tell me the truth.' > Ahmed ***told Matt to tell*** *him the truth.*

Modal passives

USE

- Use the passive form of modal verbs (eg *can, could, may, might, must, should, shall, will, would*) when the person or thing that did the action is unknown, obvious or less important than the subject of the sentence:
  Schools ***should be banned*** *from selling junk food.*
  Serious health problems like diabetes ***can be caused*** *by obesity.*

FORM

- Use a modal verb + *be* + past participle to talk about real or imaginary events in the present or future:
  Something ***must be done*** *to solve the nation's health problems.*
- Use *will* + *be* + past participle in the result clause of first conditional sentences:
  The nation's health problems ***won't be solved*** *unless the government puts a higher tax on junk food.*
- Use *would* + *be* + past participle in the result clause of second conditional sentences:
  Obesity ***would be reduced*** *if they banned junk food advertising on TV.*
- Use a modal verb + *have been* + past participle to talk about possible explanations for events in the past:
  A lot of sugar ***might have been added*** *to that fizzy drink.*
- Use *would* + *have been* + past participle in the result clause of third conditional sentences:
  Fven if they'd put a label on it, I ***would have been confused*** *by the information.*

Have/get something done

USE

- Use *have/get* something done to talk about things you pay or ask someone to do for you:
  I've had a tooth removed. (= *A dentist removed it.*)

FORM

- Use the correct tense of *have/get* + object + past participle:
  You look nice. ***Have*** *you* ***had*** *your hair* ***cut****?*
  I'm going to have *my hair* ***cut*** *tomorrow.*
  I ***had*** *my eyes* ***tested*** *last week, and now I've got new glasses.*
  I ***have been having*** *trouble with my eyes.*
  I'm having *an eye test on Friday.*
- *Have* and *get* used in this way mean the same, but use *have*, not *get*, in more formal contexts.

WATCH OUT!

The past participle comes *after* the object:

object past participle
I'm going to ***get my nails done*** *for the party.*

Futures review

USE

- Use different future forms to express different ways of talking about the future.

Present continuous

- Use the present continuous for future arrangements:
  *We're **going** on holiday tomorrow.*

Present simple

- Use the present simple for events on a timetable:
  *Our flight **leaves** at 12.*

***be going to* (1)**

- Use *be going to* + verb for future plans and intentions:
  *I'**m going to read** my book by the hotel pool.*

***be going to* (2)**

- You can also use *be going to* + verb for predictions when you can see evidence now, or have reliable information (eg statistics/research/reports):
  *According to the weather forecast, it'**s going to be** hot and sunny.*

***will/won't* (1)**

- Use *will/won't* + verb for predictions about the future:
  *I think we **will** have a fantastic holiday!*
  *We **won't** want to come home.*
- Use *will definitely* when you're 100% sure:
  *We'**ll definitely** try the local food.*
- Use *will probably* when you're 75% sure:
  *We'**ll probably** go on a boat trip.*
- In positive sentences with *will*, the adverb (*probably/ definitely*) comes AFTER *will*:
  *I'll **definitely** try surfing.*
- In negative sentences, the adverb comes BEFORE *won't*:
  *I **probably** won't try scuba diving.*

***will/won't* (2)**

- Use *will* for promises and instant decisions (made at the time of speaking):
  *I'**ll** send you an email when I get there.*

be likely to

- Use *be likely to* + verb to talk about probable events in the future:
  *We're **likely to** go walking in the mountains.*

will be able to

- Use *will be able to* to talk about future ability:
  *You **won't be able to** get any reception on your mobile phone in the mountains.*

Future continuous and future perfect

USE

- Use the future continuous to talk about things in progress at a time in the future:
  *In the future, we'**ll be living** in smaller, self-sustaining communities.*
- Use the future perfect to talk about things completed before a time in the future:
  *Fossil fuels, like petrol and gas, **will have by 2060.***

FORM

- To form the future continuous, use *will/won't* + *be* + *verb* + *-ing*:
  *I'**ll be doing** my homework at 8pm.*
- To form the future perfect, use *will/won't* + *have* + past participle. You often use *by* + time expression with the future perfect:
  *I **will have finished** my homework **by 9pm**.*

WORDS & BEYOND

WORK WITH YOUR DICTIONARY

In this book you can find tips to help you check words and use them correctly.

TIP: Use the word class (noun/verb/adjective, etc) to find the right word in the dictionary. Then use the context of the text and the examples in the dictionary to find the correct meaning.

TASK: In the description in Exercise 2, page 6, find the word *tap*.
– Look at the words around it. Is *tap* a verb or a noun?
– Find the verb or noun entry in the dictionary.
– Look at the different meanings. Find the correct meaning for this text.

tap
★★

VERB Pronunciation /tæp/

1. [INTRANSITIVE/TRANSITIVE] to touch someone or something gently and to move them slightly, or to make a soft knocking sound

Michael tapped his nose with his forefinger.
He tapped another code into the computer.

a. to touch the screen of a mobile device in order to make something happen

Tap here to activate plugin.

2. [TRANSITIVE] to use electronic equipment to secretly listen to what someone says on the telephone

3. [TRANSITIVE] to get a substance from a particular place or object

The scheme aimed to tap underground water resources.
tapping trees for rubber

tap
★★

NOUN Pronunciation /tæp/

1. [COUNTABLE] an object used for controlling how much water, gas, or liquid comes out from a pipe or container. The American word for a tap that controls water is **faucet**

There's no hot water coming out of the hot tap.

2. [countable] the action or sound of touching someone or something gently

I felt a tap on my shoulder.
A few taps with a hammer and it was fixed.

3. [countable] electronic equipment used for listening secretly to someone's telephone conversations

She suspected they'd put a tap on her phone.

Pages 6 and 7

EXTREME SPORTS

base jumping
bodysurfing
bungee jumping
free diving
free running
ice climbing
rock climbing
skateboarding
skydiving
snowboarding
tower running
windsurfing

GO BEYOND

Think of two different ways to categorise the extreme sports. Then sort the sports into the categories.

Page 10

ACHIEVEMENTS AND CHALLENGES

achieve (a dream / an ambition / fame)
attempt (a task / to do something)
encounter (a problem / difficulties)
face (your fears / a challenge / difficulties)
fulfil (your potential / a dream / an ambition)
overcome (obstacles / difficulties / problems)
reach (the top / the summit / your goal)
risk (everything / your life)
take (a risk / a chance)
take up (a challenge / an offer / an invitation)

GO BEYOND

Use the phrases to write three sentences about your life. Think about when you or someone you know achieved something or had to face a challenge.

NEW WORDS IN UNIT 1

able-bodied
abseiling
bench
circumnavigate
dance routine
hang-gliding
heights
kayaking
landing
parachute
put up a fight
ride (a wave)
spin
tap

WORK WITH YOUR DICTIONARY

TIP: When you want to know the meaning of phrases, phrasal verbs and idioms, look up the main 'content' word in the phrase in a print dictionary. For example, in *turn off* in the blog in Exercise 2, page 16, you should look up *turn* and not *off*. In an online dictionary, type in the whole phrase.

TASK: Underline the following phrases in the blog in Exercise 2, page 16: *the real world, give away, make out, out of sight*. Use your dictionary to find the meaning of these phrases.

turn off

PHRASAL VERB

1. [TRANSITIVE] to stop a piece of equipment working temporarily by pressing a button or by moving a switch

Will you turn the television off, please?

It is now safe to turn off your computer.

Pages 16 and 17

DIGITAL DEVICES

back up
click
download/upload
enter
log on/out
scan
set up
swipe
tap
turn on/off
turn up/down
update

GO BEYOND

What do you do to keep your computer and personal information safe? Write three sentences using some of the verbs.

Page 20

NEGATIVE PREFIXES: *IL-, IM-, IN-, IR- AND UN-*

illegal
illogical
immoral
impatient
incapable
irrelevant
irresponsible
unaware
unfair
unlikely
unusual
unwell

GO BEYOND

Write the opening lines of a short story called 'A bad day'. Use some of the adjectives.

NEW WORDS IN UNIT 2

advertising space
anonymous
Big Brother
brand
cashpoint
CCTV
erase
folder
get into the wrong hands
give away
issue
make out
make your case
on the contrary
out of sight
privacy
remain
reveal
tag somebody in a photo
track
unique

WORDS & BEYOND

UNIT 3

WORK WITH YOUR DICTIONARY

TIP: Your dictionary can help you to learn the most useful words: good dictionaries show frequent words in some way – for example, in red and/or with stars. Compare the words below from the film list in Exercise 2a, page 28.

storm
★★

NOUN Pronunciation /stɔː(r)m/

scientific
★★★

ADJECTIVE Pronunciation /ˌsaɪənˈtɪfɪk/

gadget

NOUN [COUNTABLE] Pronunciation ˈɡædʒɪt/

TASK: Look up more words from the film list in Exercise 2a, page 28 and find out if they're frequent words: *emotional, destroy, bury, strike, lava*

Pages 28 and 29

OUR ENVIRONMENT

avalanche
drought
earthquake
flood
hurricane
landslide
tornado
tsunami
volcanic eruption
wildfire

GO BEYOND
Write where and when these disasters usually happen.

Page 32

NOISE VERBS

bang
burst
crash
explode
groan
roar
scream
sigh
slam
smash
whisper
yell

GO BEYOND
Which words in this list describe quiet sounds? Which words describe the loudest sounds?

NEW WORDS IN UNIT 3

ash
brake
bury
community
creep
creepy
death
destroy
devastate
disaster
disease
dystopia
every cloud has a silver lining
eyewitness
fire alarm global
grab
homelessness
ignore
knock
lava
nuclear explosion
operation
rescue
simile
snap
spread
step
strike
survivor
swing
twist
tyre
utopia
war
warming

WORK WITH YOUR DICTIONARY

TIP: Use your dictionary to find out how to pronounce words. Use the phonetic symbols to pronounce sounds and find out the stress (after the /ˈ/ symbol in the word). You can also listen to the pronunciation of words in an online dictionary. Check if you need British or American pronunciation. Look at the examples below from the advert in Exercise 2, on page 39.

TASK: Look up more words from the advert in Exercise 2, page 39 and find out the pronunciation and word stress: *apprenticeship, salary, engineering, available, opportunity.*

apprenticeship

NOUN [COUNTABLE/UNCOUNTABLE] Pronunciation /əˈprentɪsʃɪp/

Pronunciation of **job**

NOUN /dʒɒb/

Pronunciation

This is the British English pronunciation of **job**.

Pronunciation of **job**

NOUN /dʒɑb/

Pronunciation

This is the American English pronunciation of **job**.

Pages 38 and 39

JOBS

accountant
app/software/web developer
beauty therapist
carpenter
electrician
firefighter
flight attendant
gardener
healthcare assistant
lighting/sound technician
plumber
veterinary nurse

GO BEYOND
What do people do in the different jobs? Write a short description of each job.

Page 42

FILM JOBS

(best boy)
caterer
cinematographer
costume designer
dialogue coach
director
editor
extra
(gaffer)
make-up artist
producer
stunt double

GO BEYOND
Write which of the jobs you would most like to do. Give reasons for your choice.

NEW WORDS IN UNIT 4

blank
clapper
crossroads
crowd scene
film credits
harmful
in a hurry
injection
journey
location
manicure
mates
outfit
paperwork
pedicure
pseudonym
salary
scheme
set
shoot (a scene)
similarity
spreadsheets
underneath
zombie

WORDS & BEYOND

WORK WITH YOUR DICTIONARY

TIP: Use your dictionary to check if a noun is countable or uncountable – or both. For example, look at the entry for *art* below. *Art* can have different meanings and can be countable and uncountable.

TASK: Look up these words from the essay in Exercise 3, page 50 and find out if they are countable or uncountable – or both: *school, graffiti, imagination.* If it's both, does the meaning change?

art
★★★

NOUN Pronunciation /ɑː(r)t/

1 [UNCOUNTABLE] paintings, drawings, and sculptures that are created to be beautiful or to express ideas
Do you like modern art?
a. something that people feel has value because it is beautiful or expresses ideas
Are these films art or entertainment?
2 [UNCOUNTABLE] the activity of painting, drawing, or creating sculptures
She devotes her spare time to her art.
3 **arts** [PLURAL] subjects of study that are not scientific, such as history, literature, and languages
an arts graduate/degree/subject
4 **the arts** [PLURAL] activities such as art, music, film, theatre, and dance, considered together
5 [COUNTABLE] [usually singular] an activity that needs special skills or knowledge
Bringing out the best in your students is an art.
art of doing something:
I have now mastered the art of letter-writing.

Pages 50 and 51

ART

collage
graffiti
installation
landscape
mural
pavement art
performance art
portrait
sketch
still life

GO BEYOND

Which of these types of art have you made, painted or done?

Page 54

WORDS TO DESCRIBE ART

average
controversial
dramatic
dull
elaborate
impressive
moving
powerful
quirky
stunning
subtle
unique

GO BEYOND

Write two or three sentences about your favourite work of art. What is it like and why do you like it?

NEW WORDS IN UNIT 5

angle
apart from
as a rule
as far as I'm concerned …
by and large
canvas
chalk
charcoal
chewing gum
comfort zone
commission
computer-generated
educate
except for
exception
fresco
functional
generally
handprint
image
imagination
ink
light bulb
mud
musical
on the whole
plaster
realistic
signature
spray paint
subtitles
territory
unfamiliar

WORK WITH YOUR DICTIONARY

TIP: Use your dictionary to find common collocations –nouns, verbs, adjectives, prepositions or adverbs that usually go together with other words. For example, *crime (in the entry below)* is often used with the verbs *commit* or *fight*, and with other nouns such as *prevention* or *rate.*

TASK: In the magazine feature in Exercise 2 on page 60, find one noun collocation for *collect*, *solve* and *catch*. Then look up these words in your dictionary and find out if there are other common collocations.

crime
★★★

NOUN Pronunciation /kraɪm/

1 [COUNTABLE] an illegal activity or action

commit a crime (=do something illegal): *She was unaware that she had committed a crime.*

solve a crime (=find out who did it): *It was a crime that would take police years to solve.*

a. [UNCOUNTABLE] illegal activities in general

fight/combat crime: *new laws to help us combat crime effectively*

crime prevention: *Crime prevention experts are helping to make the hospital secure.*

crime rate (=the number of crimes that people commit): *The crime rate in the city has risen sharply.*

Pages 60 and 61

CRIME

Crime	Criminal	Verb
blackmail	blackmailer	blackmail
burglary	burglar	burgle
cybercrime	cybercriminal	
kidnapping	kidnapper	kidnap
mugging	mugger	mug
murder	murderer	murder
pickpocketing	pickpocket	pick someone's pocket
piracy	pirate	
robbery	robber	rob
shoplifting	shoplifter	shoplift
theft	thief	steal
vandalism	vandal	vandalise

GO BEYOND

Put the crimes in order, from the most serious to the least serious.

Page 64

TYPES OF EVIDENCE

alibi
clue
DNA
fingerprints
footprints
mark
proof
remains
trail
witness

GO BEYOND

Burglars have stolen things from your house or flat. When the police arrive, what types of evidence will they look for, and where? Make a list.

NEW WORDS IN UNIT 6

at all costs
bad press
be stuck in traffic
common sense
corruption
crime doesn't pay
crime scene
figures
file sharing site
in any given situation
in real life
keep an eye on
lost property (office)
mafia boss
make headlines
neighbourhood
nine-to-five job
out of sight
owner
punishment
recreate
shopkeeper
sink
solve
take precautions
the prohibition
the small/big screen
there's safety in numbers
trouble spot
turn back
valuables
wander

WORDS & BEYOND

UNIT 7

WORK WITH YOUR DICTIONARY

TIP: Check grammatical information about verbs: Do they have irregular forms (3rd person present simple / present participle / past simple / past participle)? Are they transitive (followed by an object) or intransitive (not followed by an object)? For example, *save* in the entry below has regular forms and can be both transitive and intransitive.

TASK: Check if these verbs from the magazine tips in Exercise 2 on page 72 are transitive or intransitive or if they can be both: *borrow, spend, waste.* Which verb has an irregular past tense and past participle?

save
★★★

VERB Pronunciation /seɪv/ Word Forms

present tense	
I/you/we/they	save
he/she/it	saves
present participle	saving
past tense	saved
past participle	saved

4b **save** or **save up** [INTRANSITIVE/TRANSITIVE] to regularly put money in a bank or invest it so that you can use it later
I've managed to save almost £500 for my holiday.
save for: *Don't wait until you're 40 to start saving for retirement.*
save to do something: *We've been saving to buy a new car.*

Pages 72 and 73

MONEY VERBS AND NOUNS

bank account, debt, donate, fee, income, inherit, loss, owe, pay back, profit, raise, withdraw

GO BEYOND
Use the money verbs and nouns to make newspaper headlines related to people, countries or companies in the news.

Page 76

ADJECTIVES ENDING WITH *-FUL* AND *-LESS*

careful, endless, forgetful, helpless, hopeless, grateful, motionless, peaceful, pointless, stressful

GO BEYOND
Write sentences using the adjectives and the money verbs and nouns from the list on the left.

NEW WORDS IN UNIT 7

airmail, allowance, block, cardboard, convertible, dude, generously, goods, homeless, iceberg, it's not fair, parcel, radical, savings account, saying, sleepover, street junction, VAT, waterproof

WORK WITH YOUR DICTIONARY

TIP: Use your dictionary to check if a word is formal or informal. You can also check if words are British English (BE) or American English (AE).
For example, the word *teammate* is not informal and is used in both British and American English. But the word *mate* is only used in British English to mean *friend* and is informal.

TASK: Find out if any of these words or phrases from the photo story in Exercise 2 on page 82, are formal or informal: *wow, for ages, get on, fantastic, space, a bit, excuse*. Which one is only used in British English?

teammate

NOUN [COUNTABLE] Pronunciation /ˈtiːmˌmeɪt/
someone who is in the same team as you

mate
★★

NOUN Pronunciation /meɪt/
1 [COUNTABLE] BRITISH INFORMAL a friend
He's over there, talking to his mates.

Pages 82 and 83

RELATIONSHIPS

ask out
break up
fall out
get on
get over
get together
go out
let down
make up
put up with

GO BEYOND

Write three sentences about you or somebody that you know using some of these phrasal verbs.

Page 86

REPORTING VERBS

accuse
advise
blame
forgive
offer
persuade
refuse
remind
threaten
warn

GO BEYOND

Complete the sentences. Remember to use correct forms after the verbs.

1 I once accused …
2 I've never forgiven …
3 It's hard to persuade people …
4 I will always refuse …

NEW WORDS IN UNIT 8

a date
ashamed
bounce
budget
bully
care
challenging
clumsy
contact
depression
desperately
face to face
fault
feedback
frenemy
get down in the dumps
give somebody some space
go without
light as a feather
overhear
policy
praise
push
role model
upset

WORDS & BEYOND

UNIT 9

WORK WITH YOUR DICTIONARY

TIP: Use your dictionary to find synonyms – words with the same or a similar meaning to another word. For example, in the article in Exercise 2b on page 94, *famous* and *well-known* are synonyms – see the entry for *famous* below. (Note: in some online dictionaries you have to click on 'thesaurus' next to the word to find synonyms.) You can check if they're synonyms by replacing them in the text.

TASK: In your dictionary, find synonyms for these words from the article in Exercise 2b on page 94: *tasty, definitely, originally, come from, combination.*

famous – thesaurus entry

★★★

ADJECTIVE

1 if someone or something is famous, a lot of people know their name or have heard about them

Synonyms or related words for this sense of famous

Famous and well-known: *famous, well-known, celebrated, renowned, fabled, legendary, notorious, infamous, illustrious, the one and only...* more

Pages 94 and 95

FOOD

baked
bitter
filled
grilled
hot
savoury
sour
spicy
spread
steamed
sweet
wrapped

GO BEYOND

1. **Write one type of food that is often cooked in each of these ways: baked, grilled, steamed.**
2. **Write one type of food for each taste: bitter, hot, savoury, sour, spicy, sweet.**

Page 98

SERVICES

alter new trousers
decorate your room
deliver a pizza
do your nails
dye your hair
frame a picture
install heating
pierce your ears
repair a computer
straighten your teeth
test your eyesight
whiten your teeth

GO BEYOND

Choose four services and write the name of a shop in your area which offers that service.

NEW WORDS IN UNIT 9

artery
auditorium
baguette
bean
beef
block
blood pressure
calorie
chilli sauce
corn
crunchy
dough
fizzy drink
grain
heart disease
herbs
junk food
maintain
mineral
obesity
pastry
paté
petition
pie
playground
playing field
soy sauce
spinach
stall
trust
vitamin
voucher
weight

WORK WITH YOUR DICTIONARY

TIP: When you look up a new word in your dictionary, look at related words in the same word family. This can help you to extend your vocabulary. In a print dictionary, look at the entries before and after the word. In an online dictionary type in the first few letters to see all words from that word family.
For example, if you look for the word *entertainment* (from the descriptions of future visions in Exercise 2 on page 104), you will find these words from the same word family: the verb *entertain*, the noun *entertainer*, the adjective *entertaining* as well as the noun *entertainment*.

TASK: Look up more words from the descriptions of future visions in Exercise 2 on page 104 and find one or more related words: *create, establish, base.*

entertain | Search

entertain
entertainer
entertaining
entertainment

Pages 104 and 105

LIFE IN SPACE

atmosphere
base
colony
dome
galaxy
gravity
orbit
oxygen
rocket
spacecraft
space station
surface

GO BEYOND
Draw small pictures to show the meaning of at least three of these words.

Page 108

PREFIXES OF SIZE, QUANTITY AND DEGREE

megacity
megastore
miniseries
mini tablet
overcrowded
overspend
supercomputer
supersonic
ultra-fast
ultra-modern
underestimate
underpopulated

GO BEYOND
Use your dictionary to find one more word for each prefix.

NEW WORDS IN UNIT 10

all the best
alternatively
carbon dioxide
consist of
dust
exploration
fossil fuels
founder
futurologist
launch
mattress
pass on
pioneer
profitable
progress
rate
satellite
signal
sustain
transmit
transparent
vision

IRREGULAR VERBS

base form	past simple	past participle
agree	agreed	agreed
be	was/were	been
become	became	become
bite	bit	bitten
break	broke	broken
build	built	built
burst	burst	burst
buy	bought	bought
can	could	been able to
catch	caught	caught
choose	chose	chosen
come	came	come
cost	cost	cost
cut	cut	cut
do	did	done
drive	drove	driven
eat	ate	eaten
fall	fell	fallen
feel	felt	felt
find	found	found
fly	flew	flown
forget	forgot	forgotten
get	got	got
give	gave	given
go	went	gone
grow	grew	grown
have	had	had
hear	heard	heard
hide	hid	hidden
hurt	hurt	hurt
keep	kept	kept

base form	past simple	past participle
know	knew	known
learn	learnt/learned	learnt/learned
leave	left	left
lend	lent	lent
let	let	let
lie	lay	lain
make	made	made
meet	met	met
must	had to	had to
overcome	overcame	overcome
pay	paid	paid
put	put	put
run	ran	run
say	said	said
see	saw	seen
sell	sold	sold
send	sent	sent
sit	sat	sat
sleep	slept	slept
speak	spoke	spoken
spend	spent	spent
stand	stood	stood
steal	stole	stolen
take	took	taken
tell	told	told
think	thought	thought
understand	understood	understood
win	won	won
withdraw	withdrew	withdrawn
write	wrote	written

STUDENT A

UNIT 7 READING

Page 74, Exercise 5b

The decision

Deciding what to do with the money wasn't an easy decision for the Salwen family. It was important that they all agreed. They spent hours discussing the world's problems and how they could help. They researched causes and charities before collectively agreeing on the Hunger Project, an international development organisation based in New York City. The Salwens' money was used to sponsor health, food and other programmes for about 40 villages in Ghana in West Africa.

UNIT 7 LISTENING AND VOCABULARY

Page 76, Exercise 8

- Are you forgetful?
- What do you find stressful?
- Name one thing you're hopeless at doing.
- Could you stand motionless for one minute?

UNIT 8 GRAMMAR 1

Page 85, Exercise 6

1 Your best friend is angry with you.
2 You have no money.
3 It's really cold.
4 Your music player is broken.

UNIT 10 VOCABULARY

Page 105, Exercise 4

Read out a definition. Your partner says the correct word.

1 the air around the Earth or a planet
2 any type of vehicle that can travel in space
3 a place from which activities can be carried out
4 a gas with the chemical symbol O
5 a group of people who live in a particular place
6 the top, outside part of something

ALL STUDENTS

UNIT 4 VOCABULARY 1

Page 39, Exercise 10

THE APPRENTICESHIP GAME

1 Set a time limit for the game.
2 Each player chooses a different square/photo on pages 38–39 to start from. Take it in turns to play.
3 First, name a job in the category. Explain why you think it would be good to do an apprenticeship in the job. Score ten points.
4 When it's your turn to play again, move to the next square and repeat the tasks in 3. If you repeat the name of a job or an explanation that you or the other player(s) have already given, you lose five points. Which player has the most points at the end of the time limit?

UNIT 5 GRAMMAR 1

Page 53, Exercise 6

STUDENT B

UNIT 7 READING

Page 74, Exercise 5b

The Power of Half

The Power of Half is all about doing something with half the money, time or possessions that you could live without. Hannah doesn't expect everyone to sell their home, but she does believe that we all have something to give. If we all give something then maybe we can make the world a better place. Hannah and her dad wrote about their experience in a book called *The Power of Half: One Family's Decision to Stop Taking and Start Giving Back*.

UNIT 7 LISTENING AND VOCABULARY

Page 76, Exercise 8

- Name a place that's peaceful.
- Are you careful with your money?
- What's the most pointless thing you've ever done?
- Have you ever felt helpless?

UNIT 8 GRAMMAR 1

Page 85, Exercise 6

1 You've forgotten your new password for your social media site.
2 You have lots of homework.
3 It's really hot.
4 You're hungry.

UNIT 10 VOCABULARY

Page 105, Exercise 4

Read out a definition. Your partner says the correct word.

1 the path an object takes when it moves around a larger object in space
2 a large group of stars and planets
3 a long, thin space vehicle
4 an object shaped like the top part of a ball
5 a place where people can live in space
6 the force that pulls two things towards each other

ANSWERS

UNIT 5 GRAMMAR 1

Page 53, Exercise 5b

UNIT 6 VOCABULARY

Page 60, Exercise 6

Crime	Criminal	Verb
blackmail	blackmailer	blackmail
cybercrime	cybercriminal	
kidnapping	kidnapper	kidnap
mugging	mugger	mug
robbery	robber	rob
theft	thief	steal

UNIT 10 VOCABULARY

Page 104, Exercise 1a

Back to the Future quiz
1 A
2 C
3 B
4 A
5 B
6 C

UNIT 10 GRAMMAR 2

Page 109, Exercise 1

The futurologist said the likelihood of California becoming independent by 2112 was 8/10.

Page 109, Exercise 3b

1 8/10
2 10/10
3 8/10
4 10/10
5 2/10
6 10/10

STEP-BY-STEP PROJECTS

Download more information from www.macmillanbeyond.com

MAKE A BOARD GAME

- Find photos or draw pictures of different extreme sports – *skateboarding, rock climbing …*
- Use the pictures to make the playing board. Write the rules of your game.
- Play your board game with other students.

MAKE A CLASS LIBRARY

- Make a list of titles to include in your library in these categories – *books, magazines, albums, films, video games.*
- Choose your favourite titles and find or make covers to display in the library.
- Make cards with reviews of the books, games, etc.

CREATE A WORK OF ART

- Choose a style for your work of art – *portrait, graffiti, collage …*
- Think of a subject and create your work of art.
- Display your work in the classroom art gallery.

MAKE A PHOTO-STORY

- Think of a situation and plot for your photostory – *a school, bullying …*
- Plan the photos you need to take and write the text.
- Take the photos, print them and write your story.

DESIGN A SPACE COLONY

- Choose a planet and list the things to include in the colony – *homes, farms …*
- Draw a plan of your colony, showing its unique features.
- Present your plan to the class.

Macmillan Education
4 Crinan Street
London N1 9XW
A division of Springer Nature Limited
Companies and representatives throughout the world

ISBN 978-0-230-45592-4

First published 2015

Designed by emc design ltd

Illustrated by Peter Cornwell p64; Stephen Dew p23, 43, 54, 75 (bottom), 96, 98, 103; Mark Duffin p143; Sally Elford p6 (header), 16 (header), 26–27 (header), 28 (header), 38 (header), 48–49 (header), 50 (header), 56, 60 (header), 70–71 (header), 72 (header), 75 (top), 82 (header), 92–93 (header), 94 (header), 104 (header), 114–115 (header); Kevin Hopgood p33, 44, 69, 76, 77, 85 (bottom), 87, 107; Bob Lea p85 (top), 108; Caron Painter (Sylvie Poggio Artists) p37, 55; David Shephard (Bright Agency) p34, 88, 141

Cover design by emc design ltd
Cover illustration/photograph by Alamy/Tim Gainey, Alamy/Frans Lemmens
Picture research by Emily Taylor

The authors would like to thank all the team at Macmillan in the UK, Mexico, Poland, Spain and the rest of the world for everything they've done to make Beyond possible. Special thanks to our commissioning editor, managing editor and our publisher for their endless hard work and encouragement. We'd like to thank Studio 8 for their creative work on the drama group videos and emc for coming up with the Beyond design concept. We'd also like to thank all the teachers and other individuals who have contributed to the course whose names appear on this page. A special thank you to Tim Handford, Pinerolo, Italy for granting us the sand sculpture interview and permission to use the photos. A special thank you also to Mike Guzmán for introducing us to Mexican street food and for making the street food video. Finally, we'd like to thank our friends and families for all their support.
The authors and publishers would like to express thanks to all those who contributed to the development and formation of Beyond. In particular, we would like to thank the following teachers, contacts and reviewers: Cristina Moisén Antón, Argelia Solis Arriaga, Krzysztof Bartold, Paweł Bienert, Agnieszka Bojanowska, Samuel Gómez Borobia, Ma. Eugenia Fernández Castro, Jolanta Chojnacka, Elsa Georgina Cruz, Dominika Dąbrowska, Barbara Dawidowska, Galina Dragunova, Monika Drygiel-Kobylińska, Mauricio Duran, Natalia Evdokimenko, Maria Teresa Velázquez Evers, Marciana Loma-Osorio Fontecha, Monika Fromiczew-Droździńska, Patricia García, Axel Morales García, Miguel Angel Rodriguez García, Aleksandra Gilewska, Joanna Góra, Ewa Górka, Daphne Green, Agata Helwich, Bethsabe Ruiz Herrera, Robert Jadachowski, Patricia Guzmán Luis Juan, Anna Kacpura, Ruth Kanter, Regina Kaźmierczuk, Katarzyna Konisiewicz, Maria Koprowska, Bogusława Krajewska, Aldona Krasoń, Joanna Worobiec Kugaj, Joanna Kuligowska, Tadeusz Kur, Maria Kwiatkowska, Josefina Maitret, Javier Majul, Claire Manners, Laura Elena Medina, Carmen García Méndez, Iwona Mikucka, Talhia Miranda, Claudia Rangel Miranda, Armando Nieto, Joanna Nowak, Anna Nowakowska, Ewa Nowicka, Anastasia Parshikova, Paloma Carrasco Peñalba, Ma. Del Carmen Fernández Pérez, Joanna Płatos, Louise Emma Potter, Maria Teresa Portillo, Juan José Gómez Ramírez, Aida Rivera, Gabriela Rubio, Gabriela Bourge Ruiz, Irina Sakharova, Małgorzata Sałaj, Patricia Avila Sánchez, Jessica Galvan Sanchez, Miguel Angel Santiago, Karol Sęk, Barbara Sibilska, Tatiana Sinyavina, Agnieszka Śliwowska, Vlada Songailene, Ángela Siles Suárez, Beata Świątkowska, Ewelina Szmyd-Patuła, Agnieszka Szymaniak, Juliana Maria Franco Tavares, José Luis Vázquez, Irma Velazquez, Małgorzata Walczak, Dariusz Winiarek, Justyna Zdunek, Zofia Żdżarska, Dominika Zięba, Marzena Zieleniewska, Anna Zielińska-Miszczuk, Robert Zielonka.
The authors and publishers would also like to thank the following schools who allowed class observations – MEXICO: Centro de Formación Escolar Banting, Centro Escolar Las Águilas, Colegio América, Colegio Axayacatl, Colegio Donato Bramante, Colegio Edgar Morin, Colegio Francés Nueva Santa María, Colegio Gesi Secundaria, Colegio José Martí S. C., Colegio San Agustin, Colegio Sir Winston Leonard Spencer Churchill De México, Colegios La Salle Boulevares, Cristian Fernández de Merino, Erasmo De Rótterdam, Escuela De Ruán, Grupo Colegio Rosario Castellanos, Instituto Atenea, Instituto Crisol, Instituto Cultural Americano Mexicano, Instituto Manuel Acosta, Instituto Oriente Arboledas, Instituto Zaragoza, Liceo Americano Francés, Liceo Ibero Mexicano, Liceo Mexicano Japonés, Secundaria Simón Bolívar. SPAIN: IES Anselmo Lorenzo, IES Camilo José Cela, IES Complutense, IES Joaquín Turina, IES Laguna de Joatzell, IES Luis García Berlanga, IES Manuel de Falla, IES Máximo Trueba. POLAND: Gimnazjum nr 30, Gimnazjum nr 104 Warszawa Wawer, Gimnazjum nv120, Gimnazjum nr 141, Gimnazjum nr 145, Gimnazjum, ul. SZKOLNA 4, Publiczne Gimnazjum w Wiązownie, ZSP w Jazgarzewie. TURKEY: Ahmet Şimşek Koleji, Anabilim Koleji, Büyük Çamlıca Koleji, Doğa Koleji, Kirimli Fazilet Olcay Anatolian High School, Modafen Koleji, Sakıp Sabancı Anadolu Lisesi.

The author and publishers would like to thank the following for permission to reproduce their images
Alamy/1exposure p17(tl), Alamy/Ace Stock Limited p143(tr), Alamy/AF archive p29(bl), Alamy/Angela Hampton Picture Library p21, Alamy/Arcaid Images p115(pool), Alamy/Aurora Photos p143(5), Alamy/Alastair Balderstone p20(cl), Alamy/Brendan Bell p7(b), Alamy/Blend Images p51(10), Alamy/Adie Bush p26(br), Alamy/Caro p61(3), Alamy/Classic Image p53(cr), Alamy/Conmare GmbH p18(cl), Alamy/Cultura Creative p15, Alamy/Oliver Furrer p26(cl), Alamy/Glow Asia RF p92(a), Alamy/David J. Green p73(f), Alamy/Jim Holden p86(tr), Alamy/Iconotec p62(2), Alamy/Image Source p22, Alamy/Ladi Kirn P95(b), Alamy/Dov Makabaw p16, Alamy/MBI pp41, 92(d), Alamy/MedicImage p36, Alamy/Jonathan Miller p20(cr), Alamy/Keith Morris p6, Alamy/David Pearson pp39(b), 108(1), Alamy/Photofusion Picture Library p61(6), Alamy/Photononstop p42(b), Alamy/Purestock p143(4), Alamy/QuickImage Productions S.L p73(mansion house), Alamy/Radius Images p92(c), Alamy/Redsnapper p102, Alamy/Science Photo Library p143(br), Alamy/Dmitriy Shironosov p39(c), Alamy/Kumar Sriskandan p17(bl), Alamy/Nick Suydam p62(3), Alamy/Hugh Threlfall p114, Alamy/Jeff Wasserman p100; **BananaStock** p66(bm); **Julian Beever** p53(bottom); **Corbis** p39(f), Corbis/Mike Agliolo p32(br), Corbis/Andrew Aitchison/In Pictures p68, Corbis/Dennis Degnan p95(a), Corbis/Envision p95(c), Corbis/Fine Art Photographic Library p51(8), Corbis/O.Furrer/F1 Online p143(2), Corbis/Christian Heeb/JAI p7(br), Corbis/Hill Street Studios/Blend Images p12, Corbis/I Love Images p72(a), Corbis/Jutta Klee p78, Corbis/Don Mason p39(h), Corbis/Ron Miller/Stocktrek Images p106(background), Corbis/Moodboard p17(tr), Corbis/Trish Punch/Design Pics p60(2), Corbis/David Pu'u p143(1), Corbis/Joe Scarnici/NewSport pp7(cr), 14(tl), Corbis/Ragnar Schmuck p77, Corbis/Qilai Shen/epa p108(2), Corbis/Paul Souders p109, Corbis/Sporrer/Rupp/Cultura p42(e), Corbis/Jochen Tack/Imagebroker p24, Corbis/Ramin Talaie p106(cl), Corbis/The Food Passionates p95(d), Corbis/Viewpress Vp/Demotix p51(9), Corbis/Leah Warkentin/Design Pics p9(bl), Corbis/Ben Welsh/Design Pics p7(e), Corbis/Nick White/Image Source p51(2); **DigitalVision** p65; **Fotolibra**/Angela Hampton p18(tr), Fotolibra/Gwyn Headley p142, Fotolibra/Derek And Pam Metson p61(4); **Getty Images**/Ana Abejon p92(b), Getty Images/AFP pp32(tr), 52(tr, br), 58, 70, Getty Images/Howard Bjornson p97, Getty Images/Bloomberg p61(5), Getty Images/Bonnier Corporation pp104(a, c), 105(b), Getty Images/BrandX Pictures p39(g), Getty Images/Annabelle Breakey p80, Getty Images/Cultura/Matelly p42(d), Getty Images/Cultura RF p39(d), Getty Images/DeAgostini pp51(7), 51(3), Getty Images/Dorling Kindersley p51(1), Getty Images/drb images p73(rich girl), Getty Images/DreamPictures p56(tm), Getty Images/Richard Druryp98(tcr), Getty Images/F1online RM p7(a), Getty Images/Grant V. Faint p56(br), Getty Images/Flickr RF pp27, 33(br), Getty Images/Oliver Furrer p7(c), Getty Images/Gallo Images p11, Getty Images/Soren Hald p39(a), Getty Images/Izabela Habur p99, Getty Images/Timothy Hiatt p62(1), Getty Images/Images Etc Ltd p112, Getty Images/Image Source p110, Getty Images/Juanmonino p93, Getty Images/Michael Kurtz p49, Getty Images/Lonely Planet Images pp19, 95(e), Getty Images/Quan Long p143(bl), Getty Images/Look p118(tr), Getty Images/Bellurget Jean Louis p63, Getty Images/Roy Mehta p115(library), Getty Images/Daniel Milchev pp42(a), 143(3), Getty Images/OJO Images p39(e), Getty Images/Onoky p86(br), Getty Images/Adrian Peacock p90, Getty Images/Steven Puetzer p66(br), Getty Images/Stone p116, Getty Images/SuperStock RM p51(5), Getty Images/Tetra Images pp73(e), 98(tmr), Getty Images/Simon Watson p42(c);
Tim Handford p54(tm, tr, br); **Image Source** pp33(bcr), 40, 59; **Misty Keasler** p74(tr); **Macmillan Publishers Ltd** pp117, 119; **Masterfile**/Robert Harding Images p52(tcr); **Picture Desk**/CJ Entertainment/Doosabu Film/Polygon Entertainment p29(br), Picture Desk/Cross Creek Pictures/Dragonfly Entertainment p29(top), Picture Desk/Warner Bros p28(tr); **Plain Picture** p66(top), Plain Picture/Cultura p9(cr), Plain Picture/TatjaB p61(1), Plain Picture/R. Wolf p17(br); **Rex Features** pp8, 73(d), Rex Features/Steve Black p73(c), Rex Features/Moviestore Collection p28(br), Rex Features/Nick Rogers p14(tr), Rex Features/Sipa p10; **Scala Archives**/Photo Art Resource/Bob Schalkwijk p52(bcr); **Science Photo Library** p106(tr); **Simon & Schuster**/Courtesy of Simon & Schuster UK Ltd p31; **Soulful Creative** p51(4); **TopFoto** p14(br); **Usborne Publishing**/Cover reproduced from Future Cities by permission of Usborne Publishing, www.usborne.com. Copyright © 1979 Usborne Publishing Ltd p105(d); **Kurt Wenner**/Northwest Fantasy©Kurt Wenner p51(6).

Commissioned photography by Studio 8 Limited pp13, 23, 35, 45, 57, 67, 79, 82, 83, 89, 101, 111

The author(s) and the publishers are grateful for permission to include the following copyright material:
Material from 'Uglies' by Scott Westerfeld. Text copyright © 2005 Scott Westerfeld. Reprinted by permission of Simon Pulse, an imprint of Simon & Schuster Children's Publishing Division;
Material from 'Ashes, Ashes' by Jo Treggiari. Copyright © 2011 by Jo Treggiari. Reprinted by permission of Scholastic Inc. & Oasis Audio, LLC;
Material from article 'The Power of Half: how Hannah Salwen and her family gave half their home away' by Emily Hohler, copyright ©Emily Hohler 2010, first appeared in The Daily Telegraph 26.03.10, reprinted by permission of the publisher.

Printed and bound in India

2019
15